YOU ARE HERE

YOU ARE HERE

A Field Guide for Navigating Polarized Speech, Conspiracy Theories, and Our Polluted Media Landscape

WHITNEY PHILLIPS AND RYAN M. MILNER

The MIT Press
Cambridge, Massachusetts
London, England

This book was set in Adobe Garamond and Berthold Akzidenz Grotesk by Jen Jackowitz. Printed and bound in the United States of America.

Library of Congress Cataloging-in-Publication Data

Names: Phillips, Whitney, 1983– author. | Milner, Ryan M., author.
Title: You are here : a field guide for navigating polarized speech, conspiracy theories, and our polluted media landscape / Whitney Phillips and Ryan M. Milner.
Description: Cambridge, Massachusetts : The MIT Press, 2021. | Includes bibliographical references and index.
Identifiers: LCCN 2020007621 | ISBN 9780262539913 (paperback)
Subjects: LCSH: Internet—Moral and ethical aspects. | Social media—Moral and ethical aspects. | Fake news. | Disinformation. | Propaganda. | Media literacy.
Classification: LCC TK5105.878 .P45 2021 | DDC 302.23/1—dc23
LC record available at https://lccn.loc.gov/2020007621

10   9   8   7   6   5   4   3   2   1

To the forests of Humboldt
the skies of Los Angeles
the trails of Park City
the prairies of Kansas
the rivers of Missouri
the hills of North Georgia
the marshes of Charleston
the sunsets of Syracuse

Contents

Preface

Four years ago almost to the day, we made frantic post-election additions to our last book, *The Ambivalent Internet*. It was too late in the production process for any substantial changes, but the press did allow us to add a gobsmacked footnote about, we couldn't believe we were typing it, President-elect Donald J. Trump. From the moment we wrote that footnote to the moment we drafted the preface to this book (over Zoom), crisis after crisis has underscored the ever-increasing stakes of the present political moment.

Phillips was confronted by these stakes—certainly not for the first time, but with a different kind of urgency—in Hamburg, Germany, where she was speaking at a 2019 symposium on journalism and public discourse. Her last night in town, she went out with two other attendees, both thirty-something progressive Germans, who asked her an unexpected but poignant question: when did the United States become the United States? Phillips cocked her head. You mean like the American Revolution? No, they explained. For them, they didn't think of Germany as *Germany*—not in the way they've come to understand it—until its post–World War II reckoning. Their question was, when did that happen in the US? Phillips thought about it. The US certainly had its share of critical historical moments. But none of them struck her as *defining*, exactly, because so many of the underlying issues—particularly around social justice—remained unresolved. Then it hit her. *That's what's happening right now*, she heard herself say. *That's what 2020 is about.*

The period between the 2016 election and the 2020 election was chaos, and that chaos accelerated as we began final edits on *You Are Here* in early 2020. Things got even worse—and made questions about the character of the United States even more poignant—after we submitted the manuscript to the press in April. And now, here we sit the day after voting ended, waiting for election results.

During the past eight (quarantined, infuriating, exhausting) months, the concepts and crises most prominent in the book have expanded predictably and veered out unexpectedly. A few of them roared straight to the center of election season. QAnon, the far-right conspiracy theory megaplex, generated even more nebulous iterations, roped in even more people (including at least one future congressperson), and prompted Trump to find increasingly creative ways to promote the Satanic pedophile elements of the theory without explicitly sanctioning them (though he did come close). The COVID-19 pandemic—which we integrated into our March edits as pandemic conspiracy theories collided with QAnon conspiracy theories—also intensified. The death toll kept climbing, forcing us to make grim edit after grim edit as we wrote. It reached 35,000 by our final draft. Since then, 200,000 more people have died in the United States alone.

As it worsened, the COVID crisis affirmed the moral center of this book: me-first individualism is deadly and dangerous to democracy. This myopia animated the MAGA Right's rejection of mask wearing, twisting a commonsense public health measure into an infringement on individual choice and personal freedoms. The politicization of mask wearing was just one source of COVID information pollution; more spread as Trump, Republican politicians, and the MAGA media orbit vacillated between acknowledging the crisis, minimizing the crisis, and blaming Democrats for the crisis. The death toll kept ticking up. And then Trump got COVID. During his three-day hospitalization in October 2020, he received aggressive experimental treatment, recovered, then pointed to his recovery as proof that COVID wasn't a problem. He even sneered, during one of his mostly maskless, socially undistanced campaign rallies, that Joe Biden would "listen to the scientists" if elected. (Biden's tweeted response: ". . . Yes.")

Against the backdrop of COVID-19, the country was also rocked by massive anti-racist protests, galvanized by the murders of George Floyd and Breonna Taylor and near-fatal shooting of Jacob Blake by law enforcement—the latest in a line of systemic police brutality against Black people. These protests and the far-right counterprotests they inspired illustrate how people's deep memetic frames, drivers of belief and identity explored throughout the book, influence not just what people see in the world, but what they're inclined to do in response. The Democratic National Convention and Republican National Convention exemplified the stark differences between competing frames. At the DNC, speakers drew parallels between the Black Lives Matter movement and the Civil Rights movement. Meanwhile, the RNC gave a prime-time speaking slot to a white couple from Saint Louis, Missouri, who pointed guns at Black Lives Matter protesters marching past their house.

And then there was the 2020 election itself, which was a category 5 hurricane of grassroots disinformation campaigns, mass media amplification decisions, and social media moderation policies. Some of the news was encouraging. For instance, while right-wing media outlets continued blasting pro-Trump disinformation, many center-left outlets did their best to avoid oxygenating outright falsehoods. The press wasn't perfect; some outlets continued normalizing and both-sidesing the Trump administration's worst abuses. Still, overall, 2020 election coverage was better—more responsible, more contextualized, more patient—than 2016 election coverage. Similarly, under immense pressure not to repeat the mistakes of 2016, Twitter made a number of strong decisions about moderating election misinformation, particularly when the falsehoods were promoted by the president. Facebook made similar decisions, but ended up equivocating or backpedaling at crucial moments.

As election results trickled in, Donald Trump unsurprisingly blamed the Democrats for mail-in voter fraud. The fake news media was of course against him too, even Fox News, which provoked Trump's wrath by calling Arizona early for Joe Biden. And Twitter was flagging his lies about the voting process just to be unfair. None of these were actual conspiracies against him, but Trump made clear that his victimhood was why the Republicans had needed to fill Ruth Bader Ginsberg's vacant Supreme Court seat ASAP. The sheer number of people who emphatically supported Trump despite these falsehoods, or perhaps because of these falsehoods, further highlights the power of deep memetic frames, and what happens when those frames say: don't trust liberal institutions, don't listen to their debunks, their facts are a personal attack against you.

Whoever ends up winning, we'll have a lot to make sense of. And a lot to fix. We hope this book helps, not merely to account for what happened during Trump's (first?) term, but to account for how we got here. The question is, where do we go next? What will the United States reveal itself to be? The aftermath of the 2020 election will significantly shape the answer, with global consequences. But the results of the election won't determine the answer. Only we can do that.

Whitney Phillips and Ryan M. Milner
Syracuse, New York and Charleston, South Carolina
November 4, 2020

INTRODUCTION: MAPPING NETWORK POLLUTION

(Phillips)

That morning in 2014, I was a little late getting outside for my run. I was a lecturer at Humboldt State University, my alma mater and favorite place on earth; green and cheerful and full of hippies, the university and surrounding town of Arcata sit on the northernmost California coast, nestled among the redwoods. Normally I was out the door by 6:45, but as I didn't have office hours or class to rush to, I could dawdle. Plus there were tenure track job applications to stare blankly at, so I didn't leave my house until close to 8:00. This was fine; my studio apartment on G Street butted up against the Arcata Marsh and Wildlife Sanctuary, and on days I didn't have the time or the energy to run the mile or so up to the community redwood forest, I'd hop on the dirt trail just beyond my backyard. From there I'd trot around Brackish Pond and the various marshes, past the restored tidal habitat, up and around Mount Trashmore, and toward Klopp Lake, beyond which was Arcata Bay, beyond which was the Pacific Ocean.

The marsh was a great place to go running, and generally a great place for people to be. Once the sun was up, and especially during sunset, the whole place was golden and gentle and there were birders everywhere and people walking their dogs as grasses whispered in the breeze. Unless you knew what to look for, you'd have no idea that the marsh was a 307-acre wastewater treatment plant, one that replicated an expansive wetland environment to filter all the toxic sludge that made its way into the city of Arcata's sewage system (Mount Trashmore, indeed). Those who did know this didn't mind; the artificial marshes were constructed to do exactly what natural marshes do on their own. It was all part of the charm.

On this run, though, the marsh felt different. As the sunlight crested over the mountains, it cast a strange, yellow, gangrenous light on a wall of clouds gathering just beyond the shoreline. The result was an oddly split scene. Toward the ocean was a terraced, soupy, mustard-looming storm front, and toward the mountains, a perfectly placid everyday scene of ridges silhouetted against a calm blue sky. Because it was the way I'd been planning on going, and I suppose because it was scarier, I ran to the ocean. As I made my first turn onto Brackish Pond trail, my whole field of vision was consumed, suddenly, by a towering, vivid, sharp-edged rainbow overlaying the sickly mass of clouds. I stopped cold. Looked closer. And realized that actually, just above me, there were two rainbows, the second a faint halo above the first. I was sure I was about to be lassoed and flung out to sea.

And yet, again, I decided to keep running. Within a few minutes, the storm made landfall, sending big fat raindrops splattering at my feet, then smaller drops, faster and harder. The sky continued to darken. Salt air became wet earth. Rather than feeling distressed about being poured on, I was distressed that it had been so long since I'd been poured on. When I first moved to Humboldt as an undergrad in 2003, rainstorms were common, even incessant. It rained, and it rained, and it rained. Of course it did; California's North Coast is a temperate rainforest. But droughts engulfed the state in 2011, and so far, 2014 had been the driest year in California's history. Things were a little less bad in Humboldt than they were where I grew up in Southern California, but even in the rainforest, the rains had become fewer and farther between.

The drought would last through 2017, a crackling dryness just waiting for sparks. Those would come soon enough. I didn't know any of that then, of course. What I did know was that the storm was something to remark on—it was raining!—which I did as soon as I got home. Sopping, remembering with pained fondness what ocean raindrops tasted like, I wrote my new collaborator Ryan Milner an email describing my run and the clouds and the rainbows.

With hindsight, I've come to think of the moment I stood, agog, staring at that cloud wall as the perfect symbol for 2014's false comforts. Bigotry, lies, and harassment were growing increasingly visible, and increasingly coordinated, online. Those facing the ocean by choice or necessity saw what was gathering on the horizon. Those facing the mountains got to live a different life. They could still enjoy a perfectly normal sunrise on a perfectly normal day. Everything was fine. Everything was great, even. But that was a failure to look.

POLLUTED INFORMATION AND YOU

Phillips's story is about running through a sewer, set against the backdrop of the climate crisis. *You Are Here* is about running through the internet, set against the backdrop of the network crisis. In some obvious ways, these crises are very different: most basically, one unfolds in the natural world, and one unfolds in the digital world. But in other ways, the overlaps are striking. As Olaf Steenfadt of Reporters without Borders explains of each, temperatures are intensifying on both ends of the scale, extreme events are becoming more and more common, and the pollution that's generated does not respect territorial lines.[1]

Online, the first feature of the network crisis is hardening polarization. Masses of people didn't wake up one morning in 2016 suddenly repulsed by those with opposing political beliefs, any more than the sun rose one morning to record-breaking high and low temperatures. Polarization reflects, instead, fundamental changes in the information ecosystem. As science and technology scholars Yochai Benkler, Robert Faris, and Hal Roberts show, these changes have asymmetrically pushed the Right toward extreme ideological temperatures.[2] They've also, international affairs scholar Anne Nelson argues, occurred slowly over a long period of time.[3] One consequence is that the Left and the Right increasingly struggle to agree even on basic facts. False and misleading information only entrenches these ideological silos, as media scholars Safiya Umoja Noble, Lee McIntyre, and Francesca Tripodi each demonstrate, making it increasingly difficult for everyday people to peer outside them.[4] The problem, in other words, isn't merely polarization itself; it's the fact that polarization emerges from the world around us. More distressingly, journalist Ezra Klein explains, polarization emerges not from a broken political system but from one working exactly as designed.[5]

The second feature of the network crisis is the intensification of what social media researchers Claire Wardle and Hossein Derakhshan call information disorder, a media landscape overrun by pollution.[6] With compounding consequence and frequency, the public faces *disinformation*, false and misleading information deliberately spread; *misinformation*, false and misleading information inadvertently spread; and *malinformation*, information with a basis in reality spread pointedly and specifically to cause harm. The crash and thunder of attack after attack, hoax after hoax, manipulation after manipulation, has wrought a media landscape so inundated that it can be difficult to distinguish what's true from what's trash. As sociologist Zeynep Tufekci and legal scholar Danielle Citron each argue, the stakes of information disorder could not be higher; it threatens civil discourse, democratic participation, and a shared sense of reality.[7]

The third feature of the network crisis is its disregard for borders. Like pollution in the natural world, polluted information moves seamlessly between communities, nations, and, indeed, the very notion of an online–offline split. This too is by design; platforms encourage the fastest spread of the most information. Far-right media in Brazil provide one example of pollution's flow across national borders. As explained by Wilson Gomes, coordinator of the Center for Advanced Studies in Digital Democracy at the Federal University of Bahia, Brazilian reactionaries heading into Brazil's 2018 general election emphasized issues—like gun rights, free speech, and attacks against "political correctness"—not indigenous to Brazilian politics.[8] Instead these issues were imported from the United States via many of the platforms and tactics perfected by the Far Right during the 2016 US election. Just as Trump had done two years earlier, populist demagogue Jair Bolsonaro rode to the presidency on a wave of right-wing anger—and a campaign promise to clear-cut the Amazon, illustrating how easily online pollution spills out into offline catastrophe.

These breaches have become increasingly common and increasingly consequential—and were increasingly difficult to keep up with as we drafted this book. Our final editing push is a prime example. We submitted copyedits in April 2020, sheltered in place after the COVID-19 outbreak mushroomed into a full-blown pandemic in March. The virus was, of course, a thing in the world. But the information disorder that corresponded with its spread—exacerbated by innumerable governmental, industry, and network failures—ensured that falsehoods and half-truths about the virus themselves went viral. And globally so. People around the world didn't know whom to trust. People around the world didn't know what to believe. As a result, countless millions failed to take the threat seriously, placing countless millions more at risk. What was already clear before, COVID-19 crystalized. Polluted information is a public health emergency.

The offline consequences of polluted information are central to our study. This material emphasis—on how pollution *pollutes*—is a primary benefit of the polluted information frame. There are others. First, subsuming mis-, dis-, and malinformation under the broad term *pollution* sidesteps questions of motive, which can be especially tricky to parse online. Whether someone meant to spread a false story knowing it was false, or spread it earnestly thinking it was true, is something that, very often, only the poster knows. Motives are certainly interesting; motives are certainly important. But motives don't always matter to outcomes, and outcomes matter more than motives. The polluted-information frame allows us to table the question of intent and focus instead on how the pollution spreads, why it was allowed to spread, and what impact the pollution has both at the initial waste site and, later, downstream.

Another benefit of the polluted-information frame is that it foregrounds issues of social justice. Paralleling decades of environmental justice research, polluted information online disproportionately harms marginalized and underrepresented communities.[9] Online and off, people with less power and privilege are simply more likely to be poisoned where they live, work, and play. To add insult to injury, these communities often lack the political and legal resources, as well as the broader public sympathies, necessary to push back. Failure to act doesn't just enable the dangers these communities face; it ultimately harms everyone. Failure to act is inhumane, and puts us all at risk.

A pollution frame also redirects attention to less obvious, but just as damaging, sources of pollution. Currently—particularly in the United

States—journalists, scholars, lawmakers, and tech companies focus most intently on the most egregious offenders: white nationalists and supremacists, clickbait sensationalists, state-sponsored propagandists, and unrepentant chaos agents. Without doubt, each pumps out a great deal of muck, and each warrants targeted research, resources, and intervention. But the conversation shouldn't begin and end there. As we show throughout the book, pollution that isn't so easily traceable, from sources that aren't so obviously toxic—from everyday citizens sharing rumors about a pandemic to journalists point-by-point debunking those rumors—can do just as much damage.

These smaller sources of pollution are not wholly distinct from their more obvious, extreme, and daunting counterparts. Instead, "big" polluters and "small" polluters are fundamentally intertwined, reflecting, once again, pollution's disregard for boundaries between *this* and *that*. The everyday actions of everyone else feed into and are reinforced by the worst actions of the worst actors—and vice versa. Focusing only on the bigots, profiteers, propagandists, and chaos agents while ignoring the well-meaning citizens who inadvertently carry contaminated messages risks weakening, if not hopelessly stymieing, efforts to clean up our shared informational mess.

The problems we face, of course, are not new. For generations, around the globe, polluted information has had devastating effects on community health and safety. We foreground this point in a number of case studies from US history, including the amplification of white racial terror during the late nineteenth and early twentieth centuries and the Satanic Panics of the 1980s and 1990s. It's a profound and typically unexamined privilege to look around and be shocked by the pollution now suffusing every stratum of society.

Polluted information itself might not be new, but the hypernetworked reach of that information certainly is, as are the powerful social, technological, and political changes accelerating its spread. Again, the issue isn't *just* pollution, any more than the issue is *just* polarization. The issue is how the world around us brought us to this moment, and how information disorder reflects a system working exactly as designed.

A system that damages so much because it works so well requires broad structural solutions. Cleaning up this or that toxic waste dump isn't enough. We need corporate regulation and civil rights protections. We need to invest in jobs and education. We need to fundamentally restructure the attention economy. But many decision makers and policymakers, especially in the US, have remained in deep denial about the problem and their—often highly profitable—role in perpetuating it. Eventually, these denialists must become part of the solution. For now, we're not holding our breath for those who benefit from polluted information to do the right thing on their own.

What we're focused on, instead, is what we all can do now. And what we all can do now, what we all *must* do now, is start thinking differently about the problem. As the COVID-19 crisis shows, our economic, governmental, and technological systems have failed us. We must agitate with all our might for networks that nurture our better angels. We must agitate with all our might for technology companies committed to public health. We must agitate with all our might for economic systems that foster freedom and justice truly for all. With enough energy, enough pressure, and enough accountability, we might be able to secure a Green New Deal for the digital age. Might, or might not. Either way, the only place to start is with our own hands.

ON THINKING ECOLOGICALLY

This is not to suggest that we should venture forth into our polluted landscape as rugged individuals. The widespread belief in the West that we exist as atomistic, self-contained islands unto ourselves, responsible only for our own fates, is part of the problem. We are never alone, and our actions are always entangled with all the other actions of all the other beings all around us. The shift in focus from self to others aligns with the communitarian ethics described by media scholars Clifford C. Christians, John Ferré, and P. Mark Fackler.[10] Communitarian ethics de-emphasizes "negative freedoms," individual freedoms *from* external restriction, and instead foregrounds "positive freedoms," freedoms *for* the collective. It's the difference between asserting that an individual has the right to spew whatever poison they want without restraint, and asserting that those within the collective have the right not to be poisoned.

Communitarian ethics is perspectival; it asks that we reorient ourselves to the world around us. Reflecting on the impacts of global climate change, botanist Robin Wall Kimmerer identifies *narrative* as an especially powerful catalyst. "The stories we choose to shape our behaviors," she writes, "have adaptive consequences."[11] Stories about the natural world that restrict our focus to exploitation and commodity, Kimmerer argues, will never inspire the long-term transformations needed to address the climate crisis. We need, instead, stories that foreground interconnection and interdependence. Similarly, stories about the digital world that restrict our focus to individual people and individual rights will never inspire the long-term transformations needed to address the network crisis. Here, too, we need different stories.

To that end, we adopt throughout this book a series of grounding ecological metaphors.[12] We use these metaphors—and the stories they inspire—to encourage reflection about how deeply entwined we are with our world and with one another. Metaphors featuring actual stuff help us articulate the stakes for other actual stuff: flesh-and-blood people, mappable places, and tangible things in the world.[13]

Applying this methodology to Phillips's 2014 Arcata Marsh run serves as proof of concept; it shows how communitarian thinking helps us tell different stories, and how those different stories can inspire different actions. Offline, particularly for people who are environmentally conscious, the progression from new thoughts to new choices ("leave it better than you found it") is intuitive. But that's all the more reason to turn first to the natural world so that we can apply its lessons to the digital world.

First, though Phillips didn't encounter any other runners that morning, she was hardly alone. Standing on the trail heading toward Brackish Pond, she was physically planted in a specific location and politically situated within complex economic, ecological, and social networks. As a taxpaying, voting constituent in the city of Arcata, she, like all Arcata residents who paid taxes and voted, influenced how the city was run and therefore indirectly influenced how the marsh was managed. As a person who produced various forms of waste, she, like all Arcata inhabitants who contributed to the marsh's workflow, determined what wastewater needed treating. As a person who ran or walked in the marsh every day, she, like all Arcata visitors who wandered its trails, determined whether the land was respected or treated as an open-air trash pit.

The marsh, in other words, was everybody's marsh. Not everybody realized it, of course. Regardless of that awareness, and regardless of why residents contributed to the marsh—basic biological necessity, carelessness about what they poured down the drain, willful criminality—no one stood outside the water treatment process. If you were in Arcata, you were part of the process. We explain that connection to show how people fit within their environments and to invite, as Kimmerer says, the adaptive consequences of seeing the self as linked to so much else.[14] When we approach places like the marsh not just as a source of *our* potable water but as a water source for everyone, and not just as a calm, quiet place for *us* but as a calm, quiet place for our neighbors and our neighbors' neighbors, we're more likely to modify how we act when we're there. We're more likely to realize we need to treat it well, for everyone's sake.

Shifting focus to connection, embeddedness, and reciprocity also helps generate more thoughtful, more targeted, and more effective responses to the pollution we encounter. If the Arcata Marsh were to experience a sudden uptick in toxins, the answer wouldn't be to throw an extra bucket of chlorine into the affected holding tanks and call it good. The pollution itself is just one part of the story; treating it as *the* story means that story won't be very helpful.[15] Pollution happens and can quickly spiral out of control because of all the other overlapping variables, all the people, all the technologies, all the *everything* that filters it into the ecosystem and directs where it's able to travel. Increased toxicity would indicate something systemic: a financial shortfall, or gross mismanagement, or some shift within the population resulting in more pollutants being dumped into the water supply (the marsh is fine, though, everyone should go visit). Failure to address the underlying issues all but guarantees that the toxins will intensify.

We can—we must—apply a similar framework to polluted information online. We must begin to think differently so we can begin to act differently. The trick is to draw from ecological metaphors—above, below, and all around—to locate our own "you are here" stickers on the network ecology map. As with Phillips and the Arcata Marsh, that triangulation isn't solely based on what we, as individuals, are personally doing or seeing. We all fit within a complex tangle of ideological, social, and technological connections. Knowing where we're standing in relation to all those other forces and all those other people allows us to better understand the consequences of sharing, and even simply being, in our networked environments. Most important of all, a "you are here" triangulation reveals how our individual *me* entwines with a much larger *we*—and how the fates of both are connected.

THE CARTOGRAPHY TO COME

Polluted information is as damaging as it is perfectly calibrated to our contemporary information ecosystem. It thrives when technological and economic systems function at peak efficiency. It thrives when platforms maximize user engagement. It thrives when publications pursue clicks. It thrives when everyday people do the clicking. It thrives when everything is working well—at least working well for some.

Efficient systems have long yielded catastrophic outcomes. Offline, they're the reason we're embroiled in a climate crisis. Online, we've arrived at our present precarity because of long-established ideologies and their material consequences. Understanding that past is a prerequisite for making sense of the present, and so the first four chapters of this book consider old histories alongside the contemporary dynamics of network pollution. Not only do these histories help diagnose how we arrived at this moment, they offer new ways of imagining where we could—and should—go next.

Chapter 1, "The Devil's in the Deep Frames," explores the Satanic Panics of the 1970s, 1980s, and 1990s. The panics provide a two-pronged prehistory of the contemporary media landscape. First, they contextualize the "evil internal enemy" subversion myth central to many far-right conspiracy theories. This myth is reinforced by centuries-old *deep memetic frames*: ideological ways of seeing and being that, in the case of the panics, transformed everyday information into apparent evidence of a vast satanic conspiracy. Besides establishing continuity between conspiracy theories past and present, the Satanic Panics exemplify, and in fact emerge from, *network climate change*. Critical to network climate change was the widespread adoption of read/write media in the 1960s and 1970s, media industry and policy shifts during the 1970s and 1980s, and the political consolidation of the New Right in the 1980s and 1990s. Similar to environmental climate change, network change emerged slowly over time, as existing filtration systems became more and more taxed by more and more pollution. The result was a full-blown network crisis, making the Satanic Panics a harbinger of the disaster to come.

Chapter 2, "The Root of All Memes," draws inspiration from redwood roots systems. In digital networks, as in redwood forests, pollution introduced into one part of the grove swiftly filters out to the rest of the grove and groves beyond that. We focus on early social media, shaped by liberalism and its negative freedoms. Two powerful deep memetic frames, the white racial frame and fetishized sight, generated a deluge of pollution, then obscured the ecological consequences—at least for those shielded by whiteness and its fetishizing gaze. Many within the forest were not shielded by either; they knew what was happening and tried to sound the alarm. But they were ignored by the people who remained ensconced by such comfortable, safe, utopian frames. "Internet culture," a moniker adopted in the mid-aughts by a tangle of academics, tech industry insiders, and subcultural trolls, epitomizes this failure. Propped up by the white racial frame and fetishized sight, internet culture spread pollution far and wide, all under the guise of fun. And it was fun, for some people. As young white scholars studying this landscape, it was fun for the two of us as well; our unexamined frames resulted in years of extraordinary obliviousness. All that fun didn't stop the pollution from flowing; it just rendered the pollution invisible to those of us who weren't being poisoned by it. Yet.

Chapter 3, "Tilling Bigoted Lands, Sowing Bigoted Seeds," picks up where chapter 2 leaves off. It uses the metaphor of land cultivation to show how individual social media users influence their networks simply by inhabiting them. Whether the land a person tends is the size of a backyard garden or a factory farm, anyone can loose polluted information into whole other environments regardless of intent or awareness. As evidence, we analyze the rise of white nationalism and supremacy, along with a whole gamut of chaos entrepreneurship and weaponized disinformation, during the 2016 US presidential election cycle—not as a shocking twist to the American experience, but as a continuation of well-worn historical patterns. As has long been the case, the actions of the violent racists, chaos entrepreneurs, and disinformation agents themselves played a critical role in this rise. But so did the actions of everybody else. Center-left journalists did a great deal to amplify reactionary messages, especially young reporters raised on internet culture. Because of their online experiences, these reporters were primed to see violent ideology as "just" trolling, on "just" the internet. The roots below thus merged with the land all around, further demonstrating the need to consider exactly what we're putting into our networks—even when we're trying to help.

Chapter 4, "The Gathering Storm," tracks the weather systems that scale up and envelop the whole media ecosystem. Here we focus on some of the most ferocious storms online: the pro-Trump Deep State conspiracy theories that swirled from the earliest days of Trump's candidacy, polluted his 2019 impeachment, and undermined crucial public health warnings about the COVID-19 pandemic. Each new element of the Deep State narrative—including the responses that the stories inspired—fused with preceding elements, resulting in an ever-expanding superstorm. While the Deep State narrative is unique to the Trump era, a number of historical continuities persist between the Deep State and similar theories of the past—most notably, the embrace of the generations-old deep memetic frame known as Make America Great Again. The unique contours of the digital environment, however, from platform architecture to algorithmic amplification, coupled with growing asymmetric polarization, make modern conspiracy theories more consequential and more dangerous than ever. Failing to account for the totality of these hurricanes—including the energy we personally feed them—leaves out information essential to weathering the storms, weakens communitarian efforts to prepare for impact, and, most destructive of all, can cause the storms to grow more powerful as they travel. It's an overwhelming sight. But we must look up.

As we track how polluted information seeps through our networks, how everyday choices spread that pollution, and how overlapping energies fuel media superstorms forward, a network ecology map emerges, bit by bit, into view. Affixing our respective "you are here" stickers to that map is the next step. The final two chapters thus pivot to practice: what can, what *should*, everyday people do when confronted with so much polluted information? Chapter 5, "Cultivating Ecological Literacy," lays the foundations for an answer. A prominent call is to check facts, verify sources, and critically analyze everything we see. While these strategies can be beneficial in some cases, for some people, they aren't universally effective. In fact, they can outright backfire in hypernetworked social environments. What we need instead is an approach that works with the contours of online environments, not against them, and doesn't draw from the same taproot as the problem itself, namely, the negative freedoms of liberalism. Ecological literacy is the answer. By foregrounding interconnection, embracing positive freedoms for the good of the collective, and always considering how the things happening *here* might impact people over *there*, an ecological framework is uniquely primed to address the network crisis that threatens us all. It allows us to cultivate different fruit from a different grove.

Chapter 6, "Choose Your Own Ethics Adventure," translates theory into practice. The objective of the chapter, and indeed the whole book, is to push for long-term structural change. Those changes won't happen overnight; but they won't happen at all if we don't resolve, right now, to start working for them together. That work begins with the slow, steady task of cultivating network ethics: of telling different stories and acting differently because of those stories. Network ethics looks beyond the messages being spread and beyond the messengers who spread them and out to what communitarian effects are felt throughout the environment. Who is standing downstream; whose water supply is poisoned; whose bodies are nourished, and whose are harmed. The most obvious sources of pollution clearly still require a response. *And*, network ethics maintains, everyday actions are equally deserving of ethical reflection and intervention. The individuals responsible for small-scale pollution may not mean to cause harm. They may have the best of intentions. Even so, everyday people, without even realizing it, can still flatten the lives of others into one-dimensional pixels, sidestep consent, and cause dehumanizing damage. They can still provide industrial-grade polluters a direct line into the water supply. Network ethics is a critical bulwark against the spread of these polluted deluges, especially when that pollution is unintentional. More than that, it's key to ensuring that the pollution isn't generated in the first place.

STANDPOINT, AUDIENCE, AND AN INVITATION

The internet is global. Its problems are global. But the United States plays an outsized role in those problems, and so, as American scholars focused on US media and politics, we've applied our critique to the culture, history, and shortfalls we know best. It begins with the world's largest and most powerful technology platforms, which are based in the United States and steeped in American norms. Most consequential to global politics are free speech absolutism, an unchallenged faith in the marketplace of ideas, and an obsession with individual autonomy, all of which US companies blithely project onto parts of the word operating under totally divergent political and legal frameworks. For instance, as Julia Carrie Wong of the *Guardian* observes, Mark Zuckerberg's impassioned free speech defenses of Facebook's laissez-faire political ad policy ignores 90 percent of its global users, who are not, have never been, and will never be subject to the First Amendment but are nonetheless subject to Facebook's US-colored glasses.[16]

The United States' role in global pollution isn't limited to the norms it exports. It also flows from its cultural production—the actual stuff of media and memes. As an example that still nauseates us, we didn't merely read Wilson Gomes's conclusions about reactionary American imports to Brazil. We heard him say the words at a May 2019 symposium on memes hosted by Fluminense Federal University in Rio de Janeiro. We were the only scholars from the States in attendance, and also the only people in the room who didn't speak Portuguese; we were therefore the only snowflakes wearing simultaneous translation headphones. They set up a whole booth with two translators just for us; the symbolism was already thick. As Gomes laid out his case, we began sinking in our chairs. We had no idea. But as we soon learned, this was common knowledge. Everybody we talked to knew that US extremism and manipulation tactics and memes—so many memes[17]—had drifted south. In his talk, Gomes was gracious about this. Not once did he say out loud, not once did anyone say out loud, what we both knew to be true: the US needs to get its shit together.

We care quite a lot about the US, and all the other countries we share so much with, including our pollution. With that global ecosystem in mind, even as our cherished, deeply flawed United States lumbers large at the forefront, this book is animated by three overarching objectives that we hope will help readers no matter where they come from. The first is to present a novel framework for understanding how polluted information spreads across networks and what kinds of actions help spread it. The second is to situate the present moment within the broader arc of media history. The third is to provide all citizens of good faith, from journalists to educators to public figures to casual social media users, a set of best practices for participating in these networks as ethically, mindfully, and humanely as possible.

"Citizens of good faith" is key. Politically we are both progressives. The chapters to come draw from feminist theory and critical race theory, and the overarching ethos of the book is explicitly antifascist, with a particular focus on the dangers of white supremacy in all its forms. That said, we are not writing solely for people who think like us. Ideally, a range of people with a range of political views will read this book. Conservative readers, that means you too; we're glad you're here, because we're all living through the same crisis. What we ask from readers regardless of their politics is sincerity and the resolve to help, or at least to not make things any worse.

Citizens of bad faith, those who actively choose to sow confusion and discord for cynical, opportunistic, or bigoted reasons, aren't who we're talking to. We're not sure if any conversation could convince them to do or think otherwise. Luckily, there are more citizens of good faith than there are citizens of bad faith—evidenced, ironically, by the fact that citizens of bad faith rely on the good-faith majority to spread their toxicity.

And so we conclude with an invitation. Without question, it's difficult to linger on the chaos and uncertainty of our dizzying political moment. It's difficult to linger on rancor and abuse. It's easier to look away, or at least to point our fingers elsewhere, to social media companies, to media manipulators, to bigots, to politicians, to journalists, to the people we disagree with. We invite you, instead, to run toward the storm. To reflect on roots connecting to soil connecting to sky, and all the overlapping energies that collapse one thing into another. To situate yourself within the network map, one ever-moving dot among hundreds of millions of other ever-moving dots, all feeding into and being fed by social media companies and media manipulators and bigots and politicians and journalists and people we disagree with. To consider your responsibilities to your neighbors and your neighbors' neighbors.

We hope you'll join us. Because together, we're the best hope we've got.

1 THE DEVIL'S IN THE DEEP FRAMES

The story was shocking, breaking just days before the 2016 US presidential election. As revealed in a cache of emails stolen by the Russian government and published by WikiLeaks, Hillary Clinton's campaign chair John Podesta had ingested breast milk, semen, menstrual blood, and urine during a bizarre occult ritual known as a "spirit dinner." A shadowy cabal of high-profile figures had attended the satanic smorgasbord. As if anyone needed any more proof, the Clinton campaign was, *dramatic pause*, in league with the devil.

So the story went, anyway.

The reality of the spirit dinner is much more banal (save for the fact that the emails were procured through a coordinated effort by a hostile foreign power to subvert American democracy, but that's just details). John Podesta had received a message from his brother Tony, an art collector. Tony told John that performance artist Marina Abramović—a friend of Tony's—had invited him and John to a "spirit cooking" dinner. "Spirit cooking" was a reference to Abramović's 1997 art installation of the same name, which featured, among other jarring imagery, recipes written on gallery walls in what appeared to be blood. John never responded to the invitation. A later exchange between Tony and John revealed that John hadn't attended the dinner, but that didn't matter. The story was out: John Podesta was a devil worshipper. This was news to Abramović, who later explained that the dinner, which again, John Podesta did not attend, featured "just a normal menu. . . . We just call things funny names, that's all."[1]

That particular fact check is only the tip of the iceberg; spirit cooking wasn't a one-off conspiracy theory specific to the 2016 election. Clinton and her associates had been accused of various degrees of devil worship for decades.[2] Months before the spirit dinner story broke, for example, Ben Carson—the brain surgeon turned Trump booster later turned Housing and Urban Development Secretary—asserted that Clinton was an agent of Lucifer himself.[3] That Carson's statement was forgotten almost as quickly as he said it shows how normalized the Clinton-is-a-devil trope had become.

The satanic conspiracy narrative is much older and broader than Clinton's career, of course. Its existence within the contemporary political landscape stems from a centuries-old belief that embedded within every rung of society are demonic elements whose sole, nefarious purpose is to undermine Christianity and, indeed, Western Civilization itself. Online, the narrative remains doggedly resonant within far-right circles. This chapter traces the historical origins of the narrative and shows how modern media have ensured its continued circulation. In particular, we focus on the Satanic Panics, which began fulminating in the United States in the 1960s and reached their peak (or, perhaps more appropriately, their nadir) in the late 1980s and early 1990s.[4] Drawing from decades, even centuries, of cultural precedent, these panics reflected growing concerns about Satan's influence on secular society and on impressionable youths in particular. The panics included efforts to exorcise the demonic forces believed to be lurking in a range of media, including television, books, rock music, and role-playing games like Dungeons & Dragons.

The panics also focused on exorcising the demonic forces believed to be embedded in local communities. Some of these efforts centered on actual violent crimes that had, or were publicized as having, occult elements. Others centered on accusations of satanic abuse based on "recovered memories," resulting in dozens of criminal trials. A networked combination of Evangelical church leaders, clinical psychologists, law enforcement officers, and concerned parents worried about the spirit dinners of their day all played critical catalyzing roles.

Besides contextualizing reactions to Abramović's party plans, the Satanic Panics illustrate two concepts at the heart of this book. First, the panics emerged from a *deep memetic frame* at the core of Evangelical Christian theology. Deep memetic frames grow forth from what we're taught, what we experience, and how we're conditioned to interpret information. They shape our realities, and by extension our actions, so thoroughly and so seamlessly that the people peering out from behind them likely have no idea the frames even exist. *This is just how the world is*; the epistemological equivalent of breathing.

Second, the Satanic Panics thrived because of *network climate change*, which was brought on by a series of shifts within the media environment. These include the emergence of easily recordable, remixable, and shareable read/write media beginning in the 1960s. Read/write media allowed more people from more walks of life to shape their networks to more ambivalent ends. A formidable far-right broadcast media ecosystem also emerged in the 1960s, and was energized by the political rise of the so-called New Right in the 1970s. Fundamentalist media and right-wing political networks were further boosted by industry deregulation and the advent of cable television in the 1980s.

Polluted information certainly existed before these shifts. However, it had never been able to flow at anywhere close to the speed and scale afforded by the changing network climate. The Satanic Panics didn't just epitomize these changes; they emerged from them. The panics therefore provide a crucial, if unexpected, window into the full-blown network crisis we face today. Only by studying these origins can we fully appreciate the mess we're in. And only by fully appreciating the mess we're in can we hope to begin cleaning it up.

DEEP MEMETIC FRAMES

Understanding the tenacity of the Satanic Panics requires an understanding of deep memetic frames. The meaning of the term, and the influences informing it, can be broken down word by word.

First is the notion of *frames*. Sociologist Erving Goffman, folklorists Jeffrey Victor and Bill Ellis, and linguist George Lakoff writing with philosopher Mark Johnson all describe frames as sensemaking mechanisms that allow people to tell coherent stories about the world.[5] Lakoff and Johnson go so far as to call frames the "metaphors we live by"; they're so integral to human cognition that they shape what a person can see.[6] Philosopher Sandra Harding's work on feminist standpoint theory adds a crucial contour to this discussion. As Harding asserts, a person's relationship to power—the result of their race, gender, class, ability, the list goes on—establishes where they're positioned in the world. This standpoint, in turn, directly influences what's visible to that person, which in turn directly influences what they know.[7]

These frames reflect fundamental ideals and can cohere an entire lifetime of choices, beliefs, and experiences. In short, they run *deep*, to a person's very core. We borrow this term from sociologist Arlie Russell Hochschild's account of the "deep stories" that animate the political ideologies of Louisiana conservatives.[8] As Hochschild explains, the deep story these conservatives tell is one of "traditional" American values—hard work, independence, Christian faith—being trampled by "line cutters" who take what these conservatives believe to be theirs. In this case and others, deep stories are the paradigms through which we viscerally experience everyday life. We feel our way into deep stories; those same feelings form the core of deep memetic frames.

Finally, our inclusion of the term *memetic* signals the reciprocal social sharing that allows deep frames to spread. They're memes in Milner's articulation of the term, a modification of the concept introduced by evolutionary biologist Richard Dawkins: ideas moving back and forth between collective norms and individual actions, evolving as they travel.[9] From this view, deep memetic frames aren't bestowed from on high, a way of seeing that somebody assigns to you. Instead, they're maintained through what we do and say, and what others do and say, within our networks—as well as the cultural cross-pollination that occurs between networks. All that social participation—some direct, some indirect—spreads deep frames between this person and that person, between this group and that group.

Memetic spread is further propelled by the persistent churn of catalyzing and stabilizing cultural forces. Stabilizing forces are institutional and mainstream. They codify norms and maintain the status quo within a particular cultural tradition. Catalyzing forces, on the other hand, are vernacular and grassroots. They respond to, play with, and often subvert stabilizing forces using alternative communication channels. Sometimes these communication channels exist wholly outside mainstream reach. Sometimes they're repurposed by institutions. No matter how they're communicated, deep memetic frames circulate through a blend of both.

The deep memetic frames at the heart of the Satanic Panics did exactly what present-day deep memetic frames do: they established ethical and ideological ways of being in the world. In the process, they didn't just direct what people saw (or thought they saw); they shaped what people believed should be done in response.

"For We Wrestle Not against Flesh and Blood . . ."

Fears about a Satanist lurking under every bed are not unique to the United States nor to the 1980s. Instead, the Satanic Panics trace back centuries to a cluster of deep stories that Jeffrey Victor calls *subversion myths*, also known as *secret conspiracy myths*.[10] Subversion myths, Victor explains, boil down to the fear of an evil internal enemy. The myths are grounded in Christian theology, specifically Satan's rebellion against God. Having fallen, the story goes, Satan spends his days attempting to destroy God's creations; that fall, and all of Satan's subsequent scheming, forms the foundation of the Western ideology of evil. It's also the foundation of Christian threat assessment. Instead of facing adversaries of "flesh and blood," Ephesians 6:12 of the King James Bible warns, Christians are locked in a battle "against principalities, against powers, against the rulers of the darkness of this world, against spiritual wickedness in high places."

Even when subversion myths sidestep specific references to Christianity, these myths still draw from Christian roots; as religious studies scholar Julie Ingersoll argues, fears about conspiratorial subversion aren't framed by believers as conflict between specific human actors at specific moments in history. Rather, they're seen as clashes between Good and Evil.[11] Even more distressing to those believers, it's not just that *they* are coming to get *us*; *they* are already here, hiding in plain sight.[12]

A related predecessor to the Satanic Panics is the *blood ritual myth*, in which a group of malevolent strangers stealthily kidnap and murder children, then use the children's blood and body parts in occult ceremonies.

The blood ritual myth fused with satanic subversion myths in the eleventh century, when they were lobbed (falsely) by the Catholic Church against religious dissidents in Orléans, France.[13] Similar accusations were made (also falsely) against the rebellious Cathars in the thirteenth century and the economically powerful Knights Templar in the fourteenth century. From the thirteenth century onward, accusations of occultism became a preferred religious justification for decimating enemies. Case in point is the *blood libel myth*. This myth shares features with the blood ritual myth but was specifically deployed starting in the thirteenth century to demonize Jews, who were said to be sacrificing Christian infants and using their blood in rituals.[14] The blood libel myth is a cornerstone of modern anti-Semitism.

A third foundational myth implicates the Illuminati, an organization founded in the mid-eighteenth century. The brainchild of Bavarian revolutionary Adam Weishaupt, the Order of the Illuminati opposed organized Christianity and sought to seed rationalist, pro-Enlightenment ideals across the West by infiltrating powerful institutions and effecting change from within. In this sense, the Illuminati really was a subversive organization, as opposed to being a paranoid figment of the Church's imagination.[15] The Order of the Illuminati eventually aligned with another fraternal organization, the Freemasons, inspiring fears about which Masonic lodges may have been infiltrated.[16]

Wherever they might have been lurking, members of the Illuminati were said to be society's puppet masters. Throughout the nineteenth and early twentieth centuries, these suspicions were increasingly directed at Jews, who were accused of hatching a variety of nefarious plots from the shadows—including efforts to rule the world through communism. Fascist propagandists and, later, anticommunist crusaders, ran with this association. It wasn't long before the so-called Jewish conspiracy, dovetailing with communist infiltration paranoia, was said to extend to Satan himself.[17]

The alleged links between Satanists, Jews, and the Illuminati fed right into the twentieth century's Satanic Panics. Some of the most prominent far-right conspiracy theorists in the 1960s and 1970s explicitly connected the Illuminati and Satanism to "the Jewish influence," while others played up the connection between the Illuminati and Satanism but downplayed specific references to Jewish people.[18]

Whatever their level of implicit or explicit bigotry, the flood of anti-Illuminati articles that circulated through conservative and Evangelical media platforms during the early 1970s codified satanic Illuminati subversion, a connection that persisted well into the 1990s.[19] Influential televangelist Pat Robertson, for example, argued in his 1991 book *The New World Order* that the Illuminati's "atheists and Satanists" were the masterminds behind the formation of the United Nations. "The New Age religions, the beliefs of the Illuminati, and Illuminated Freemasonry," he wrote, "all seem to move along parallel tracks with world communism and world finance."[20] Though they might seem divergent—for the uninitiated, what the Illuminati has to do with Satan has to do with the United Nations is, let's say, opaque—all these conspiracy theories replicate the same age-old subversion myth and its warnings about the world.

The satanic subversion myth fueling the Satanic Panics tended to cluster around specific demographic groups. First, with rare exception, the Satanic Panics unfolded in small towns and rural communities. As an explanation, Victor cites the economic anxieties present in these areas during the 1980s and 1990s, as well as growing concerns about teenage drug use, crime, and depression.[21] Also relevant, Victor argues, is rural America's pervasive Evangelical religiosity. Strong Christian faith wasn't the sole precursor for belief in a satanic conspiracy, but belief in the devil incarnate both provided a basis for credulity and was statistically concentrated in rural areas.

The Satanic Panics weren't just a predominantly rural phenomenon. They were also a predominantly *white* phenomenon. Tracing a rumor that spread through his local community in western New York in 1988, during which many townspeople were gripped by fears that satanic cult members were planning to kidnap and sacrifice the town's blond, blue-eyed children, Victor notes that local Black folks showed little interest in the story—likely because the threat was, very pointedly, white supremacist.[22] It simply wasn't directed at nonwhite children; Satan didn't want *their* souls. Anthropologist Phillips Stevens Jr. emphasizes a similar racial discrepancy, which he attributes to the more nuanced role Satan plays in many Black Christian churches.[23]

Specific religious traditions are, of course, variable across and within communities. However, as religion scholar Yvonne P. Chireau explains, subtle differences between Black Christianity and white Christianity help contextualize the devil's respective roles within Black and white churches. These differences have deep—and deeply violent—historical roots.[24] Namely, the stark distinction between Good and Evil and emphasis on original sin, among other characteristics of white European Christianity, were not indigenous to African religious practices. Enslaved African people in the United States were prohibited from practicing their own religions and were forced to adopt Christian traditions—which they did, with some adjustments. One of many consequences was that existing deities were mapped onto the figure of Satan, who would have been broadly recognizable to white Christians as "their" Satan but also retained many African folk elements.[25] That Satan posed its own threats. The white Christian Satan did too, and when white Christians steeped in apocalyptic dualism began seeing those threats in their own communities, it didn't take much kindling for the panics to catch fire.

Satan Satan Everywhere

In his analysis of the panics, Bill Ellis argues that the satanic subversion myth was a cultural grammar for believers; it connected dots across events, allowing people to explain what was happening (or what they thought was happening) in the world.[26] Jeffrey Victor likewise observes that the satanic subversion myth helped believers interpret the deluge of threatening information about Satanism that emerged during the 1960s and 1970s. Fundamentalist media already had plenty to say about the devil, of course; but satanic mythology and iconography also grew increasingly prominent in mainstream popular culture.[27] The 1980s and 1990s were even more saturated with Satan, from occult mass media to crimes with satanic elements to nonbelievers' constant jokes about Satanism. These decades were therefore even more primed for subversion mythmaking.

For people who didn't see through the satanic conspiracy frame, the occult elements pushing their way to the forefront of popular culture were disconnected curiosities. They were sources of entertainment and humor, if they were given any thought at all. For people standing behind the satanic frame, in contrast, there was nothing disconnected about any of it. It proved, instead, the undeniable existence of the conspiracy. Given all the evidence, or more accurately, all the phenomena perceived as evidence, there was no other reasonable explanation: demonic forces were on the march, and they were coming for your soul.

These forces cleave into two basic categories. First, there were empirically true occurrences: things that were actually happening in the world. Second, there were things that believers experienced as real, cohered by the deep memetic frame of satanic subversion. Our distinction between *true* and *real* draws from Buddhist psychologist Tara Brach, who illustrates how thoughts and beliefs—particularly those related to "bad" others—function as navigational maps. Those maps guide a person's journey through life, but they don't necessarily correspond to the actual topography of the land.[28] The difference between true and real thus helps explain how false beliefs take hold—and what can (and can't) be done to counter those falsehoods. At the same time, there can be, and often is, uneven overlap between the true and the real. During the Satanic Panics, plenty of empirically true occurrences were experienced as real evidence of demonic subversion—a parsing that depended almost entirely on the map a person happened to be holding.

The Truth about Satan

The first empirical truth inspiring the panics was the rise of the radical counterculture in the 1960s. Historian Richard Hofstadter argues that the "cosmopolitan" ideologies at the heart of the counterculture catalyzed widespread right-wing conspiracy theorizing.[29] Second-wave feminism, civil rights activism, and antiwar protests were regarded as especially threatening.[30] At the time, conservative paranoia hinged on the perceived threat of communist infiltration. It was the communists, the story went, leading the youth, and indeed everyone unaware of the threat, astray—all part of their plot to destroy America from within. As worries about communists became for many conservatives increasingly interchangeable with worries about Satanists (in both cases often serving as thinly veiled anti-Semitic attacks), hippies and activists became a natural, existential, and downright spiritual threat.

It didn't help that some corners of the counterculture actively, often gleefully, associated themselves with New Age religious movements and occultist iconography.[31] During the height of the Vietnam War protests, for example (already an affront to conservatives), activist demonstrators associated with the Youth International Party, also known as the Yippies, led an exorcism designed to levitate the Pentagon (and also designed to be a good photo op).[32] The Women's International Terrorist Conspiracy from Hell, or WITCH, likewise played with occult themes to publicize its unabashedly feminist social justice agenda.[33] Famously, on Halloween 1968, members of WITCH marched down Wall Street, hexing the stock market; they followed up the stunt with many other "guerrilla theater" efforts to curse the evil twins of capitalism and patriarchy.

The actions of the Yippies and WITCH emerged against a backdrop of rising neopagan spirituality strongly associated with what's now called "the Left." New Age religious movements, particularly those based in California, came to be known broadly as "hippie cults."[34] Of course, not all countercultural religious movements were leftist; the Church of Satan, founded in 1966 San Francisco by former burlesque performer and carnival barker Anton LaVey, was libertarian, white supremacist, and utterly disdainful of hippies for their peace-and-love messaging.[35] What the Church of Satan lacked in goodwill, however, it made up for in public relations prowess; LaVey staged a series of media spectacles that gave the people, journalists in particular, the satanic iconography they longed to see, or simply longed to scream about (which sold just as many papers). Through these spectacles, LaVey ensured that the church and its head showman would remain in the headlines for a decade. They also helped establish many of the motifs that would become tethered to Satanism in the 1970s and 1980s.[36]

That Anton LaVey was cast as Satan in Roman Polanski's hit 1968 film *Rosemary's Baby* foreshadowed the Church of Satan's wide-reaching pop cultural influence.[37] But LaVey and his church were just drops in the occultist bucket. Subsequent years saw a slew of television shows, movies, and documentaries sympathetically portraying the occult. Sociologist Marcello Truzzi, writing in 1972, charted this burgeoning play with the mysterious, demonic, and paranormal, deeming it part of an "occult revival"—a phrase *Time* magazine also used in a 1972 cover story.[38] This play was a prominent element of youth counterculture, and young people were frequently the target audience and narrative focus of occultist media; many universities started teaching courses about the occult, and new occult bookstores tended to crop up around college campuses.

According to Truzzi, colleges weren't the only hotbeds of occult activity at the time; a "sexy fad" of "suburban witches" also emerged.[39] These dabblings in the demonic were often more aesthetic than theological. Still, they were a surefire way to get asked to parties, which, as Truzzi noted in the *Sarasota Herald-Tribune*, pretty much summarized the appeal of suburban occultism.[40] The growing popularity of J. R. R. Tolkien's *The Lord of the Rings* trilogy, which introduced millions of readers to wizards, magic, and other fantasy staples, further entrenched interest in the occult, as did the Tolkien-inspired world of Dungeons & Dragons.[41] A veritable deluge of satanic imagery in mass-market films and books—along with a thriving underground market for occultist splatter cinema—continued growing in popularity, and profitability, throughout the 1970s.

The ubiquity of occult pop culture provided ample fodder for teenage rebellion into the 1980s, resulting in what Jeffrey Victor calls the "Satanic symbolism fad."[42] As communication scholar Kembrew McLeod—who was himself a teenager and occult symbolism-dabbler at the time—explains, the exoticism and darkness of pentagrams and hooded figures, coupled with the general ease with which they could freak out the olds, provided a compelling alternative to "a world of strip malls and monotonous minimum wage jobs."[43] The appeal of satanic symbolism also helps explain why so much petty teenage crime at the time—and even some outright violent crime—featured satanic imagery.

Satanism and the occult were also front and center in many high-profile news stories, which brought true visibility to satanic subversion myths, regardless of how real audiences thought the stories were. A rash of cattle mutilations in the 1970s, for example—or what appeared to be cattle mutilations; by all scientific accounts, the animals died of natural causes—spurred a media-fueled panic, prompting many to blame satanic ritual bloodletting.[44] While the specific allegations made in these stories often tested the limits of empirical truth (and that's being generous), they were a predominant, quantifiable element of the cultural landscape. They also intermingled nicely with the more mundane elements of the occult revival. No matter what you believed, one thing was undeniable: Satan sure was in the news a lot.

The darkest side of satanic symbolism soon entangled with a range of "sex-and-ritual-murder" stories linked to the so-called hippie cults that, until the 1970s, many outside the fundamentalist Right had regarded as benign or even attractive. The murder/Satanism trend first emerged in the wake of the Manson Family murders. Reports of extensive ties between Manson Family patriarch Charles Manson and the Church of Satan weren't true, but made for compelling headlines nonetheless.[45] Fears of satanic violence were compounded by the spate of serial killers that began making headlines in the 1970s. Notable cases include the Zodiac Killer, Ted Bundy, John Wayne Gacy, Jeffrey Dahmer, and the "Son of Sam" David Berkowitz, who ultimately cited a range of satanic influences for his crimes. "The Night Stalker" Richard Ramirez eventually joined their ranks in the mid-1980s, flashing a pentagram on his palm at trial and declaring "Hail Satan!" during sentencing.

A series of "confessing Satanist" narratives circulating in the 1970s further boosted the visibility of Satanism. One of the most prominent confessing Satanists was Mike Warnke, whose 1972 book *The Satan Seller* chronicled his professed experiences working for, essentially, a multilevel satanic marketing scheme. Warnke would later become a frequent guest on national television programs.[46] Equally notable was John Todd, who began giving lectures detailing his time as an "ex–Grand Druid" within a "Satan-type church" in the early 1970s.[47] And then there were the self-proclaimed satanic ritual abuse survivors. One of the first, and arguably the most influential, was Michelle Smith. In her 1980 book *Michelle Remembers*, Smith described, to much fanfare and media attention, being raped by snakes, having devil horns surgically attached to her forehead, and being rubbed with the bisected halves of ritually murdered babies.[48]

Michelle Smith wasn't alone. Throughout the 1980s, hundreds of public accusations were made by women and children claiming to have been victims of satanic ritual abuse—abuse that included, among other alleged horrors, blood sacrifices, the forced ingestion of bodily excretions, sexual violence involving sharp foreign objects, and participation in infanticide. The "atrocity stories," as Victor calls them,[49] at the heart of these accusations resulted in dozens of criminal trials, as well as countless reams of newspaper copy and television coverage that beamed the stories into millions of American homes. The most high-profile of these trials centered on alleged satanic ritual abuse at day care centers. One particularly infamous case was the 1983 McMartin preschool trial, which took place in Manhattan Beach, California. The story told by the alleged victims' parents, child welfare advocates, and self-proclaimed satanic abuse experts was that over a period of five years, 360 children were subjected to "extremely bizarre sexual acts,"[50] as well as baby killings, cannibalism, and animal mutilations. Michelle Smith consulted with the parents of the allegedly abused children and, according to the first prosecutor in the McMartin trial, helped shape the children's testimony.[51]

None of the satanic ritual abuse alleged during these trials was ever substantiated, even after intense investigations by law enforcement. Moreover, the accounts of satanist media boosters like Warnke, Todd, and Smith have since been exposed as questionable at best and demonstrably untrue at worst.[52] But no matter how false the claims might have been—whether they were born of cynicism or delusion or misdirected trauma—their consequences were still true. They could be outright devastating, particularly for the dozens of innocent people who were brought to trial, some of whom were convicted.[53] And then there were the broader consequences for public opinion. All the publicity around all these stories provided Satanism an enormous amount of visibility.

National television played a particularly important role. Geraldo Rivera's now-infamous 1988 NBC special "Devil Worship: Exposing Satan's Underground" employed absurd levels of hyperbole, shouting, and weaponized quotation to further the satanic subversion myth. In one instance, after the camera zoomed in on the business card of a Kansas serial killer, Rivera proclaimed that the card "seemed straight from hell!"[54] Rivera's program was especially shrill, but it was just one among many exploitative, aggressive, and often shockingly lurid prime-time specials overhyping satanic threats. During one Sally Jessy Raphael special in 1989, for example, a self-professed satanic ritual abuse survivor described the various rapes and pregnancies satanic cultists forced her to endure so that they could use her children as sacrifices. In one case, the woman claimed, the cultists ate her baby.[55]

Inspiring and inspired by national television coverage, local newspaper coverage kept the devil omnipresent in the small-town and rural communities inclined to believe satanic subversion myths. This coverage played a much different role than national news coverage. Rather than redirecting focus to what was happening elsewhere (a basic hallmark of the national news), local reporting grounded satanic rumors within specific geographic areas and therefore sustained interest in satanic conspiracy stories. As Victor notes, the people being quoted in local news stories tended to be locals themselves, including cops, community leaders, and members of the clergy—lending even more credence to the subversion myths for people already inclined to believe.[56]

Real but Not True

To true believers reading the headlines and following the ritual abuse trials, the threat of Satanism took the form of fears about—obviously—Satan. But fears about Satan went much deeper than Satan himself. Instead, the Satanic Panics epitomize digital media researcher Nancy Baym's observation that moral panics are "representative anxieties" about social change.[57] The fears at the heart of this panic, like any panic, thus unearth deeply held ideals about how the world should be—ideals shaded by the deep memetic frames that adherents stand behind.

Throughout the Satanic Panics, the underlying subversion myth reflected anxieties about the decline of "traditional values" and the nuclear Christian family central to those values. Maybe that family never existed the way people thought it did. Maybe "traditional values" were only ever code for patriarchy or white supremacy or any number of other oppressions. That didn't matter. The perception among many conservative Americans was that the droves of women entering the workforce, the droves of parents who chose to practice alternative religions or no religion at all, the droves of children shuffled off to day care and teenagers coming home to empty houses, represented an existential threat. "Satanism," sociologist David G. Bromley notes, "constitutes a metaphorical construction of a widely experienced sense of vulnerability and danger by American families."[58] The creeping sense that something bad is going on here, something *evil*, must therefore be understood as cultural commentary as much as religious lamentation.[59] Seeing through this particular frame, seeing so much evidence of so many threats, how could a person *not* panic?

Understanding how and why the Satanic Panics reflected broader cultural tensions demystifies believers' most baffling claims. It also contextualizes how the panics could persist in the absence of empirical proof. In the case of satanic ritual abuse allegations, no credible evidence of anything even close to a national network of satanic abusers was ever produced. In some of these cases, sexual and physical abuse likely had taken place. But a conspiratorial cabal of Satanists was not responsible.

What persistent claims to the contrary show is what happens when the real clashes with the true. For believers, satanic ritual abuse was—that is to say, *felt*—very real because a number of co-occurring, even seemingly contradictory, cultural forces helped position the believers behind the deep memetic frame of satanic subversion. That frame, in turn, helped translate true information into perceptions into evidence.

One of the most robust planks of that frame was shifting attitudes within psychiatry toward the sexual abuse of women and children. These changes emerged from a newfound understanding of the psychological effects of trauma, stemming from research into post-traumatic stress disorder after the Vietnam War. Work done by feminist survivor advocacy groups also contributed to the growing body of knowledge about trauma.[60] This research informed how sexual abuse accusations began to be handled. Historically, when women and children alleged abuse, they were not believed, and in fact were frequently discouraged from making such accusations. Efforts to right this wrong were appropriate and sorely needed. They also primed many social workers not just to believe ritual abuse narratives, but in many cases, to actively seek those narratives out—creating an odd, slim, short-lived overlap in the deep memetic frames of feminists and the deep memetic frames of conservative Christians. Both groups were looking through their own respective portals, for their own respective reasons. It just so happened that when it came to ritual abuse, they saw, for a brief moment, the same thing.

Second, in reframing their understanding of, and therefore their responses to, patients' trauma, many psychologists—particularly within the burgeoning "Christian therapy" movement—began employing multiple personality disorder (MPD) as a diagnostic tool.[61] MPD was said to be the result of trauma so unbearable that the sufferer quarantines their memories of the experience within an entirely different personality. MPD diagnoses, which were reclassified as "dissociative identity disorder" in the fourth edition of the *Diagnostic and Statistical Manual of Mental Disorders*,[62] have since undergone significant scrutiny and are now as controversial as they are rare.[63]

However, in the early 1970s, MPD diagnoses experienced a sudden uptick, both as a response to patients' existing claims about ritual abuse and as a tool to coax out new claims. Indeed, most women who professed to be survivors of satanic ritual abuse were diagnosed with MPD, the first being none other than Michelle Smith, author of the MPD archetype *Michelle Remembers* and, later, consultant on satanic ritual abuse cases. Smith wrote her book with her former therapist—and later husband—Lawrence Pazder. Pazder was, unsurprisingly, a vocal proponent of MPD diagnoses and, through the publicity surrounding the book, became the clinical face of satanic ritual abuse. Tellingly, he is credited with the first recorded use of the term, invoking it during the 1981 meeting of the American Psychological Association.[64]

Using MPD to codify accusations of satanic ritual abuse was a logical, if misguided, extension of efforts to correct the systemic dismissal of women's and children's experiences. Whether the victim was an adult woman or a child, not remembering abuse provided, within the MPD frame, evidence that the abuse had in fact occurred. It had just been pushed down so far that it needed to be coaxed out by a psychotherapist.

Other external forces influenced allegations of satanic abuse. Victor describes the recovered-memory sessions that children were subjected to as a process of joint storytelling. This process, Victor explains, drew equally from mass media—including films and television, as well as the stories told by Michelle Smith and other first-wave satanic ritual abuse survivors—and folklore about witches, black magic, and devil worship. It easily veered toward priming; the child would be coached, however subtly, into telling the story they knew the investigator wanted to hear.[65] Adult women diagnosed with MPD claimed similar experiences and told stories similar to those told by children—so similar, in fact, that the stories could be outright interchangeable.

For MPD proponents, the similarities between these stories pointed to their truth. For MPD critics, the similarities pointed to deep methodological flaws. Most troubling was the frequency with which MPD therapists used the atrocity stories told by women to corroborate, and even to help extract, the atrocity stories told by children, and vice versa.[66] Anthropologist Sherrill A. Mulhern sums up the problem: it wasn't just that the alleged victims of satanic cults were saying the same things; it's that they were being heard in the same ways.[67]

Many of these women and children were unquestionably at risk. Many had spent a lifetime not being believed. Many genuinely needed protecting. The satanic subversion frame took all these empirical facts and transformed them into evidence of another reality entirely. True dangers became real myth. That myth, in turn, created a whole host of imaginary evils—evils that, for believers, needed exorcizing.

Concerns about the deluge of satanic influences in popular culture were similar to ritual abuse allegations. In both cases, panicked citizens pointed to things that were truly there and reframed them as evidence of something else. Anti-Satanist activism focused in particular on identifying and eradicating presumed demonic influences—which included, most basically, any presence of magic—in children's programming, with cartoons like *He-Man* singled out by Evangelical conspiracy theorists.[68] Children's toys inspired the same alarm, as exemplified by Christian writer Phil Phillips. Phillips's books, including *Turmoil in the Toybox* and *Saturday Morning Mind Control*, augmented mainline Christian concerns about secular culture with claims that children's toys were conduits for actual demons.[69] The belief that children's souls were at risk, and not just metaphorically, also resulted in widespread book bannings in public schools and libraries.[70]

Anti-occult activists weren't just worried about elementary-age children. Teenagers were thought to be particularly susceptible to pop Satanism, with rock music pegged as the ultimate highway to hell. Jack Chick, author of popular fundamentalist direct-mail comics known as "Chick tracts," addressed the threat in the 1978 tract *Spellbound?*. The comic chronicles how powerful occultists infiltrated the music industry.[71] To produce rock songs, the tract explains, druids play melodies from ancient manuscripts, and witches overlay them with lyrics hiding coded spells. Rege, one of Satan's top demons, is then summoned to curse the final record.

No matter the empirical truth of Rege's hellish production schedule, the subversion myth informing it was experientially real enough to hold tangible sway. Indeed, many people outside the Chick tract distribution network believed that something sinister was happening in the music industry. That underlying fear was front and center in Geraldo Rivera's 1988 "Exposing Satan's Underground" special. In front of a live studio audience, he grilled Black Sabbath frontman Ozzy Osbourne about the prevalence of Satanism in heavy metal music. Osbourne, utterly baffled throughout the interview, was far from the only musician sucked into the Satanic Panic orbit. Organizations as high-profile as the Parents Music Resource Center, established in 1985 by the wives of prominent American political figures, had long railed against the presumed dangers of hard rock music, triggering congressional hearings about the threat. Notably, the organization charged concerned parents and educators fifteen dollars for "Satanism Research Packets."[72]

Relying on similar tropes, anti-Satanists also targeted the fantasy tabletop game Dungeons & Dragons, claiming that D&D uses mind control, causes teens to kill themselves and others, and generally lowers their spiritual defenses against demonic influence.[73] Such was the argument of Bothered about Dungeons & Dragons (BADD) founder Patricia Pulling, who blamed her son's 1982 suicide on a curse he received during a D&D session.[74] As writer Paul Corupe notes, many D&D players were amused by anti-D&D advocacy, acquiring and circulating anti-D&D literature—including a Chick tract titled *Dark Dungeons*—as high camp.[75]

For non-Christians and Christians whose relationship with Satan was more metaphorical than literal, satanic conspiracies made little sense, veering between derangement and comedy. For believers, however, the power of the Satanic Panics was how *logical* they were—at least based on the maps believers were holding. The claims were also, as Bill Ellis emphasizes, unfalsifiable, which just added to their explanatory power.[76] There was nothing anyone could argue to definitely prove that Satan *wasn't* secretly pulling the strings. That was the teflon of anti-Satanism advocacy. Efforts designed to fact-check the conspiracy or make fun of the conspiracy (cue *Saturday Night Live*'s Dana Carvey in full Church Lady drag imploring, "Could it be . . . *Satan*?") didn't just amplify the message; they provided further support for the theory by looping the attempted debunker into the *them* of the conspiracy itself. Denying Satan's existence is exactly what a Satanist would do. The harder *they* resist the truth, the more proof it provides *us*.

The Satanic Panics were not unique in their imperviousness to fact checks. Ellis maintains that all subversion myths are similarly impenetrable, with similar outcomes for those who try; for true believers of any of the myths, the more emphatic the debunking, the more likely it is that the debunking will backfire. Nor were the Satanic Panics unique in the cultural issues they raised. As is always the case with moral panics, they weren't "just" about what they were about. Satan may have been at the center of the story, but he was, himself, a minor player in the drama. The panics were able to grow when they did, as they did, with whom they did, because of the social and technological forces at the heart of American culture. Much has changed between then and now. Simultaneously, much has remained the same—affirming novelist Hunter S. Thompson's observation that "yesterday's weirdness is tomorrow's reason why."[77]

NETWORK CLIMATE CHANGE

When considering the spread of polluted information, it's tempting to point to social media and other recent communication advancements as the reason things have spun so desperately out of control. The problem, goes the lamentation, is what's happened in the last few years. It's all Facebook's fault!

This claim holds some basic truth: without the proliferation of social media, there wouldn't be so damn many places for pollution to flow. Recent history, however, is not the root cause of network pollution, as the Satanic Panics underscore. That root cause extends, instead, to network climate change, which first took hold in the 1970s and 1980s. Just like the ecological climate crisis, the network crisis emerged from the buildup of wide-reaching, often overlapping forces, including the introduction of new communication technologies, changes within the media industry, and the rise of the political powerhouse known as the New Right. Each of these forces map directly onto the Satanic Panics, illustrating its slow, steady burn toward impending disaster.

New Kinds of Media, New Kinds of Pollution

The first shift contributing to network climate change was the mass adoption of read/write media. These media included home video cameras, audio recording devices, and electronic photocopiers, whose output could circulate through distributed publishing and broadcasting channels. Thanks to read/write media, the number of mediated messages everyday people could spread increased exponentially. Catalyzing cultural forces—which accrued energy from the things everyday people were saying and doing—could also set agendas across and between networks with much greater ease. Just as the Industrial Revolution led to a rise in environmental pollution, the network revolution led to a rise in polluted information.

Of course, everyday people—at least some of them—could contribute to their information landscapes long before read/write media. The advent of the printing press in the fifteenth century, for instance, opened up media production considerably, certainly compared to the centuries before, when literacy was exceedingly rare, and professional scribes were responsible for cataloging most information. Over the next few centuries, an increasing number of well-to-do amateurs and small-time professionals were able to produce limited runs of their own commentary. The early days of electronic media, from high-speed telegraph lines to amateur radio broadcasts in the late nineteenth century and early twentieth century, gave even more users even more agency, even more choice, and even more ability to make their voices heard in their networks.

However, the commercial and technological trends that made mass media big business in the first half of the twentieth century ensured that the everyday people who had access to daily newspapers, broadcast networks, and movie theaters were typically end users, not producers—and certainly not owners. A smattering of hobbyists may have homebrewed amateur media, but the average global citizen didn't have a publishing house or pirate radio station in their basement. In short, while communication innovations throughout the nineteenth century and the early twentieth century resulted in an increasingly nuanced relationship between everyday people and their media, the vast majority of folks remained vastly reliant on corporate institutions for news and entertainment.

Read/write media, which emerged slowly in the 1960s and more quickly by the 1970s, rewrote that equation. More people could now create and distribute a variety of media content from their basement, office, or a public television studio a few blocks away. The information landscape was fundamentally and irreversibly altered as a result. This was a boon for democratic participation. It was also a boon for polluted information.

The "media-enhanced conduits" of Evangelical Christianity, which directly fueled the Satanic Panics, are a case in point.[78] Particularly significant was the emergence of Charismatic Evangelicalism in the late 1960s and its broader acceptance within the Christian mainstream throughout the 1970s. Charismatic Christianity focused on the "charismata," or "gifts of the spirit," including speaking in tongues, prophetic ability, and powers of exorcism. It shared tenets with the deliverance ministry movement, which held that true believers could cure diseases, cast out demons, and otherwise perform miracles. Both maintained that Satan and his demonic influences were everywhere, including within some human beings, who had made a pact with the devil through active choice (including blood pacts and witchcraft) or inadvertent consequence (including contact with the occult). It was extremely easy to be exposed to satanic influence and, through that exposure, to "infect" family members and children.

Adherents of Charismatic Christianity and the deliverance ministry were linked together through networks of folk media, including newsletters, direct mailers, comic tracts, transcribed sermons, and spoken-word records. After the introduction of VHS tapes in the late 1970s, videotaped sermons and alt-Christian films, including fear-the-reaper titles like *Exposing the Satanic Web*, added to the prevalence of Evangelical grassroots media.[79] Although they often emerged on the religious fringes, charismatic and deliverance ministry messages about the reality of Satan's earthly influence were shared so often, across so many religious networks, that they became increasingly common within mainstream Christian circles.[80]

The confessing Satanist and "ex–Grand Druid" John Todd, for example, employed Christian media networks to spread, and in the process normalize, his exceedingly tall satanic tales. Todd began giving lectures about his professed experiences in the early 1970s. Over time he amended his narrative to include elements of the Illuminati myth, additions he pilfered from other fundamentalist media, including records and books (among them Mike Warnke's *The Satan Seller*).[81] Todd then recorded his remixed reflections on cassette tapes and distributed them through vast anti-occult networks.[82] Todd's folk media content subsequently caught the attention of Jack Chick, who drew from Todd's accounts to write his most popular Chick tracts. These homebrewed, catalyzing forces, created by people working out of their own garages, were quickly sucked into established networks of professionals with institutional backing. As these stabilizing forces played catch-up with catalyzing forces, and catalyzing forces added fuel to what had already been stabilized, the stakes became increasingly apocalyptic, at least for the people who saw Satan everywhere they looked.

As the Media Landscape Turns

Read/write media did not emerge in a vacuum; nor did the Satanic Panics. Both emerged, instead, in the context of much broader changes within the media environment. These changes helped empower the Evangelicals pushing the panics. They also precipitated the network spread of far-right fearmongering. The consequences of both would reverberate for decades.

The most structural of these changes was the development of an increasingly professionalized Evangelical media ecosystem, which allowed Chick tracts, bootleg sermons, and other grassroots charismatic media to trickle into ever-widening networks.[83] This ecosystem thrived, first, because mainstream corporate media in the mid-twentieth century began shying away from explicitly religious programming, rankling audiences who wanted God on the airwaves. Relatedly, Evangelical media thrived because fundamentalist Christians were growing increasingly wary of creeping cultural secularism and innately mistrusted the professional news media's role in that process.[84]

For these overlapping reasons, Evangelicals began building their own communication channels. Most notably, vast Christian radio networks began cropping up in the 1950s, an outgrowth of the small fundamentalist stations that had peppered the country for decades.[85] Christian radio filled a cultural void for listeners resistant to secularized mainstream media, and Christian television wasn't far behind. By 1961, Pat Robertson—who would go on to author the antiglobalist, anti-Satanist, anti-Illuminati manifesto *The New World Order*—began airing religious programming on his new television station, WYAH. WYAH grew exponentially over the next few years, rebranding as the Christian Broadcasting Network (CBN), and by 1975 was beaming via satellite to millions of viewers across the world. By the time Robertson cemented his Evangelical legacy in the mid-1980s, CBN was the third-largest cable network in the United States, trailing only CNN and ESPN.[86]

The rise of fundamentalist broadcast media was not merely the result of available infrastructure and interested audiences. Deregulation was another catalyst. For most of the twentieth century, a Federal Communications Commission directive called the Fairness Doctrine had been a stumbling block for fundamentalist media.[87] The doctrine mandated that broadcast stations devote airtime to matters of public interest and that they present diverse perspectives on those issues. Personal attacks required free airtime for the aggrieved party to reply, and specific political endorsements required free airtime for opponents to say their piece. As media scholar Heather Hendershot explains, the Fairness Doctrine didn't keep fundamentalist firebrands off the air and didn't extinguish their conspiratorial messages.[88] It did, however, incentivize the stations carrying them to vary their programming and kept fundamentalist programs from diving directly into electoral politics.

By the 1980s, however, the Fairness Doctrine was dying a slow death. For one thing, the FCC dismissed most complaints without much investigation.[89] For another, the rise of cable television undermined the doctrine's usefulness. The growing number of specialized cable networks ensured that there were, ideally at least, plenty of places to get plenty of perspectives. Crucially, these networks weren't licensed like broadcast stations and therefore weren't subject to the Fairness Doctrine anyway. Enforcing the doctrine only on the broadcast stations that were now a smaller part of the mass-media landscape seemed increasingly moot, and in 1987 Ronald Reagan's FCC decided that the free market could regulate broadcasting well enough on its own.[90]

And regulate itself the market did. Free from even the shakiest Fairness Doctrine guardrails, networks could be as hyperpartisan and hypertargeted as they wanted. In fact, demographic laser focus was a safe way to turn a profit in an increasingly noisy business. Within the mainstream, cable networks and establishment broadcast outlets competed for attention through entertainment stories, human interest stories, and satanic Geraldo spectaculars. Anything to keep audiences glued to the television.

For the Christian Right, Anne Nelson argues, these industry shifts launched an outright bonanza.[91] Fundamentalists were now free to express their Christian nationalist subversion myths unfettered. The televangelists and fundamentalist media figures pursuing American theocracy no longer had to worry about even pretending to care about other perspectives. Why would they? This was, from their frame, a holy war. The only broadcaster to lose a license under the Fairness Doctrine had defended himself on precisely those grounds. When you're giving God's point of view, he'd argued before the FCC in 1972, why would you give free airtime to Satan?[92] By the late 1980s, the devil was no longer owed his due—and increasingly, neither was a shared universe of accepted facts. Your preferred frame was only a dial spin away.

Hypernetworked Evangelists

A third factor contributing to network climate change was the rise of the radical Christian political movement known as the New Right.[93] Christening itself as America's "moral majority," the New Right sought to restructure US culture by restoring it to a halcyon yesteryear of patriarchal, white Protestant domination. Equally impressed and distressed by the grassroots successes of the labor, feminist, and civil rights movements, Anne Nelson explains, fundamentalist operatives in the 1960s sought to counter those successes by pushing Christian churches toward conservative political activism.[94] By the end of the next decade, Evangelical Christians and the Republican Party had essentially become one and the same. To mobilize this newly coalesced Evangelical voting bloc, the New Right established a complex matrix of organizations, linking local and national politicians, community leaders, and churches.[95]

Through the New Right's organizational, political, and communication infrastructures, fundamentalists across the nation received marching orders about perceived threats and policy initiatives.[96] Unsurprisingly, one of the core grievances of the New Right was that secular media, with all their occult undertones, were undermining everything that made white Christian America great. This particular affront generated increasing political energy with the 1980 presidential election, and found an unexpected ally in presidential candidate Ronald Reagan, a secular divorcé from California. Despite a fairly moderate reputation and tone, Reagan happily courted Evangelicals and happily parroted fundamentalist talking points as he did.

Reagan's decisive victory was yet another coup for the New Right; it was the perfect realization of a long-standing effort to purge moderate voices from the Republican Party. After all, the New Right's frame naturally transformed anyone who opposed its policies into an enemy—and a spiritual enemy at that. From this perspective, even mild dissent was tantamount to, as Nelson describes it, "Satanic agitation striking back at God's natural order."[97] Moderates did not have a seat at that table. You were either with us or in league with the devil.

To purge moderates from the broader cultural landscape, the New Right cultivated strategic alliances with Christian media companies, whose owners were already firmly embedded within New Right networks (relationships that persist to this day, as Nelson exactingly maps).[98] Through this synergy, Christian cable outlets like CBN and Christian radio networks like Salem Radio wielded more and more influence, and the New Right's messages were able to spread farther and farther, helping to stabilize what had once been wholly grassroots Evangelical messaging.

Although Evangelical messages were, of course, targeted toward Evangelicals, they didn't remain perfectly confined to Evangelical networks during the Satanic Panics. Instead, these messages were able to filter into contiguous networks when a person with one foot in Evangelical circles had another foot in secular circles. The people carrying the messages from Evangelical networks to secular networks may have been oblivious to their role in the filtration process. Still, cross-pollinating Evangelicals did a great deal to spread the panics far and wide. Loose connections across multiple networks were all it took to bring the devil to secular doorsteps.

For example, bolstered by the New Right's growing political clout, organizational sophistication, and Evangelical media wraparound, a cadre of overwhelmingly white, overwhelmingly male, overwhelmingly conservative Christian law enforcement officers began rooting—or at least trying to root—violent satanic elements out of local communities. These officers were known colloquially as "cult cops."[99] As there were no actual violent, child-sacrificing occultist networks to prosecute, cult cops instead employed community policing methods designed to "manage deviance," that is to say, zero in on the community's most visible outcasts.[100] Cult cops also hosted frequent cult seminars attended by local educators, social workers, mental health personnel, victim advocates, corrections officers, and clergy. Cult seminars linked a variety of symbols—including the peace sign, as well as all sorts of supposedly atypical behaviors, like listening to heavy metal or wearing black clothes—with violent criminality.

Cult cop seminars weren't the only opportunity for anti-Satanism professional development. Multiple personality disorder training seminars and conferences, at which MPD therapists and self-proclaimed survivors would attest to the absolute truth of the survivors' claims, were another (seemingly) official source of satanic rumors.[101] Although these proceedings were neither released publicly nor subjected to peer review, some of the talks and workshops were bootlegged and shared across other networks. Because they had a professional air, they were then accepted as scientific fact by interested cult cops, mental health professionals, and child welfare organizations, eventually spreading all the way back to the ministries that had carried the ideas to prominence in the first place—ministries that were, in turn, validated by all the secular professionals saying the same thing that they were.[102]

Specific participants within specific networks didn't necessarily know about all the other networks propagating the panics. Nor was there necessarily any coordination between groups that fell outside the New Right; individuals were, as Victor emphasizes, "usually unaware of the broad scope of the collective organizing process going on."[103] In some cases, obscuring certain connections to certain networks was a deliberate communications strategy. It's why, for instance, so many organizations linked to the New Right falsely presented themselves as nonpartisan and secular. The result was to bolster the credibility and potency of the subversion myths. When what the cops were saying lined up with what the psychiatrists were saying lined up with what the pastors were saying lined up with what the television was saying, each claim sure seemed to reinforce the next.[104]

As the messages pinged between networks, accruing with each turn what looked like corroboration, believers—along with people who might otherwise have discounted Satan's material influence—didn't see those network machinations at work. They only saw what was right in front of them. And what was right in front of them didn't just look like evidence. From their vantage point, it *was* evidence, as real as the day was long. The New Right didn't have to lift an organizing finger for this to happen. A slowly intensifying network crisis did the work for them.

THE RISING TIDE OF POLLUTION

The problem of network climate change is not, in itself, the shift from one media ecology to another. This is especially true considering how restrictive the previous ecology could be: restrictive of diverse access, restrictive of diverse expression, restrictive of diverse representation.

The problem of network climate change is, rather, just how easily contemporary networked media facilitate, and even outright encourage, unstoppable flows of raw sewage. The infrastructures established by the previous regime simply aren't equipped to filter such an overwhelming, incessant deluge of pollution. Just like the natural environment, the media environment has become stressed beyond capacity. Polluted rivers spread sludge to other regions, to other ecosystems, to other water tables. Polluted networks do the same.

Of course, the Satanic Panics emerged at the outset of network climate change, not at its pinnacle. Falsehood might have spread far and wide throughout the 1970s, 1980s, and 1990s. But network flows had their limits. One of the most conspicuous was that people within the mainstream—including mainstream journalists—were broadly oblivious to the growing influence of Evangelical media and the growing political power of the New Right.[105] These folks may have been aware of the brewing "culture wars," and may have heard some jokes about televangelists, especially the ones caught up in sex scandals, but the twain of Evangelicalism and mainstream media had little reason to meet. The adherents of each were standing behind totally divergent deep memetic frames; the vistas they saw and even the air they breathed were simply different. As a result, many on the Left, who tended to live in more secular, urban areas, had no reason to dip a single toe in any Evangelical media circles—which was just fine with soldiers of the New Right, who took active measures to bypass traditional, secular, unchristian media.[106]

A similar gap existed between local newspaper coverage and national newspaper coverage. National newspapers—unlike national cable television—showed little interest in satanic conspiracy theories, certainly when compared to their small-town counterparts. When they did report on Satanism-related stories, national papers tended to report on them as skeptical outsiders.[107] It may have been that the reporters and editors at national newspapers weren't aware of the panics unfolding in rural areas because they were headquartered in metropolitan cities. It may have been that the publications were aware of the localized panics but chose not to amplify them because these reporters, from their more secular, left-leaning vantage point, thought the rumors were silly. Either possibility points to the growing disconnect between rural and urban, a gulf that would continue to widen in the US over the coming decades—to explosive effect during the 2016 election.

The lack of widespread national newspaper coverage also shows that, at the time, local rumors could still remain local, even as certain elements of those rumors were stabilized nationally through broadcast news, popular movies, and high-profile court cases. Indeed, different Satanic Panics could be unfolding just a few towns apart from each other, without either town realizing another panic was happening in its own backyard. While conducting research into satanic cult abduction rumors in Jamestown, New York, for example, Victor was shocked to learn that many similar but independent rumors existed within a 250-mile radius covering western New York, northwestern Pennsylvania, and eastern Ohio.[108] Information could still remain quarantined, even as the same deep memetic frame pervaded multiple locations.

The Satanic Panics, in short, highlight a landscape with increasingly porous network boundaries. That permeability didn't stop the Far Right and the mainstream from building out their respective Galapagos Islands of communication media. For decades, they remained separated by a vast ideological gulf, and were free to cultivate their own norms. When some messages, or at least some parts of some messages, traveled upstream from the fundamentalist Right to the mainstream, it was easy enough for the mainstream to filter those messages out. They could be ignored or laughed at or sensationalized for ratings and then forgotten. The fundamentalist Right, in contrast, had always been down current from the mainstream, and had always been aware of the messages emanating from Ungodly Island; all that refuse was precisely why Evangelicals tried to bypass the mainstream's influence in the first place.

Digital networks ensure that any clear-cut separation between the mainstream and the Far Right is no longer possible. In our fully realized network crisis, filtration barriers between local and national networks, between rural and urban populations, between the pluralistic mainstream and the MAGA Right, have weakened and in some instances dissolved entirely. Informationally, the two islands now find themselves linked.

Research published by Viktor Chagas, project lead of the coLAB research group at Fluminense Federal University in Brazil, illustrates the contemporary dissolution of network barriers.[109] Chagas and his team focused on the rampant spread of polluted information via WhatsApp in 2018. They found that pollution flowed seamlessly between large, diverse Brazilian influencer networks and smaller, more homogeneous, local Brazilian networks. Using these data, Chagas and his team then mapped the Brazilian disinformation ecosystem. The results show the fundamental permeability of networks. When the information that spreads is helpful and true, free-flowing channels can be crucial. When the information is destructive and false, free-flowing channels can trigger a public health crisis.

John Podesta's supposed demonic diet, a story cherry-picked and grossly misrepresented from the 2016 WikiLeaks email dump, is a case in point. None of the lurid details were new. Podesta participated in satanic rites? *Been there.* He drank blood and semen and urine? *So eighties.* He's part of a secret cadre of devil-worshipping elites calling the shots from the shadows? *When's lunch?* We have all, deliberately or through cultural osmosis, watched this movie before. But the seamlessness with which those lurid details could travel across and between networks: *that's* what was new. The checks and barriers that had in the past generally kept this thing over here and that thing over there now carry polluted information to entirely new shores. Not every shore is blanketed evenly; that's not how pollution works. Still, as we'll see in the coming chapters, when pollution is introduced—about Clinton's satanic leanings, about secret cadres of child-molesting globalist elites within the government—those currents can be so strong that pollution can filter straight into the presidency itself.

It took some time for the Podesta allegations to travel to the center of US politics, of course. That filtration process began with the far-right conspiracy factory InfoWars, which first floated the spirit dinner story. Such a narrative fit right in with InfoWars' steady stream of refuse; in the previous month, for instance, InfoWars' host Alex Jones had asserted that Hillary Clinton, along with US president Barack Obama, was an actual demon. "And they say 'listen,'" Jones explained, "'she's a frickin' demon and she stinks and so does Obama.' I go, 'like what?' 'Sulfur. They smell like hell.'"[110] InfoWars' publication of the Podesta spirit dinner story triggered, in turn, coverage by more widely established conspiracy-adjacent outlets like the Drudge Report, which triggered even more coverage by even more established outlets like Fox News, which triggered Twitter's algorithms to push #SpiritDinner to the top of the day's trending topics list, which triggered wall-to-wall coverage by mainstream news organizations. More and more people, conservative and progressive, piled on and piled on, ensuring increasingly dizzying, and increasingly expansive, spread. The *Washington Post*, for example, doing its best to stand above the fray (but not quite succeeding), lamented, "Oh, Cool, Now the Campaign Is All about Charges of Satanism."[111]

Like the Satanic Panics, the uproar over John Podesta's unanswered email points to much larger shifts within the media climate. Thanks to all the changes—political and technological and regulatory—that began in the 1960s, there's now no longer such a thing as a purely local story. There's now no longer such a thing as geographic or ideological quarantine. The network crisis makes sure of it. The next chapter shows how quickly, and indeed how stealthily, pollution travels across all these interconnected networks of networks. It focuses in particular on what happens when the people doing the sharing have no idea that the things they're posting, remixing, commenting on, and laughing at are contaminated. This particular iteration of the Satanic Panics may have passed, but when pollution enters the system now, we all have hell to pay.

2 THE ROOT OF ALL MEMES

Very little sunlight makes it to the redwood forest floor. Even on clear days, but especially when it's cloudy, a grayness suffuses. The grayness is dark but also green. It's veiled but casts no shadow. It's a quality of light but clings to your skin, as a mist. In the grayness, in the greenness, mist melts into branch, and branch into trunk, and trunk into dirt. All pours onto the redwoods' woven roots, as much above ground as below, tangled and tumbling off the sides of embankments, jutting up from fallen old growth, crisscrossing like veins across the trail. There's a sense, in the forest, that what happens over there, beyond this tree line or gully, has everything to do with the *here* where you're standing. Biologically, it does. Dense networks of fungi and roots link this tree to that tree to another and another with such efficiency, and such robust energetic exchange, that distinguishing one tree from the next becomes mere semantics. They are, in every way that matters, the same tree. What happens right here is what happens over there. Connection to the point of unity.

The internet as we know it is designed to enable precisely the intertwine seen in the redwoods. Information seeping from here to there with ambient ease is the point; content flowing from amateurs to professionals then back again is the point; expression spanning the globe in previously unimaginable ways is the point. All the network enclosures that kept polluted deluges like the Satanic Panics relatively confined in the 1980s and 1990s have grown increasingly permeable as roots have fused with trunks have fused with branches have fused with mists. Our problem now is not that things have gone unexpectedly wrong. It's that they've gone exactly as they were designed to go—with profound consequences for how much pollution is generated, where it travels, and whom it affects.

This design is rooted in liberalism. "Liberal" in this sense does not necessarily mean "politically progressive" or "morally permissive," as the term is often used in contemporary US politics. Instead, liberalism as a political philosophy extends all the way back to the Enlightenment of the eighteenth and early nineteenth centuries and back farther still to the scientific revolutions of the sixteenth and seventeenth centuries. Claimed in different combinations by a broad range of political perspectives, liberalism enshrines individual freedoms like free speech, a free press, property rights, and civil liberties.[1] Liberalism informs libertarianism, which places particular emphasis on personal autonomy, as well as neoliberalism, which places particular emphasis on free-market capitalism.

Online, liberalism is most clearly articulated through the maxim that "information wants to be free." This sentiment reflects liberalism's staunch defense of negative personal freedoms: freedom *from* external restriction.[2] John Perry Barlow, cofounder of the Electronic Frontier Foundation, soaringly affirmed the negative freedoms of online spaces in his 1996 essay "A Declaration of the Independence of Cyberspace." Barlow's essay does exactly what its title suggests. It's *our* internet, Barlow argued; the government can jump off a cliff.

Barlow was hardly alone in his resistance to government intervention or his celebration of negative freedoms. As technology historian Steven Levy explains, freedom of information was foundational to the computer revolution of the 1960s, 1970s, and 1980s,[3] and science fiction writer Bruce Sterling proclaimed in 1993 that freedom to do as one wished was one of the main draws of the early internet.[4] Unsurprisingly, libertarianism was a dominant political philosophy among early internet adopters.

All these negative freedoms fundamentally shaped the digital landscape. First, freedom from censorship ensured that the maximum amount of information—regardless of how harmful, dehumanizing, or false—roared across the landscape. Freedom from regulation encouraged what journalism professor Meredith Broussard calls "technochauvinism," the overall sense that if something can be done, that's reason enough to do it.[5] Build the website. Share the information. Thus spoke Mark Zuckerberg: move fast and break things.[6]

This origin story is only partial, of course, a history written by the victors. As technology reporter April Glaser chronicles, Barlow's 1996 declaration was one of many network possibilities.[7] Indigenous antiglobalization activists in Mexico, for example, were simultaneously building a very different sort of digital community. They may have shared some ideals with the likes of the Electronic Frontier Foundation, but their focus was on *positive* freedoms: empowering marginalized communities for the good of the collective, not merely protecting individual rights for the benefit of those individuals. Many leftist organizers followed the same path. Liberalism's negative freedoms, however, were what attracted neoliberal entrepreneurs to the fledgling internet; communities to be cultivated became markets to be tapped.

We have the forest we have because *freedom from* won. Those who moved fast and broke things, who found increasingly ingenious ways to ensure that information wouldn't just be free but also profitable, didn't think about the toxins their social platforms might filter into the forest. Nor did they think about the toxins they themselves were spreading. In an impassioned 2019 acceptance speech for—appropriately enough—an Electronic Frontier Foundation award named after John Perry Barlow, sociologist danah boyd highlighted these toxins, particularly the industry's normalized misogyny, racial exclusion, and tolerance of sexual predators. "These are the toxic logics that have infested the tech industry," boyd stated. "And, as an industry obsessed with scale, these are the toxic logics that the tech industry has amplified and normalized."[8]

Decision makers within the tech sector aren't the only contributors to the internet's polluted outcomes; the millions of its early adopters who structured their lives around the jubilant cry *don't ever tell me what to do* also sidestepped the toxins they carried. Neither group thought about the ecological consequences of their actions, because they didn't have to. They were positioned behind a set of deep memetic frames that kept them safe, happy, and utterly oblivious as pollution coursed through the forest's roots.

One of these frames was the *white racial frame*, which allowed participants to—among other things—heed Barlow's utterly Cartesian proclamation that the internet is the "new home of Mind" and that cyberspace "is not where bodies live."[9] Any harassment directed at people of color, any hate speech, any harm, that wasn't *real*, it was just the internet—an easy thing to say when you're not the one being targeted.

Another frame poisoning the forest was *fetishized sight*. As in our previous work, we use the term *fetishization* to label the tendency during online interaction to fixate on the object you're looking at—just the GIF you're sharing, just the post you're reading, just the tweet you're replying to—without considering the very real people represented in or producing or affected by those objects.[10] When everything is flattened to pixels on the screen, it's easy to forget the people standing behind those pixels, how being flattened might hurt them, and how our everyday actions might make that hurt worse. Fetishization, as we will see, is supercharged by the white racial frame, and the white racial frame is supercharged by fetishization.

Tangled up with both frames is what came to be known as "internet culture." A jumble of sites, memes, and aesthetics that exploded to prominence in the mid- to late aughts, this culture maintained close ties to the tech sector and was a product of liberalism through and through. Its emphasis on fun and funny negative freedoms—share that meme, troll that stranger, joke about Hitler, *it's your right*—downplayed the destructive, antidemocratic, and deeply polluted dimensions of fetishized sight. Its adherence to the white racial frame muted diverse ideas and experiences, erroneously claiming online spaces for white people, and in particular white men, whose centrality was taken as a given.

The compounding myopias of content producers, platform designers, and everyday social media users—each tapping into the roots of all the others—normalized a deeply detached, deeply ironic rhetorical style that created space for white supremacist violence to flourish a half-decade later. It also silenced the alarms being raised by the people who didn't just see the poisons bubbling up, but were themselves being poisoned, and who cried for help but were ignored—or were punished for their effort.

The political and ethical failures at the heart of so-called internet culture makes tracing its roots uncomfortable. And we mean personally uncomfortable. The two of us were ourselves part of that culture, as were many of our friends and colleagues. We all bear responsibility, and all must face what boyd describes as a "great reckoning" for the toxicity we collectively helped normalize.[11] This toxicity wasn't restricted to our own insular circles. Instead it helped wedge open the Overton window—the norms of acceptable public discourse—just enough for bigots to shimmy through in 2016. Their deluge of hate, falsehood, and conspiracy theory ripped the walls right off. But first came the absurdist, loud, silly fun that flourished a decade before. The pollution cast off by all that fun percolated underground, intensifying with each passing year. It may have emerged unnoticed by many. Ultimately it was felt by all.

INTERNET CULTURE, OR HOW WE FED THE FETISHISTIC GNARL

At first glance, the term "internet culture" seems like it should be highly inclusive. Based on the assumption that internet culture is, well, culture on the internet, what on the internet *wouldn't* be internet culture? That broad sense of the term, however, wasn't the one that emerged in the mid-2000s to describe the slew of remixed jokes, jargon, and folk art occurring on sites like Something Awful, 4chan, and eventually Reddit and Tumblr.

We say "sense of the term" rather than "definition" because internet culture was never fully defined, not exactly. The people creating and remixing all that content certainly talked about a thing called "internet culture." But just as often, they called it "meme culture" or even just "The Internet," without explaining what they meant. These same people—many of whom called themselves "internet people"—explicitly and enthusiastically identified with it and actively contributed to it, with *it* best summarized by a shrugged "I know it when I see it." Even researchers who studied this *it* could waffle on the name and description. In a 2012 article coauthored with fellow internet researcher Kate Miltner, for example, Phillips blithely described the *it* as "early meme/ROFL/internet culture whatever."[12] Here we've settled on "internet culture," because that was the term we encountered most often.

No matter what they labeled it, internet culture participants sorted themselves into a highly insular clique, with a highly recognizable aesthetic. In addition to embracing fetishized sight and irony as a mode of being, members echoed a familiar set of attitudes. The internet was a cordoned-off playpen that severed memes from consequences. All these memes were free to spread widely and *should* be free to spread widely; if you didn't like something, you should just log off (also lol it's just the internet). Being able to do or make or mock something was justification enough. Even participants who had little sense of what liberalism was—other than being broadly in favor of their own free speech—drew from and reinforced centuries-old liberal roots.

Internet People, Internet Ugly

The most basic feature of internet culture was the people who embraced it. This included, first, everyday meme enthusiasts active on popular platforms like 4chan, Reddit, and YouTube. Meme enthusiasts employed by media and entertainment platforms like Urlesque, BuzzFeed, Gawker, Rocketboom, and Know Your Meme formed a crucial subsection of this group. Another group comprised employees of the social platforms that internet culture depended on, as well as people working for social-media-savvy marketing and advertising agencies like the Barbarian Group and Wieden+Kennedy. Rounding out these prominent early adopters were academics at institutions like MIT, Harvard, and NYU, which were home base for many internet people and actively supported conferences and talks related to internet culture.

The boundary between these groups was highly permeable; members of one group often knew members of other groups personally, professionally, or both. Phillips, for her part, was friends with a number of people within the BuzzFeed / Know Your Meme orbit, which introduced her to other media and entertainment circles, which looped back around to the academic circles Milner traveled in. People also frequently moved between groups, like those who started graduate school after working for media and entertainment companies or those who got jobs at social platforms after finishing their PhDs.

The preeminent internet culture conference, ROFLCon, epitomized this blur. It was held in 2008, 2010, and 2012 at MIT, with additional off-year summits in New York City and Portland, Oregon; Phillips was a conference attendee in 2010 and 2011 and a speaker in 2012. The overwhelming majority of its organizers were students affiliated with MIT or Harvard; attendees included everyday meme enthusiasts, largely students from Boston-area universities, and media and tech sector professionals. The Barbarian Group sponsored the first ROFLCon in 2008, Wieden+Kennedy sponsored the Portland summit in 2011, and Harvard's Berkman Klein Center for Internet and Society sponsored the 2012 conference.

And then there were the trolls. In contemporary parlance, "trolling" is used as a blanket label for just about any undesirable thing someone could do or say, from being an ass on Facebook to being a bigot in person. Back then, the term wasn't such a broad catchall.[13] The trolling that overlapped with internet culture traces back to 2003, when an American fifteen-year-old named Christopher "moot" Poole created a simple image board called 4chan. Although the online sense of the term *troll* long predates 4chan, it took on a newfound and highly specific meaning as more and more participants, particularly on 4chan's /b/ (or "random") board, began calling themselves trolls and behaving in highly recognizable, highly idiosyncratic ways. After incubating for a few years, subcultural trolling enjoyed a golden age from about 2008 to 2012, the same as internet culture more broadly—a parallel that derived, most basically, from just how seamlessly trolling subculture fed into internet culture writ large.

This tangle is illustrated most clearly by the fact that Poole helped organize the ROFLCon series and spoke on several ROFLCon panels throughout the conference's four-year run. True to trollish form, Poole's "ROFLTeam" profile image in 2010 and 2012 featured a Black man— Poole is white—wearing a leather jacket, holding a lightsaber, and standing in someone's messy living room. Beneath the photo, the caption reads, "Moot Mootkins is part of the ROFLTeam. He is a motherfucker."[14] The line references the then-popular "Epic Beard Man" meme, which was based on cell phone footage posted to YouTube then shared on 4chan. In the video, an older, white, bearded man clad in a shirt reading "I am a motherfucker" violently assaults a Black man.

Poole's invocation of Epic Beard Man was indicative, not just for the racist wink of the joke. One of the most basic markers of subcultural trolling during this time was the incessant creation and circulation of internet memes. As danah boyd explains, 4chan's design primed it to become internet culture's first meme factory.[15] Because Poole didn't have enough server space for everything being uploaded to 4chan's various boards, he built the site so that it would delete older posts to make room for new ones. Users were frustrated when their favorite content would disappear, so they would frequently repost images, often after altering them slightly.

4chan's content didn't stay confined to 4chan. Instead the memes enjoyed by trolls and the memes enjoyed by broader internet culture were strikingly symbiotic. Several factors contributed to this blur. First and foremost, the memes emerging from internet culture circles often *were* trolling memes, created and spread by trolls on 4chan. Either the trolls themselves were publicizing their own content off-site, or the trolls' work resonated strongly with 4chan's more casual visitors, who carried the memes beyond the site's borders. Poole spoke to this dynamic during a 2010 ROFLCon panel titled "Mainstreaming the Web," asserting, uncontested, that 4chan created the memes that everyone else on the panel—including representatives from internet culture hotbeds like Know Your Meme and the Cheezburger Network—studied, collated, and profited from.[16]

Even when memes hadn't originated on 4chan, the aesthetic overlap between trolling subculture and internet culture was so pronounced that a meme from one could easily be mistaken for a meme from the other. They looked the same and did the same things with the same sense of humor.

Nick Douglas, a blogger who has written for internet culture publications like Urlesque, the Daily Dot, and Gawker, calls this unifying aesthetic "Internet Ugly."[17] As the moniker suggests, Internet Ugly is a "celebration of the sloppy and the amateurish" and describes apparent aesthetic misfires like rough editing, bad grammar, and a whole lot of shaky, freehand mouse drawing.[18] The title of Douglas's article on the subject, "It's Supposed to Look like Shit," pretty much sums it up.

Like boyd, Douglas traces the rise of Internet Ugly to 4chan's platform architecture.[19] Because threads on 4chan were deleted so quickly, sometimes within minutes, posters needed to act fast. The images posted quickly enough to be seen by others tended to be the most haphazard, slapdash, and outrageously non sequitur. Polished work, "good" work, simply took too long. As more and more people inside and outside 4chan replicated the aesthetic, the logistic necessity of Internet Ugly gave way to an established social norm. It entered the taproot of the network.

In a 2013 PBS *Idea Channel* video, Mike Rugnetta elaborates on the Internet Ugly aesthetic, which he christens "glitchy art."[20] For Rugnetta, the popularity of "malfunction-esque" content could be attributed, at least in part, to millennial nostalgia. As he explains, the technologies that kids (some kids, anyway) played with in the late 1980s and early 1990s, including 8-bit sound and video, magnetic tapes, and VCRs, were often unreliable and unpredictable. The resulting "ballet of mistakes" at the core of the busted-media look, Rugnetta argues, "sends you, or me at least, careening back to childhood." The implication is that internet culture's affection for weird, broken, ugly shit stems, perhaps counterintuitively, from comforting warm fuzzies.

Douglas similarly links Internet Ugly to personal experience.[21] When internet people reacted with nostalgic glee or absurdist delight (or both) to Internet Ugly, or when they fell back on the "I know it when I see it" explanation, those reactions were a knowing wink, one that communicated "I am one of you; I am aware of all internet traditions." Laughter was, by extension, an act of "laughing with," performing for an audience who understood and appreciated a given message and were able to reciprocate in kind—not just by laughing back but by sharing their own absurdist fun.

As much as internet culture participants *laughed with* one another, however, they also *laughed at* others. The weaponization of laughter was most apparent on 4chan's /b/, championed by participants—and by Chris Poole—as a free speech stronghold. Activity on /b/ could be so outrageous, so disruptive, and so aggressively transgressive that digital media scholar

Finn Brunton described the board in 2011 as "the most broadly offensive artifact that has ever been produced in the history of human media."[22] Anthropologist Gabriella Coleman likewise highlights the offensiveness of the site, adding that trolling subculture was replete with "terrifying" and "hellish" elements, particularly when trolls used what they called "life-ruining tactics" to terrorize their targets for months or even years on end.[23] As Phillips recounts, these same trolls regularly framed their activity as a kind of public service, one that helped protect, of course, free speech (exactly how this worked was never made clear). Trolls also claimed that their attacks encouraged people to think more critically, an outcome they prodded along by taunting, gaslighting, and deceiving targets. Many joked that they deserved a thank-you for their efforts.[24]

Although their targets could be quite diverse—at the time, trolls gleefully singled out women, progressives, and people of color, as well as Republicans, Christians, and white people generally[25]—trolling participants were unified by a particular kind of laughter. Described by trolls as "lulz," this laughter celebrated their targets' distress while simultaneously policing the boundaries between *us* and *them*. The trolling *us* laughed. The targeted *them* did not.

Trolls may have been especially ruthless in their attacks. Their laughter may have been especially loud, and their understanding of free speech especially myopic. However, the pursuit of lulz was endemic to broader internet culture. Exemplifying this register was the common call to "learn how to internet." Learning how to internet meant knowing how to replicate or at least decode the internet culture aesthetic, to respond to memes "correctly," and, most important of all, to not take anything too seriously. The result was to cleave the *us* who knew how to internet, who got the jokes, who responded to things with a troll face, from the *them* who didn't or couldn't or wouldn't. For internet people, feeling distressed online—because someone saw something unseeable, because someone clicked a link they shouldn't have, because someone fed the trolls—was a self-inflicted wound. Certainly not something to start censoring platforms over; that would ruin everything.

Douglas emphasizes the boundary policing behind "learning how to internet" in his discussion of "fail content,"[26] a staple of Internet Ugly that highlights mistakes, bad ideas, and anyone accused of fucking something up. The laughter generated by fail content was directed at unfortunate souls on the other side of the *us/them* line, either because they were the supposed fuck ups, or because they were clueless outsiders who didn't get the joke. A related target of uproarious derision was "bad" media. Phillips describes this derision by using the Japanese word *kuso*, which loosely translates into "ha ha, awesome, this is terrible."[27] The *kuso* response accompanies a range of content, Phillips writes, from poorly executed images to glitch art remixes of videos from the 1980s and 1990s to "the online obsession with failure generally, which worships at the altar of ineptitude and technological incompetence."[28] Very often, *kuso* responses were framed as a strange sort of fandom. The laughing *us* didn't hate the thing they were actively mocking; they loved it—never mind that proclamations like "I sure enjoy reveling in your humiliation" aren't exactly compliments. That, of course, didn't matter to the *us*. They could point and laugh, and that freedom was reason enough to do it.

Bringing Fetishized Sight into Focus

Whether internet people talked about *kuso*, Internet Ugly, or lulz, whether they were malicious or jovial, the result of their fun was to flatten wholes into parts; all the surrounding context might as well not have existed (to them, anyway). Fetishized sight was so pervasive within these circles that it constituted a deep memetic frame; it made the world make sense to those seeing through it.

The act of cleaving digital text from broader context is, on one level, a feature of online play, reflective of the affordances of digital media. *Affordances* are simply what technologies allow people to do with them; they're why people do what they do, because that's what they *can* do. Most basically, digital media allow people to alter, edit, and remix content; manipulate parts of that content without disrupting the original; and save, store, and easily access the content later.[29] The result is decontextualization: stuff that's not connected to where it originated or what it started out as.

The simple fact that these actions can be undertaken and therefore are undertaken is not what creates fetishized sight. For the frame to flourish, a number of additional factors must converge. One of the most critical is the sharing imperative: that social media companies encourage their users to post, comment on, and generally spread as much content to as many people as possible. As media scholar Siva Vaidhyanathan argues, this impulse is quite literally coded into platform design.[30] When bad information ends up mixing in with the good, the directive from corporate headquarters is not to quiet down and proceed with caution. It's to post even *more* information as a corrective. This remained Mark Zuckerberg's rallying cry straight through 2019, when, during a speech at Georgetown University, he doubled down on what Vaidhyanathan describes as his company's "nineteenth century view of speech."[31] More memes, more comments, more pixels on the screen, faster and faster, across and between an ever-widening vortex of participants free to duke it out to their hearts' content—democracy in action, right?

Maybe for some. Others, who find themselves trampled and dehumanized as a result, employ a different calculus informed by different frames. In her 2019 Electronic Frontier Foundation award speech, danah boyd lamented everything the tech sector lost by refusing to give these others—women and people of color and gender-nonconforming people and disabled people—a seat at the user design table.[32] Those who were at that table, particularly as internet culture blossomed, were overwhelmingly white, male, and upwardly mobile. Historically, that's the demographic least likely to experience persistent, coordinated abuse, certainly not by reactionary bigots or violent misogynists. Consequently, the lead developers and top managers at social media companies didn't have much reason to scan the forest for these specific risks. They had the luxury of emphasizing freedom *from* over freedom *for*.

As a consequence, rather than building platforms that protected users against the dangers of fetishized sight, and rather than seeking out, listening to, and learning from people who had been targeted, these developers and top managers built platforms that *streamlined* fetishized sight and encoded their own myopic frames into user experience. In short, because they only saw versions of themselves, only listened to versions of themselves, and only respected the experiences of versions of themselves, they all but invited the deluge of abuse, harassment, and manipulation that was soon to overrun their sites—a deluge they never saw coming, because they didn't think they needed to look.

Assessing the platform's long-standing failures to curb abuse and harassment, Twitter's cofounder Ev Williams admits as much. "Had I been more aware of how people not like me were being treated and/or had I had a more diverse leadership team or board," he explains, "we may have made it a priority sooner."[33] Charlie Warzel, writing for *BuzzFeed News*, further links Twitter's "abiding commitment to free speech above all else" with the homogeneity of the company's top decision makers. As one former senior employee told Warzel, "The original sin is a homogeneous leadership. This is part of what exacerbated the abuse problem for sure—because they were often tone-deaf to the concern of users in the outside world, meaning women and people of color."[34] Tarleton Gillespie echoes a similar point in his study of how platform moderation policies shape social media. Many of the platform designers he interviewed were surprised by the levels of hatred and obscenity that so quickly overtook the networks they had created.[35] They assumed, as one content policy manager explained, that the people using the sites would be like them, and designed their policies and tools accordingly.

Internet culture—and all the *kuso*, Internet Ugly, and lulz it incubated—grew out of this myopia. The resulting jokes and fun and jargon were *just* jokes and *just* fun and *just* jargon with few consequences for the internet culture clique. Grinning, clueless participants who had learned how to internet got to flatten entire lives into dehumanizing memes. They got to reduce misfortune, pain, and tragedy to lulzy punch lines. They got to comfortably cavort within a smug, self-satisfied *us*.

And by *they*, of course, we mean *we*.

In our early work, especially when we were graduate students, we were absolutely, undeniably guilty of seeing the world with fetishized sight. We didn't know each other yet—we wouldn't be introduced until 2012, after we'd both received our PhDs—but we got the same things wrong, evidencing our shared standpoint behind that frame.

For Milner, fetishized sight came in the form of a permissive attitude toward the jagged edge of the visual internet, itself a reflection of liberal assumptions about the inherent democratic good of unrestricted speech. As he wrote his dissertation on internet memes in 2011, Milner paid little attention to the very real people represented in the images he was including in its pages. He dropped in pictures of children in their homes, activists at protests, and "fail" after "fail" without ever stopping to think about how the people he included might feel about snapshot moments of their complex lives being enshrined in the academic pantheon for time eternal. He never asked anyone's permission to let Google Scholar catalog and index that one time some kid fell off a trampoline, maybe breaking their leg, maybe bankrupting their parents. Who knows, who cares; the GIF was funny. "It's already on the internet," Milner said with a shrug. "It's already public data." Years later, a reviewer called him out for treating people like pixels, cautioning him to carefully weigh the costs and benefits of what he amplified. His immediate reaction was to get defensive. "Progress at any *cost*," he bellowed, until he heard himself say that out loud, stopped, and said, "I guess I hadn't thought of that before."

For Phillips, fetishized sight came in the form of a permissive attitude toward the concept of harm on the internet, itself a reflection of John Perry Barlow–esque assumptions about online disembodiment: the internet was not where the body lived. Not only *could* you separate who people were offline from what they did online, but you *should* consider any bad behavior online in the context of subcultural norms. Trolls were playing a role, duh; that play was the thing to focus on. For example, as Phillips began working on a journal article about trolling on 4chan in 2009, she included example after example of trolls' attacks, including their "jokes" about pedophilia, without reflecting on the embodied harm the trolls' actions cause, or the fact that their "jokes" were based on all-too-real traumas. For her, these aggressions were just subcultural play, just trolls being trolls. Violence was an object of research interest, not something to worry about amplifying. One of the article's reviewers critiqued her on that point, reminding her that pedophilia was not a funny joke on the internet; it destroyed lives, and further, attitudes like hers were what helped normalize violence. Like Milner, her immediate reaction was to get defensive. "Normalizing violence, that's stupid, I'm a *folklorist*," she snorted as her face grew hot, which at first she thought was anger, then realized was embarrassment. She also hadn't thought of that before.

We should have thought of that before. We should have seen the embodied consequences of what we shared without having to be told. That we didn't is a personal failing. It also reflects something bigger: that we were seeing what our accepted frames encouraged us to see. Or encouraged us *not* to see, as was more often the case. We were far from alone in that myopia. What we missed, what so many other people missed, and more importantly *why* we missed it, emerged from something deeper than the digital tools we were using and deeper than the platforms we were posting on. Our fetishized sight emerged from yet another outcropping of liberalism and the Enlightenment before that: structural white supremacy. Or described another way, freedom for white people: white lives, white liberty, and the pursuit of white happiness at the expense of everyone else.

The extraordinary freedoms of whiteness, our own very much included, didn't just allow pollution to seep into the public square. The freedoms of whiteness rendered that pollution invisible to the people peering out through the internet's most carefree frame.

THE UNBEARABLE WHITENESS OF INTERNET CULTURE

As our burgeoning cast of characters so far attests, the *what's what* and *who's who* of internet culture was as much about bodies in the world as it was about pixels on the screen. All those pixels would not have been represented, remixed, and mocked as they were without all those bodies doing the fetishizing. The resulting fun, or at least what seemed like fun for the people in on the joke, muted some while amplifying others, further entrenching the line between the *us* who laughed and the *them* who did not. Whiteness snaked across all of it, leaching assumptions, minimizations, and subtle (and sometimes not so subtle) aggressions into the root system.

Muted Bodies, Muted Groups

In some ways, the demographics of early internet culture were straightforward: the people who participated in, studied, and otherwise policed the boundaries of "The Internet" were overwhelmingly white and majority male. The actual internet has, of course, never been exclusively or inherently white. In 2013, for example, as internet culture began to catapult into the mainstream, the Pew Research Center reported that people of color were marginally *more* likely to use social media than white folks.[36] Whiteness as default, however, was baked into the "internet culture" narrative. It was the unexamined *us* against which all other people, and all other forms of expression, were measured.

ROFLCon is a case in point, both for how it reinforced the white majority and for the ambivalence at the core of that majority. Throughout the conference's multiyear run, attendees skewed *very* white and *very* male, a point that ROFLCon's founders Tim Hwang and Christina Xu admit somewhat sheepishly in a 2014 interview with the *Journal of Visual Culture*.[37] This imbalance existed even though the ROFLCon organizing committee was racially diverse and in some years supermajority female. The question was, Why? What accounted for the striking difference between conference organizers and conference attendees?

Xu pins the discrepancy on the stereotypes tangled up with early internet culture, which equated being computer savvy with being a straight white dude. As she explains, unless you actively describe a space as being for "girl geeks" or "Black nerds," those groups won't think the space is for them and consequently won't come to your event. Assumptions about who and what counted, and therefore who and what belonged, influenced the *we* the conference indirectly constructed. This *we*, in turn, played an implicit game of boundary policing. Excluded most stringently, even if inadvertently, was content popular within Black communities, which ROFLCon all but ignored in 2008 and 2010.[38] "It's not the internet culture I grew up on," Xu admits of Black memes and influencers; "but that doesn't make it not a part of it."[39] This realization, Xu says, prompted ROFLCon organizers to take more active steps in 2012 to emphasize inclusiveness.[40]

Still, the overall issue persisted. Conference attendees remained overwhelmingly white, and the whiteness of internet culture remained a normative default. ROFLCon 2012's "Choose Your Own Adventure" event program booklet, for instance, paired conference panel descriptions with related campy 8-bit stock images of people sitting at computers and generally having fun. Tellingly, throughout the ninety-five-page program, there wasn't a single pixelated figure obviously of color.[41] Maybe this was meant to be an ironic send-up of the (presumed) homogeneity of internet culture. No matter the motive, the art, like so much else about the conference series, signaled that white attendees were the welcomed, privileged *us* and everyone else was the invisible, second-class *them*. There was nothing surprising about the resulting conference demographics.

As Xu's admission about ROFLCon's *we* underscores, issues of inclusiveness (or lack thereof) were bigger than the conference itself. The problem exemplifies, instead, the pervasive, unexamined whiteness—and very often default maleness—at the core of internet culture. Race and technology scholar André Brock's 2012 study of Black Twitter highlights that default.[42] Writing concurrently to the ROFLCon series, Brock chronicled how Black Twitter then—just like Black Twitter now—was buzzing with memes and jokes and was every bit the generator of internet culture that "internet culture" was. But, Brock explained, unlike what white folks were doing online, what Black folks were doing wasn't granted legitimacy, if it was noticed at all, by the mostly white, mostly male gatekeepers laying claim to "The Internet."[43] One of the specific gatekeepers Brock cited in his 2012 piece was none other than Internet Ugly's own Nick Douglas, who in 2009 contrasted how Black people use Twitter with the "correct" ways "normal" people use Twitter. For Douglas, Brock explained, "normal people" translated to "white guys with collars and spelling."[44]

Feminist and critical race scholars have long underscored Brock's point.[45] So have scholars who study internet cultures outside the United States.[46] As these scholars attest—along with an entire subdiscipline of scholars focused on online communities in North America—queer people, people of color, and indigenous people have gifted digital spaces with boundless creativity, ingenuity, and playfulness.[47] Even when, as Brock explains of Twitter, they're using a technology "that wasn't originally designed for us."[48]

That these stories and these researchers are frequently omitted from what white scholars call "internet culture" is one more example of how underrepresented groups are culturally muted. For decades, communication research has emphasized the pervasiveness of such omissions in offline spaces.[49] People from underrepresented backgrounds have always had things to say, and have often put themselves at great risk to speak. But historically they've struggled to find a broader audience. That is, they've struggled to find white people willing to take a few steps back and hand over the microphone—or even just to listen.

To this point, Black feminists Moya Bailey and Trudy underscore the frequency with which Black women in particular are erased, ignored, and plagiarized online.[50] They call this phenomenon *misogynoir*: anti-Black misogyny, a term they coined in 2008, for which they regularly go uncredited. That Black people, and Black women in particular, have been erased *and* plagiarized is a paradox as old as America. Commenting on the frequency with which white people have come to appropriate Black Twitter's jokes, memes, and slang, critical race scholar Meredith Clark zooms out to the much broader historical pattern. "Black culture has been actively mined for hundreds of years for influences on mainstream American culture,"[51] she states; the insult of plagiarism only deepens the injury of muting.

The muting and appropriation that pervade online spaces, both within internet culture and more broadly, are the result of what social theorist Joe R. Feagin calls the white racial frame: a fetishistic worldview that normalizes the oppressions of people of color.[52] While the white racial frame often manifests as outright prejudice, discrimination, and racist violence, it's also an everyday mental tool kit for navigating the world, one that privileges white bodies and white lives over the bodies and lives of people who aren't white. Muting is one of the many actions within this frame that's not obviously or physically violent but still enacts symbolic violence.[53] Violence is still violence—still dehumanizing, still marginalizing, still harmful—whether symbolic or physical. The difference is that symbolic violence can be, and frequently is, perpetuated by people who replicate racist frames without ever considering themselves racist, and indeed, who might out-right denounce racism.[54]

Media scholar Richard Dyer explains how the white racial frame is reinforced symbolically through images and ideas.[55] For Dyer, whiteness is, obviously, a skin color. Beyond that, something can be socially white or representationally white, whiteness can be a characteristic of people and texts, and it can broadly be considered a quality.

According to Dyer, the first marker of symbolic whiteness is that it establishes and jealously guards its own centrality, a point underscoring sociologist Tressie McMillan Cottom's observation that whiteness defends itself against a whole host of truths.[56] Second, whiteness asserts power and control to maintain that centrality. Third, whiteness separates the lived experiences of the body from the abstract ideas of the mind, in the process downplaying the embodied consequences of whiteness. Together, these tactics reinforce structural white supremacy. They're how white people have for centuries kept themselves in positions of power and privilege.

Online, the white racial frame likewise keeps whiteness the default center and norm. It enables white folks to pick and choose whom and what they pay attention to, to assume speech always works for the good (meaning *their* good), and to fetishize the nonwhite *them* for the benefit of the white *us*. And more often than not, white people are oblivious to all of it. They might not be the only group in the forest; indeed, they might be a minority in the forest. But the whole forest still feels the effects of their whiteness.

Whiteness in the Meme Factory

The subcultural trolling that flourished during the aughts perfectly entwines fetishized sight and the white racial frame. The connections are so complete that Dyer's characteristics of symbolic whiteness are exactingly, even uncannily, replicated within early trolling norms. Trolls vigorously and often violently maintained the centrality of whiteness on 4chan's /b/ board. They reveled in asserting control over others through off-site raids and on-site boundary policing. They erased their own embodied experiences by obsessively maintaining their own anonymity—while at the same time abstracting the violence they committed against others as a fun, consequence-free source of lulz.

If a clear barrier separated subcultural trolling and internet culture, these critiques would begin and end with the trolls themselves. That, however, is not how the forest works. Instead, the two sets of roots are tangled, with widespread consequences for the surrounding grove. A MemeFactory showcase, hosted by NYU on October 9, 2009, and then uploaded to Vimeo, epitomizes how seamlessly the fun of early internet culture gnarled up with trollish fetishization, and how seamlessly fetishization gnarled up with the white racial frame. It also illustrates the crucial role that laughter plays in sustaining deep memetic frames and in spreading pollution far and wide.

MemeFactory was a performance trio featuring Stephen Bruckert, Patrick Davison, and Mike Rugnetta, the eventual host of *Idea Channel*; Davison and Rugnetta also wrote for Know Your Meme. Like Know Your Meme, MemeFactory sought to archive internet culture for internet people and translate popular memes for audiences outside the esoteric forums and niche networks where the memes were created. MemeFactory's highly choreographed, highly energetic live shows featured internet memes projected rapid-fire onto three separate screens. At times, text appeared on one screen to comment on the images featured on the other screens, or to undercut something Bruckert, Davison, and Rugnetta were saying. The result was dizzying and perfectly replicated the glitchy, ugly, breakneck, and, of course, lulzy feel of internet culture.

Unsurprisingly, many of the images featured in MemeFactory's NYU performance originated on 4chan. Some were flagged as trolling memes, but many were not. Bruckert, Davison, and Rugnetta also spent a great deal of time discussing the ins and outs of 4chan, its various boards, and its decree that nothing should be taken seriously. As within internet culture more broadly, trolling played a foundational part in the show.

Unlike 4chan's trolls, the MemeFactory performance didn't outwardly weaponize or revel in the traps of whiteness. However, those traps were still scattered throughout. In the intervening decade, Bruckert, Davison, and Rugnetta—all of whom are white—have reconsidered many of the assumptions they once made about the impact, politics, and ethics of memes. Davison, for instance, told us that he "CRINGED" (caps lock his) when he reread the research he'd done during his MemeFactory years.[57] In that research and more broadly in his life, he explained that he was content to "bull-china-shop through issues of image-based sexual violence, of racism both implicit and explicit, as well as tons of other terrible mindsets." Davison did not mince words in explaining why. "My social and political irresponsibility come from having been a cis white middle class dude in his mid-20s, plain and simple," he said. "I was an incredible embodiment of privilege at the time."

Thinking back on his own MemeFactory experience, Rugnetta echoed Davison's all-caps CRINGE.[58] "When MemeF (and even Know Your Meme, depending) comes up now," Rugnetta told us, "I want to gesture to all my current work as a way of saying OK BUT IT'S DIFFERENT NOW"—a reflection of the fact that in the years after MemeFactory, Rugnetta turned a pointedly critical eye toward internet culture, trolling very much included, through his work on *Idea Channel*. Bruckert, too, looks back with deep discomfort, noting how his assumption at the time— that lampooning white supremacy would weaken white supremacy—only outfitted white supremacists with the plausible deniability of "just trolling."[59] He recalls satirically pantomiming bigoted ideologies in MemeFactory performances, Stephen Colbert–style, to show how ridiculous and wrong those ideologies are. The problem was that those jokes often failed as jokes and in their overarching mission. They just reinscribed the bigotries they had set out to critique, and spread them to new audiences.

It's not that Bruckert, Davison, and Rugnetta were wholly unaware of the problems pervading early internet culture during MemeFactory's heyday. As Davison explained to us, the trio did think about the impact and content of their shows, and they did have an ethics. The issue, he observed wryly, was that it was a "*naive and myopic*" ethics (italics his).[60] Rugnetta underscored this point, telling us that he assumed the MemeFactory audience *knew* what the bad things were. He also assumed that the people targeted by the most harmful memes would understand their intentions, which were not to hurt anybody. They shared the bad things because they had a responsibility to tell the truth about internet culture.

It was in this spirit that the MemeFactory trio offered a disclaimer at the outset of their 2009 NYU performance, acknowledging that the show would feature a great deal of racism, sexism, homophobia, and violence. They did not condone any of it, they explained. But they had to include it, because that's what the internet is; pretending otherwise would be to misrepresent the culture. The presentation then proceeded to mix all that racism, sexism, homophobia, and violence in among a deluge of more innocuous, absurd, and often laugh-out-loud funny memes. So many images were flying across the screen, so many ironic captions were clattering against whatever was being said, and so much laughter was echoing across the auditorium, that it was difficult to zero in on any one meme, let alone form a critical response to any of them.

The argument that you risk misrepresenting a culture if you don't illuminate its harms dovetails with the assumption that, in order to understanding something, you have to hold it up to the light and properly dissect it. At the time, these assertions were common within internet research circles. For some, they remain common, an extension of even deeper liberal ideas about free-flowing information and unrestricted speech. Bad speech isn't the real danger, the argument goes. Censoring bad speech is. Similarly, ignoring the harms inherent to a particular culture means having less robust, less accurate, and less valuable discussions about that culture.

The basic sentiments might be true; how could a person talk about the harms of trolling, for instance, without talking about trolling itself? However, when all that harm is publicized as it's analyzed, and more importantly *laughed at* as it's analyzed, the argument becomes a tougher sell. It also becomes a tougher sell when considering the experiences and basic sense of safety of the people whose bodies are being targeted. Accurately representing a culture might be the goal. However, when that culture pushes already marginalized people farther to the margins, clinical analyses risk replicating the same marginalizations and contributing to a public square where fewer people feel safe and are safe. All because their bodies and comfort and overall wellness matter less than clinical accuracy.

One segment of the MemeFactory performance epitomized this myopia and the white racial frame at its core. It featured the "O RLY" meme, which originated on 4chan in 2005 with an image of a screeching snowy owl, captioned with the letters "O RLY?" (shorthand for "oh really?"). As memes do, the O RLY owl inspired countless variations. At the NYU show, a number of examples flashed rapid-fire across the screen, including a black owl captioned with the phrase "NGA RLY." The crowd roared with laughter. Just as suddenly as it appeared, the image was replaced with another, and then another, and then another, as unmoored pixels flew everywhere, here and then gone and then onto the next bit of fun.

Watching this 2009 moment ten years later was jarring. Not because the MemeFactory performance was unique in its juxtaposition of fun memes and dehumanizing memes. Recall, for instance, how 4chan's Chris Poole casually referenced the racist Epic Beard Man meme in his ROFL-Team profile page. As was so common within internet culture circles at the time, violence against a Black body was just another funny ROFLCon joke, a barely registered shrug, even with Harvard sponsoring the conference.[61]

Nor was the MemeFactory "O RLY" moment unique in its universalization of a white *us*, epitomized by a room full of mostly white college students laughing uproariously because that picture up there, did you see it, it made the black owl say the N-word lol. How it might feel for a Black person to sit in that auditorium and be inundated by laughter directed quite literally at blackness, how it might feel to be reminded that the N-word is a hilarious punch line to lots of white people, was not part of that discussion.

Indeed, what was most jarring about this moment was that it *wasn't* unique. What was jarring was thinking back and remembering how common that kind of imagery and those kinds of reactions were at the time (like when Phillips attended a MemeFactory performance in person in 2010 and laughed so hard she cried). Those images and reactions weren't a bug in the MemeFactory performance; they were a feature of internet culture. They certainly were a feature of our early research. In public presentations she gave between 2008 and 2010, Phillips would regularly include similarly jarring juxtapositions in her slides. She didn't include those images to be provocative. She included them because she *didn't* think they were provocative. She, like the MemeFactory trio, assumed that everybody knew that racism was bad, so if you saw something racist, then it was obviously satire. And if it was satire, then what harm could it possibly do to surface it, or even laugh at it? Anyway, it was normal to collapse terrible things with funny things, that was just how the internet was, and I'm here to tell you about the internet, why are you looking at me like that?

For Milner, the same juxtapositions were front and center in his 2012 dissertation. Many of the images he chose to analyze were explicitly racist or sexist and often appeared on the same page as funny animal pictures and non sequitur absurdities. Sometimes Milner would comment on that racism or sexism, but all too often he would ignore it to focus on what *really* fascinated him, because look at how the position of the captions in figure 2.1 creates a visual ellipsis, thus indicating a punch line, isn't that *cool*? That's what memes were to him: just academic abstractions, just points of clinical interest. Racism was a by-product of the shock humor, not something his white body ever had to worry about.

Plus, Milner figured, echoing a point Rugnetta raised when reflecting on his MemeFactory days, the whole reason to do this work was to show how important internet culture was, to prove to his colleagues and classmates and uncles at Thanksgiving that memes were worthy of study. For Milner and Rugnetta, taking seriously the ugliness of so many memes risked—in their minds, anyway—undermining the claim that memes mattered. And so they foregrounded the beauty of the collaboration and the creativity and, as Rugnetta explained, "the potential (utopian only, please) futures this activity might suggest."[62] The resulting defense, Rugnetta continued, could be summarized as "I mean yeah some of it is racist but like, OTHER THAN THAT, how great is it?"

When confronted by all this racism, Milner in turn defaulted to the same disclaimer included at the start of the MemeFactory performance. Analyzing something did not mean you *liked* that thing. You were being a researcher, and what researchers do is explain what's true. However, along with Phillips, along with Bruckert, Davison, and Rugnetta, along with so many of the other people we worked with and laughed with and were friends with at the time, Milner missed an important detail. You can't argue that you're making a careful analytic critique when at the same time you're setting people up to enjoy the things you're critiquing.

Irony and the Guffawing Us

The dangers of collapsing fun into ugliness and ugliness into fun were especially prominent during MemeFactory's 2009 segment on "fail" content. Throughout the night, the NYU crowd reveled in unfortunate misspellings, professional faux pas, and people simply struggling to behave "correctly." Failures at life, you could say—someone's version of life, anyway.

The rollicking guffaws that followed these fails were not single-handedly conjured by the MemeFactory performance. Bruckert, Davison, and Rugnetta might have teed up the punch lines, but they couldn't force the audience to laugh. Yet laugh the audience did, uncontrollably, reflecting the norms the audience carried into the room with them—norms that simultaneously universalized the experiences of an implied *us* and demeaned the implied *them*. Look the right way, according to *our* standard. Talk the right way, according to *our* standard. Act the right way, according to *our* standard. Laughter, in those moments, was an act of naming and shaming difference. As was so often the case within internet culture, *difference* meant anything that deviated from white, middle-class, cisgender, straight, male norms. People who fit those norms provided nothing to laugh at, nothing to meme, so they were spared the fetishized trampling.

Among those not spared during the MemeFactory performance were several internet-infamous young white women who had inspired widespread mockery online. These young women, Bruckert, Davison, and Rugnetta explained, were known as "camwhores." On 4chan, the slur described women who revealed their bodies on the site. At one point in the show, an image of one of these young women, a teenager, was projected onto the screen. The crowd exploded in boos and hisses. "KILL HER!" one man in the audience shouted.

Davison offered up an even more telling example from another Meme-Factory performance. Late in the show, Davison explained, the trio had displayed a screenshot taken from a daytime talk show. The guest on the show was a very large Black woman. Someone had added the text "A

WILD SNORLAX APPEARS"—"snorlax" referring to a type of oversized Pokémon. This slide, Davison explains, got the biggest laugh of the whole performance, so much so that it interrupted the flow of the script, compelling the three men to turn around to check what on the screen was causing such a ruckus. Part of him still wants to believe, Davison admits, that the audience was reacting more to the fact that anyone would *say* something like that—that it was metacommentary on the cruelty of the caption. And yet, Davison concedes, "I have to acknowledge that really, we were just telling our audience a fat joke that someone else had come up with, and they were laughing at this woman's expense."[63]

Obviously destructive, unabashedly dehumanizing trolls taking active, gleeful steps to harm others are easy to condemn; that's a no-brainer. But the audience members who howled with laughter in response to these "failed" women did the same basic thing. They disconnected their laughter from its consequences for these particular women, and indeed for all the women, Black and white and brown, daily poisoned by violent misogyny and compoundingly poisoned by racism. The laughing *us* sidestepped all that. Instead they approached the targets of their amusement as punch lines, as pixels, as objects that never learned how to internet, never learned how to act right or look right. They did so because they could, because they were both willing and able to see lulz instead of people.

This willingness and ability to disregard consequences highlight the hazards of ironic fetishization. They also highlight its causes. As literary scholar Christy Wampole explains, arm's-length, giddily ironic reactions—like the ones on display during the MemeFactory performance, across internet culture more broadly, and throughout our own early work—are a luxury enjoyed only by people who also enjoy an excess of comfort and lack of risk.[64] For ironists, life is negative freedom: freedom to do and say what you please simply because it pleases you, without having to pay a price for any of it. Why not laugh; why not play; nothing matters. Conversely, where there is suffering, where there is injustice, where bodies bear the scars of violence and dehumanization, there is no irony, because there is no freedom. No freedom to go about your business unmolested, and no freedom from the harms bearing down on your body. The only thing that's laughable is the idea that nothing matters.

Research published in 2019 by Stop Online Violence against Women, an inclusive public affairs initiative, underscores the consequences of the ironic, fetishizing fun of internet culture.[65] By 2012, Black women on social media were ringing the alarm bells about harassment campaigns that employed trolling tactics and internet culture aesthetics to demean and dehumanize Black women.[66] Russian disinformation agents later replicated the same tactics and aesthetics to suppress the Black vote during the 2016 US presidential election. As part of these campaigns, bad actors essentially trained social media algorithms to accept bigoted content as normal. In the process, they trained white eyes—often already more than willing—to accept it as normal too.

Recontextualizing Laughter

When reflecting on internet culture, especially with ten years of hindsight, it's easy to succumb to despair, coupled with a creeping sense of shame, over how terrible everything on the internet is—at least that's how we often feel. That said, fetishized sight is not inevitable and doesn't characterize every instance of online play. Decontextualization might be inevitable, the result of digital affordances. Fetishization, however, is something else entirely. It's a deep memetic frame—one not everyone is looking through. Internet researcher An Xiao Mina, for instance, highlights memetic play in China that doesn't rely on fetishization.[67] When Chinese citizens critique government oppression with protest memes, Mina explains, they can be just as slapdash, quippy, and Internet Ugly as their American counterparts.[68] The difference is that the punch line *is* the broader context: the state's autocratic control, satirized with messages of resilience and resistance.

Leftist Brazilian memes evidence a similar dynamic, a point Viktor Chagas emphasizes in his analysis of the activist "struggle memes" shared across Brazil on WhatsApp and Facebook.[69] Like Chinese resistance memes, struggle memes hinge on the context of political action within an increasingly repressive state. Through these memes, citizens gain a more holistic understanding of the political landscape and its stakes for everyday people.

The memes described by Mina and Chagas—which have parallels around the globe, including some pockets of the United States—can still be funny. They can still be glitchy, non sequitur, and downright obscene. But they are not animated by aloof, nihilistic irony. And that makes all the difference.

The danger, in other words, isn't the specific act of creating or sharing memes, of having fun on the internet. The danger is the perfect, even symbiotic, gnarl of fetishizing ideologies, fetishizing technologies, and fetishizing actions. Early internet culture epitomized this intertwine. Groups who found themselves muted or targeted by so much dissociated laughter, and all the streamlined sharing that carried it forth, could have foreseen the effects. Those who couldn't, whose entire life got to be laughter, would not have known to heed Wampole's stark warning, issued in 2012, that irony at these levels creates an ethical vacuum in the individual and collective psyche. "Historically," Wampole explained, "vacuums eventually have been filled by something—more often than not, a hazardous something."[70]

A HAZARDOUS EVERYTHING

Until 2010, the laughter ricocheting through subcultural trolling and internet culture circles remained relatively quarantined to those circles— less quarantined than the subversion myths at the heart of the Satanic Panics, but still somewhat bounded within groups of internet people. As it accelerated, network climate change ensured that these boundaries would dissolve. By 2012, Christina Xu explains, "an industry had sprung up" around internet culture, so much so that she and ROFLCon cofounder Tim Hwang decided that 2012 would be the last conference.[71] "In 2012," Hwang says, "we were on the phone with Grumpy Cat's agent, and it was like, 'this cat has an agent.' I think that fact alone is a really big indication of how the space of internet culture had changed in a four-year time period."[72]

This shift occurred for many reasons, as Phillips chronicles.[73] First, the introduction of content generating sites like Meme Generator and Quickmeme in 2009 and 2010 allowed users to instantly create memes without knowledge of the photo-editing software that had been a barrier to internet culture contribution. Compounding shifts in memetic production was the family-friendly Cheezburger Network's 2011 acquisition of Know Your Meme. Cheezburger's acquisition injected corporate capital into the site and, in the process, helped draw an even wider audience—including advertisers and marketers—to its growing meme database. Efforts to "memejack," in which marketers would attempt to harness internet culture output, became increasingly common and drove increasing attention to specific memes and the communities that spawned them. An uptick in news coverage about the latest memes, including the exploits of trolling subculture on and around 4chan, also spurred the mainstreaming process.

Much more subtle but just as significant was the increasing, interconnected influence wielded by prominent internet people. As Davison underscored, it was weird how insular that world was. It was weird, he continued, that we—referring to Phillips and the whole network of academics and media types in the New York internet culture orbit—were all at ROFLCon. It was weird, Davison said, that he met Chris Poole several times. It was weird that Andrew Auernheimer, the notorious white supremacist and violent misogynist known as "weev," attended the first MemeFactory show at NYU. At the time, however, Davison didn't think about who was who and what was what. Everybody just stumbled around making and sharing content.

The issue was that this "everybody" was already on a fast track to success. Many, including ROFLCon's organizers and superparticipants, attended some of the most prestigious universities in the world, and after college they accepted positions at some of the most prestigious media and technology companies in the world. Their voices, their jokes, and their frames tangled even more tightly with industry. Even as everyday enthusiasts produced a dizzying stream of content, the fact that the most prominent behind-the-scenes influencers were friends, or at least friends of friends, who actively promoted one another's work across and between high-profile platforms, helped cohere that content. It also helped that content stretch its tendrils out to further mainstream attention.

Before long, the jokes, memes, and overall aesthetic of internet culture, including many elements of trolling subculture, were showing up on television and in movies. Trolling and meme merchandise was everywhere, in malls, at Target, and even on floats in the Macy's Thanksgiving Day parade. In just a few short years, internet culture hadn't just gone mainstream. It had come to define popular culture—a popular culture steeped in the idea that the more information there is, the more memes people share, the more people comment, the more pixels people flatten, the better things are. For some. Certainly for the titans of liberalism who found ways to monetize all those memes, comments, and pixels while doing everything possible to avoid restricting speech. For them, it wasn't just that information should be free; it's that free information was a gold mine.

And so the pollution embedded within internet culture became more potent as it seeped through ever-broadening swaths of the forest. The most obvious references to trolling subculture might have been minimized or simply forgotten as that taproot fed into so many others. Still, lulz became a dominant register, not just among extremely online influencers, but also among people who had no idea what forest they were even in, let alone how deep down the roots went. This included many journalists, as we'll see in the next chapter, and, we're certain, many people reading this book.

The resulting chorus of ironic, nihilistic, fetishistic laughter created the perfect conditions for bigotry to spread stealthily, tucked away within things that didn't seem polluted at all. That seemed, instead, like harmless fun. As so many otherwise well-intentioned people watched, seeing nothing, trolls and lulz and glitchy art melted into supremacist hatred, like mists melting into branches melting into roots. Once there, its poison could spread, unfettered, from this tree to that, gathering more strength with each turn. Soon it couldn't be contained and burst up through the sidewalk, into the public square. This process took time, but it wasn't difficult; internet culture and white supremacy share the same frames. The difference is that white supremacists *know* they're sowing poison.

The next chapter chronicles how bigots exploited these frames throughout the 2016 US presidential election cycle. The story of early internet culture helps ground that conversation. It also serves a more prescriptive function, underscoring that while our present troubles have grown from the seeds we've planted, they shouldn't be seen as inevitable. Fetishized sight and the white racial frame are potent and, for white people in particular, difficult habits to break—or even to recognize as habitual. But it's still possible for all of us to turn our heads, take in more of the landscape, and take seriously what too many among us haven't noticed before. This is our first line of defense against the spread of bigoted pollution. It's not a guaranteed fix. But if we don't try, the forest may never recover.

3 TILLING BIGOTED LANDS, SOWING BIGOTED SEEDS

The farmhouse sits left of center in the worn, gray image, dated about 1935.[1] "This photograph shows an approaching dust storm in Morton County, Kansas," the Kansas Historical Society caption reads, and does it ever.[2] There are a few other objects in the frame, set back about a quarter mile: possibly a car or set of cars, possibly a shed or set of sheds, possibly a tree or set of trees. Otherwise, all that surrounds the house is dirt. Crumbling, dry, dirt on the ground, and darkening, billowing, dirt in the sky, a hundred feet up, maybe higher, like a mountain range roaring toward the farm. For the Morton County homesteader who worked that farm—and indeed for everyone in the Southern Plains region—this looming dust storm, and the other looming dust storms that plagued the Dust Bowl throughout the 1930s, must have felt like divine retribution.

In some ways, it was. Rather than being purely natural phenomena, the storms were the result of terrible meteorological luck combined with social, political, and technological forces all colliding with the Great Depression.[3] One of these forces was the influx in the 1920s of "suitcase farmers" lured West by the promise of easy money, then lulled by the yields of an unusually rainy decade. Very often these farmers knew very little, or cared very little, about sustainable agriculture; they just planted and planted and planted and harvested and harvested and harvested. Another prelude to disaster was the widespread adoption of mechanized farming, which allowed farmers to till massive swaths of native grasslands with unprecedented ease and speed. New tools plus a farming boom plus all that rain led to an overproduction of wheat, fueling an inevitable price drop. The less wheat was worth, the more wheat had to be produced to turn a profit. To meet that need, farmers tilled even harder, exposing even more soil to the winds. And then, just as the Great Depression had fully enveloped the region, the rain stopped. Not for one year, not for two. For ten. The plowed lands cracked and fell barren. Into the winds the dry dirt went. Houses filled with it. The sky filled with it. All there was was dirt.

Heading into the 1930s, land conservationists knew full well that the "reckless and haphazard" farming practices of the 1920s, as Kansas representative Clifford Ragsdale Hope described them, were a catastrophe in the making.[4] Convincing farmers to prevent the impending ecological disaster was a hard sell, however. For one thing, unless *all* farmers planted cover crop or roughened exposed soil, erosion relief efforts were of little use. No matter how well you maintained your fields, if your neighbor's topsoil was loose, their dirt would blow onto your land—making you, suddenly, part of the problem. When strong winds blew, and they always blew, the result was devastating. Crops failed, farms collapsed, and people caught in the storm suffered a host of health problems, from long-term respiratory illness to death by suffocation.

The Dust Bowl illustrates how profoundly human cultivation shapes the environment. Ecological cultivation and digital cultivation unfold, of course, in vastly different contexts. But in both cases, individual choices affect the entire ecosystem.

Online, users with large platforms have a particularly deep footprint, but those with the smallest audiences also shape the landscape. Network climate change makes sure of it. Big pollution is pushed to small places, and small pollution is pushed to big places, sending gusts every which way. In some cases, pollution is introduced through willful destruction, the digital equivalent of someone razing massive plots of native grassland, fully aware of the consequences. In other cases, pollution results from inadvertent harms, the equivalent of learning how to grow crops but not learning how to manage soil. In our hyperconnected online ecosystem, even seemingly helpful actions can contaminate the environment, the equivalent of working the land as hard as you can so that you can grow extra food for your worse-off neighbors. The dust still flies, regardless.

At the heart of this chapter are the dust storms of white supremacy, white nationalism, and broad-spectrum bigotry that, long accumulating in the soil, roared forth anew during the 2016 US presidential election cycle. As these pollutants clouded online platforms, everyday politics, and seemingly the whole country, many citizens expressed shock that such storms were even possible. Many more remained oblivious to the dust they were themselves kicking up.

A basic catalyst for these storms was, of course, the white nationalists and supremacists and broad-spectrum bigots themselves, who trampled through everyone else's fields, throwing fistfuls of dirt into the air and whooping with delight. But other more well-meaning groups fed those same storms. In particular, journalists, tillers of the land by trade and regularly pressured to overproduce, blanketed the fields with dirt. Uniquely susceptible within these ranks were the mostly young and mostly white reporters raised on internet culture. As far-right reactionaries weaponized internet culture's lulzy ethos and fetishized sight, reporters raised on those same norms were more likely to dismiss dehumanizing attacks as just trolling as usual, just edgy internet fun. They may not have meant to, but these journalists, along with so many others, tilled the lands and sowed the seeds for bigots. Once the soil was primed and the winds began to blow, it was only a matter of time before the sky went dark.

THE TRUTH ABOUT THE ALT-RIGHT, OR LOOKING BEYOND THE USUAL SUBJECTS

On August 11, 2017, white nationalists and neo-Nazis descended on Charlottesville, Virginia, for the two-day Unite the Right rally, organized in response to the planned removal of a statue of Confederate general Robert E. Lee. The screaming white men who marched through the streets wore no hoods and made no apologies. Their hateful motives were reflected in torch-lit Nazi chants calling for the eradication of people and perspectives they feared would replace them. Counterprotesters resisted; one, Heather Heyer, was murdered.

For many observers, the Unite the Right rally was synonymous with, or at least was the brainchild of, the "alt-right," a euphemism for white nationalism and supremacy. Although the term quite literally whitewashed hate, many journalists and everyday citizens had adopted it heading into the 2016 election cycle. Even after the Unite the Right rally's howling white supremacist violence, national news outlets persisted in using the term, often right in the headline or lede. Sometimes those stories quoted white supremacists who described themselves as "alt-right." More often, the stories applied the label themselves.

On the one hand, it was true that the Unite the Right rally was an "alt-right" event. On the other hand, the alt-right didn't exist—at least not in the way it was so often framed. Teasing this point out means identifying what was true, and what was not, about the alt-right.

Here are some true things.

The term *alt-right* can be traced back to 2008, when white nationalist Richard Spencer first sought to rebrand white nationalism for a more refined audience. As political scientist George Hawley explains, Spencer's alt-right—however sanitized it pretended to be—drew from the staunchly isolationist, anti-immigrant, and antiglobalist paleoconservatism movement; radical libertarianism; and white supremacist groups like the Ku Klux Klan and the Aryan Nations.[5] The term gained some initial traction and then went into a kind of hibernation; it persisted within certain circles but was not widely known otherwise.

This changed in 2015, when, as Hawley notes, the term came in vogue among reactionary conservatives online.[6] This reemergence coincided with what Jacob Davey and Julia Ebner, researchers at the Institute for Strategic Dialogue, called a "fringe insurgency" of global right-wing extremism.[7] While the nationalist and supremacist core of the alt-right remained the same, the nature of its supporters began to shift, and the term broadened with them. Media scholars Alice Marwick and Becca Lewis chronicle this evolution.[8] By 2016, the "accommodatingly imprecise" label was embraced by, or at least was being used to describe, a panoply of "conspiracy theorists, techno-libertarians, white nationalists, Men's Rights advocates, trolls, anti-feminists, anti-immigration activists, and bored young people."[9] It also became tethered to the candidacy of one Donald J. Trump, who never publicly embraced the term but didn't outright reject it, either—and certainly didn't reject the supporters who embraced alt-right ideals, even if those supporters didn't actively identify as alt-right.

Baked into this Trumpian iteration was a very particular aesthetic predicated on irony and lulz. People operating under the "alt-right" mantle imprinted this aesthetic onto a nonstop deluge of internet memes, which they gleefully described as "pro-Trump shitposting." Communication scholars Heather Suzanne Woods and Leslie A. Hahner explore how alt-right memes shaped public discourse during the 2016 election cycle.[10] While memes were not the only weapon deployed by the alt-right during the election, Woods and Hahner argue, they were particularly effective bludgeons. "Ironic" memes, in which a bigoted position was couched behind a trollish wink, were especially common.

A leaked style guide for the Daily Stormer, a white supremacist website, illustrates the coordinated strategy behind reactionary meme use.[11] The style guide encourages prospective writers to hijack existing memes, whatever their origins, with the rationale that memes are familiar and fun and naturally lower their audience's critical defenses. Funny memes, the guide's author explains, are also much easier for mainstream journalists to report on than flat-out bigotry. First, reporters have a compulsion to report on funny memes, and second, funny memes are more digestible for their readers, for whom outright bigotry is almost always, the guide concedes, a turnoff.

The pervasiveness of reactionary memes during the election points to another truth about the alt-right: its relationship, even its interchangeability, with the term "troll"—evidenced by the fact that, during the 2016 election cycle, mainstream articles about trolling frequently used "alt-right" synonymously, and articles about the alt-right very often used "trolling" synonymously. *Vox*'s Aja Romano wrote an article in 2017—"How the Alt-Right Uses Internet Trolling to Confuse You into Dismissing Its Ideology"—that exactingly diagnosed the problem.[12]

Like "alt-right," "troll" was accommodatingly imprecise to the point of nonsense, allowing the term to function as convenient shorthand for a whole host of malignancies. At times, "troll" was used to identify irony-poisoned aggressors associated with sites like 4chan, 8chan (an even more aggressive 4chan spin-off), and parts of Reddit and Twitter forwarding a pro-Trump, anti-PC, anti-"social-justice-warrior" agenda. At other times, "trolling" described the white supremacists and neo-Nazis that populated hate sites like the Daily Stormer. At still others, it labeled the activities of far-right outlets like InfoWars, Ending the Fed, and, most conspicuously, Breitbart, all of which harnessed and commoditized Trump's MAGA base. "Troll" was also used to label Russian disinformation efforts, and the Internet Research Agency—Russia's notorious propaganda outlet—was explicitly dubbed a "troll farm." Additionally, "troll" was used by supporters and detractors alike to characterize media personalities who either self-identified or were otherwise associated with the alt-right, notably Richard Spencer, former Breitbart editor Milo Yiannopoulos, and of course Trump himself, who was often crowned as the biggest troll of them all.

The final, starkest truth about the alt-right is that the people who adopted the term, or at least who were called alt-right by outside observers, committed violence. Some was physical. Some was mediated. All of it—all the racism, all the misogyny, all the transphobia, all the nativism—scarred the landscape and its inhabitants in demonstrable ways.

Layered atop the things that are true about the alt-right are things that are misleading.

The first and most basic misconception is that the term *alt-right*—and its frequent bedfellow *trolling*—ever referred to a clear, coherent movement. The accommodating imprecision of both terms meant that neither had to describe a clear coherent *anything*. In fact, the linguistic ambiguity of both terms was a convenient rhetorical escape hatch. "I'm not alt-right!" was a common sneer among those who had been labeled as alt-right by journalists, particularly after the Unite the Right rally. "I was just trolling!" was another, particularly among those who didn't like it when their racist messages were accurately described as such.

The second misconception was that the alt-right was a wholly organic, stand-alone movement. As Woods and Hahner highlight, it instead derived strength from the signal-boosting energy of its detractors.[13] Alt-right memes, for instance, were used to cohere a knowing, snickering in-group. But they were also used, actively and deliberately, to antagonize liberal and progressive audiences into responding. In so doing, liberals and progressives carried those memes well beyond the circles that created them. Had participants not provoked amplification beyond their own ranks, these memes and their underlying messages would have remained confined solely to reactionary silos. Participants would also have had far less incentive to keep making them, at least for external propaganda and recruitment purposes.

The most consequential misconception of all, however, was the claim, frequently repeated in news articles, on social media, and even within some academic circles, that "alt-right trolls" were central to Trump's 2016 victory. *They* were the ones, this story went, who had shifted the Overton window so far to the right. *They* were the ones, as *New York Magazine* reporter Jesse Singal argued, who won the election.[14] The narrative that alt-right trolls fundamentally rerouted the course of American politics is compelling, even intuitive; it serves as the backbone for a number of books and articles, including Angela Nagle's bestseller *Kill All Normies*.[15] But just because a narrative is compelling and intuitive doesn't make it true.

In chapter 1, we discussed how certain beliefs can be *real* in the sense that they are perceived as real, and therefore really shape the world, without being objectively *true*. The idea that the alt-right gifted the nation President Trump walks a similar "real but not true" tightrope. The alt-right was undeniably real in that it was, as a concept, central to 2016 coverage and commentary. As a concept, it was a point of identification for many Trump supporters. As a concept, it benefited Donald Trump's campaign.

Yet, at its core, the "alt-right" was a meme—a very successful meme, but a meme nonetheless. Its influence on the election thus reflects a kind of self-fulfilling prophesy: the more that people said the alt-right was influencing the election, the larger the idea of the alt-right became. And the larger the idea of the alt-right became, the more that idea shaped news coverage and social media commentary. With visibility begetting participants begetting visibility all the while; reality feeding into truth.

The claim that the alt-right won the election for Trump fails to account for this nuance. To the extent that it ever was one, the alt-right as an entity didn't do very much—not on its own, anyway. In ways big and small, public and private, the everyday actions of everyone else were just as important to the alt-right cause as the alt-right ever was. This was something that the industrial grade polluters lumped under the "alt-right" label understood and giddily harnessed. Just like Kansas in the 1930s, the 2016 election was an ecological catastrophe in the making.

THE NEWS FILTER

When considering the polluted fruits of that catastrophe, establishment center-left news outlets warrant particular scrutiny.[16] An August 2017 photograph of the street outside the Charlottesville General District Court epitomizes center-left journalism's signal-boosting power. The picture, taken by Getty photographer Chip Somodevilla, is an aerial shot, likely captured from an upper-story window of a building facing the courthouse.[17] It shows a member of the neo-Nazi Traditionalist Workers Party surrounded by fifty or so clamoring journalists, some extending recording devices for audio, some typing notes on their phones, and some pointing their cameras as close to the center of the fracas as possible. Had the neo-Nazi been speaking into the open air on that sidewalk, his words wouldn't have carried farther than fifteen feet. Thanks to all the cameras and microphones crammed in his face, those words ended up traveling to national and global audiences.

Yochai Benkler, Robert Faris, and Hal Roberts zero in on the amplification powers of center-left news media.[18] They argue that during the 2016 election, far-right media, from small extremist blogs like *RedState* to larger outlets like Breitbart, unquestionably influenced their sympathetic base. However, these outlets simply didn't have enough clout to shift the national conversation themselves, and the base they were energizing certainly didn't have enough votes to win an election. For their ideologies to spread from sea to shining sea, right-wing reactionaries needed establishment outlets. Reckoning with this reality is an essential first step in adopting more effective soil erosion plans.

The Oxygen of Amplification

To assess how journalists themselves felt about the relationship between news reporting and the mainstreaming of far-right reactionaries, Phillips conducted dozens of interviews with staff writers, editors, and freelancers at center-left outlets large and small, legacy and niche, including the *New York Times*, the *Washington Post*, CNN, the *Atlantic*, *Slate*, *Wired*, *BuzzFeed News*, and *Vice*.[19] The journalists Phillips spoke to affirmed at least the baseline assertion made by Benkler, Faris, and Roberts: during the 2016 election, establishment journalists gave right-wing reactionaries an enormous platform.[20] The most emphatic of these reporters asserted, without reservation, that journalists were responsible for helping create the world that white nationalists and supremacists said existed—namely, a world that was *theirs*. Other reporters were more measured, hypothesizing a chicken-and-egg relationship between coverage of bigotry and acts of bigotry. Coverage gave bigotry a larger platform, these reporters conceded, and that platform ensured there would be more bigotry to cover. But news reporting didn't *cause* bigotry to appear out of thin air.

Wherever they may have fallen on the spectrum, a majority of these reporters expressed at least some degree of ambivalence about their role in amplifying the Far Right. Many questioned whether they should cover white nationalist personalities, bigoted harassment campaigns, and dehumanizing propaganda at all. Writing these kinds of stories, after all, gives reactionary ideologies more oxygen, and that oxygen has consequences. It grants legitimacy to false beliefs and harmful ideologies. It encourages retaliatory harassment. It incentivizes future harmful behaviors.

After a pause, the same reporters would often begin listing out the dangers of saying nothing. Not amplifying polluted information risks creating space for worse pollution to take its place. It misses an opportunity to correct the record and educate the public. It allows pollution to flourish. It doesn't mean that the issue, whatever it is, will go away.

Not all the reporters Phillips spoke to were so reflective. This was a point many of the reporters themselves raised. Individual journalists, these reporters explained, vary greatly in their motives, ethics, and competencies. Many reporters and many newsrooms tried to be careful during the election, but many reporters and many newsrooms did not, either because they didn't feel the need to be, or because they weren't in the position to make those decisions. Some newsrooms, for example, couldn't afford *not* to publish sensationalist clickbait, and some reporters, particularly freelancers, couldn't afford to turn down even the most grievous assignment. Regardless of the why, bad reporting made it increasingly difficult for thoughtful reporters to keep the dust out of their own work. If some rival outlet is covering a story, however questionable that story might be, then yours will have to cover it too. You might even feel pressured to preempt bad stories with your own, better stories—an especially pressing concern when those worse stories would be coming from the other side of your newsroom, overseen by editors whose judgment you don't trust. It's better to tell a bad story carefully, several of these reporters sighed, than to let someone else screw it up worse.

Right-wing reactionaries were delighted by the resulting debris flying across the news ecosystem. The *New York Times'* Alan Rappeport, for example, reported that white supremacists were "thrilled" by the coverage precipitated by Pepe the Frog, a meme strategically adopted as a winking racist dog whistle within pro-Trump circles.[21] Gaby Del Valle of the *Outline* noted Breitbart writers' glee over *BuzzFeed News'* nonstop coverage of "alt-right" personalities.[22] The *Guardian's* Lois Beckett highlighted just how positively neo-Nazis responded to news reports about resurgent bigotry during the 2016 election.[23] As Beckett reported, one white supremacist gushed of center-left reporters, "All the things they're doing are so good."

The "good things" were, of course, only good for the reactionaries and chaos agents. Regardless of what reporters hoped to accomplish, their incessant coverage of bigoted messages sandblasted that bigotry far and wide, carving several deep contours into the landscape.

First, center-left coverage stabilized white nationalism and supremacy as a mainstream fixture. It did so, most basically, by lumping disparate personalities, groups, and motivations under the banner of the "alt-right" and then poring over the everyday minutiae and palace intrigue of the people sorted into that camp. This created an illusion of coherence, prominence, and influence, which the "alt-right" was subsequently able to grow into, at least from a PR perspective—certainly with more deftness than the often motley, often fledgling, often fractured groups of white nationalists and supremacists could have accomplished on their own. Relatedly, thanks to the constant use of the otherwise meaningless umbrella term, news coverage helped streamline "alt-right" recruitment efforts. Joining a group is much easier when the group has a name, particularly when the initiation process, including where to go and what to do when you get there, is laid out step by step.

Second, "both-sides" coverage of white nationalists and supremacists helped legitimize their violent ideologies. This "both-sides" impulse reflects the principles enshrined in the Fairness Doctrine, the mid-twentieth century policy requiring broadcasters to cover controversial issues equitably. While the journalistic impulse to provide equal coverage to conflicting perspectives isn't inherently harmful, it becomes so when one of those sides is destructive, dehumanizing, or steeped in bullshit. The reactionary Right is all three. Consequently, reporting on violent bigotry simply because it was opposed to human rights didn't make for fair and balanced coverage. That might have been the goal for many journalists, but the result was to elevate and normalize bigots' false, degrading, and antidemocratic messages. That's what equal airtime between unequal positions does: it creates a false equivalence in which the moral urgency of addressing an existential threat is reduced to a matter of opinion.

A segment on Jake Tapper's CNN show in November 2016 illustrates how "evenhanded" coverage of bigotry can legitimize that bigotry.[24] During the segment, host and guests were discussing Richard Spencer's racist rhetoric. One of the guests read a comment in which Spencer asked if Jewish people "are people at all." The producers of the show subsequently flashed a chyron at the bottom of the screen that read, "Alt-right leader questions if

Jews are people," and the CNN panel took up the debate. Whether Jewish people are people is not a point of discussion. By taking the question seriously enough to discuss it on air and then visually reinforcing it with that chyron, CNN implied that questioning Jews' humanity was one side of a conversation worth having.

Allowing white nationalists and supremacists to breeze into the public square as the moral equivalent of *not* being a white supremacist had a third effect: normalizing violence against people of color and women. It did so by reframing bigoted harm in ways that directly benefited attackers. Most conspicuous was taking bigots at face value when they contorted their dehumanizations into defenses of free speech. Ceding this frame—and ignoring the fact that bigots don't care about the free speech of the people they attack—minimized the impact their dehumanizations had on the people they targeted. It also falsely equated harassment with mere name-calling, or proof of oversensitivity, or an occupational hazard of life online that targets just needed to learn how to deal with. The dust kicked up by all that dehumanization, the dust that scratched at people's eyes and burned in their lungs, became, over time, an everyday part of life on the farm for far too many.

The contours carved by the center-left's "alt-right" coverage were unique, reflecting the uniqueness of our current media ecosystem. That doesn't mean that what happened during the election had never happened before. As unique as these contours might have been—because of digital media, because of who was running for president, because of a host of other factors stemming from the overarching oddity of the 2016 election cycle—they had ample historical precedent. Generations ago, the landscape was ravaged by a similar erosion process, to a similarly devastating effect—a legacy we're still digging out of.

The More Things Change

It's comforting, in a way—at least it can be for many white people—to imagine that today's bigotry is both new and marginal, certainly "not who we are." Unfortunately that's not the case; bigotry extends deep into the bedrock of US history. The longstanding relationship between mainstream journalism and white supremacists provides a pointed example.

And so back in time we go, to 1860, when public leaders in Charleston, South Carolina, propelled their state toward white supremacist secession from the Union. As journalist Paul Starobin chronicles, Northern outlets saw Charleston's secessionist frenzy as an exciting opportunity to sell papers.[25] Secession was such a hot topic that editors at the *New York Tribune* sent reporters down to Charleston, secretly embedding them at the offices of the *Mercury*, a rabidly anti-Union newspaper. Northern readers were enthralled by the coverage. According to Starobin, these stories presented Charleston secessionists, who, it must be emphasized, were deeply committed to owning other people, as "unhinged—but in a benign sort of way."[26] By framing secessionist white supremacy as an amusing curiosity, Northern papers filtered Southern propaganda out to their audiences—not as presaging national catastrophe, but as something entertaining to read.

That national catastrophe could have been a wake-up call, but it wasn't; white Northern journalists followed a similar template after the Civil War. In particular, Northern reporting on the white terrorist organization known as the Ku Klux Klan, which rose to national prominence between 1866 and 1871, loosed an utter deluge of pollution into the mainstream.

As historian Elaine Frantz Parsons argues, two Ku Klux Klans existed during this time: the actual Klan, which comprised thousands of violent racists who sought to destroy the bodies and the resolve of freedpeople and their allies, and the imagined Klan, created largely through white Northern news coverage.[27] The origin of both Klans began not with a bang but with the chortles of a group of financially comfortable white men in post–Civil War Pulaski, Tennessee, who created the deliberately silly-sounding social club because they were bored. As they evolved over the next few years, both the actual Klan and the imagined Klan were malignant; both crusaded for white dominance and Black hopelessness. The actual Klan was the most imminently dangerous; it was a physical, roaring-in-the-night manifestation of the cultural psychopathy that is violent white supremacy. But it could not have existed as it did, when it did, and as powerfully as it did, if the Northern press had not told such a compelling story about the imagined Klan.[28] This coverage paralleled coverage of Trump-era white nationalists and supremacists.

First, echoing contemporary coverage of the "alt-right," national stories responding to the emergence of the Klan stabilized the haphazard, localized white racial terror that had exploded following the Civil War. Those acts of terror were very real, and there had been very many of them. But white vigilantes during those early days, Parsons emphasizes, weren't communicating across regions, weren't organized in their efforts, and, other than a broad sense of racist grievance, weren't acting under any formal banner.[29] Northern coverage began tying all those disparate actions together under a coherent organizational umbrella. This allowed the Klan to coalesce not just as a movement but as a national brand. As it did, that brand inspired more and more free-agent vigilantes to take up its moniker. In an act of life imitating news, the newly knighted "Ku Klux," as individual members of the Klan were then known, began coordinating in earnest.

That they did so hinged on the second parallel to modern coverage of reactionaries: how frequently Northern reporters relied on "both-sides" framings of the Klan. Journalists regularly mined Ku Klux for comment and regularly printed their constant, head-spinning, pathological lies about what they did and what it all meant. The most egregious of these lies was that the Klan didn't even exist but rather was a hoax created by freedpeople looking for sympathy, politicians looking for votes, and newspapers looking for sales. This position was forwarded as a counterpoint to the verifiable existence of the Klan.[30]

To be clear: the claim that the Klan was an invention by freedpeople and Northern politicians was racist propaganda. The claim that the Klan was invented by Northern newspapers was more nuanced. It was objectively false in that the actual Klan was all too real, and all too dangerous, to freedpeople and their allies. Ku Klux were domestic terrorists, period. But there were echoes of truth in the claim as well: the imagined Klan was indeed very good for business, prompting newspaper owners to publish story after story. White racial terror certainly would have persisted had the Klan not coalesced. But it wouldn't have had a national propaganda apparatus to build on—a propaganda apparatus that meant more visibility, more growth, and therefore more danger.

A third parallel to modern news coverage is that Northern coverage of the Klan normalized its white supremacist violence. This coverage did so, most strikingly, by indulging the Ku Klux's winking irony and self-aware theatricality. From its nonsense name to its cartoonish robes to the carnivalesque elements of its attacks, the Klan had a flair for staging violence as comedy. As they had done when covering the Charleston secessionists, Northern papers covering the Klan took the bait, publishing reams of wry articles chronicling the group's "grotesque idiosyncrasies" as a perhaps disruptive but ultimately amusing farce.[31] The victims of these "farces" were almost never mentioned, and if they were, their political perspectives, violated bodies, and lost lives mattered very little compared to the racist stars of the show. As Parsons chronicles, white Northerners loved these wild and crazy Klan stories. Racist violence made for great copy.

By 1871, however, as the actual Klan bottomed out, the imagined Klan did too. That didn't mean journalists stopped signal-boosting white supremacy, though. As media historians Juan González and Joseph Torres note, Northern newspaper editors remained "obsessed" with lynchings through the turn of the century.[32] Even when coverage in the North was sharply critical (very few papers in the South leveled even the slightest critique), stories published in papers like the *New York Times* presented every gory, graphic, excruciating detail, sometimes subtly or not so subtly rationalizing the practice and replicating racist tropes about the people who had been murdered. The popularity of lynching stories stemmed from their newsworthiness; and their newsworthiness, communication scholar Richard Perloff argues, stemmed from the fact that they "could be guaranteed to contain information that would arouse prurient interests, engage racist citizens, and uphold a social order that was dependent upon the systematic oppression of Blacks by Whites."[33]

Needless to say, the underlying spirit of the Klan hadn't gone anywhere—for one thing, it had been systematized through Jim Crow segregation laws—and by the 1920s, both the real and imagined Klans had staged a full comeback with the rise of the "second Klan." Media historian

Felix Harcourt chronicles this rise, particularly how white Northern news coverage solidified the second Klan as an "Invisible Empire." Northern newspapers did so by highlighting the "weird," "spectacular," and even "ghostly" elements of Klan activities and also by poring over the workaday details of the Klansmen's (as they were by then known) extracurricular lives, including their charitable works.[34] Once again, white Northerners gobbled up all the Klan coverage they could get their hands on, something the Klan correctly identified as a ripe opportunity for media manipulation. When Klansmen weren't busy intimidating, attacking, and murdering Black people, Mexicans, and Jewish and Catholic immigrants, they actively played up the "weird" elements of their organization to reporters and staged increasingly elaborate media spectacles. Such displays of strength would simultaneously generate more coverage, make the group seem less threatening, and, of course, pique even more interest.

When the coverage was bad, that was fine too. The media-savvy Klansmen understood that having their name in the paper, regardless of the reason, only served to boost the Klan's visibility and membership. After a scathing serialized investigation of the Klan by the *New York World* in September 1921, for example, Klan membership skyrocketed. Exactly how many people were convinced to join the Klan solely because of what they read in the *World* is an open question. What's not is the symbiotic relationship between the Klan and the publications that continued gifting it all the publicity it could ever hope for—an outcome Klansmen were quick to brag about.[35]

Exceptions Proving the Rule

Not all journalists played the Klan's game. Many Black newspapers in the 1920s employed strategic, defiant silence in response to white racial terror.[36] If they did publish stories about the Klan, they did so to highlight conflict within the Klan's organization and other embarrassing information, like canceled rallies and member resignations.[37] Many Jewish publications were equally reluctant to afford the Klan any oxygen, a position summed up by the American Jewish Committee's Louis Marshall, who argued that Jewish coverage of the Klan would only "increase the numbers of the Klan."[38] Jewish community groups reiterated this stance in the 1960s when they successfully convinced many journalists to "quarantine" the violent anti-Semitism of the American Nazi Party by not covering it. Like Klan ideology, Nazi ideology was, for these groups, more dangerous than it was newsworthy. Areas where the American Nazi news quarantine was implemented, in turn, saw lower violence and lower white supremacist recruitment.[39]

In these cases, hate was deoxygenated, at least within certain communities, by decisive editorial action. The expanding influence of network television in the 1960s also hindered some white supremacist messaging, at least for a time, most basically because television was so beneficial to the civil rights movement. Every night, media scholar Aniko Bodroghkozy chronicles, broadcast news beamed images of racist violence into American homes, spurring many white people to action—or at least increased awareness.[40]

Recognizing that television was a crucial front in the war for white sympathies, some segregationists did their best to harness the medium for their own purposes. For example, in 1962, Sheriff Laurie Pritchett of Albany, Georgia, decided to use television cameras against civil rights protesters, and against the news media more broadly. Pritchett knew the Northern reporters gathered in Albany were there to film scenes of police brutality. Until that point, most Southern law enforcement had been happy to oblige, either because they couldn't help themselves or because they didn't fully grasp the power of those images. Maybe both. Pritchett, however, had his own game to play. So he responded to nonviolent protesters with nonviolent arrests, making sure the cameras were rolling while he did. The resulting images perpetuated the lie of a kinder, gentler segregationist. They also proved to be deeply concerning for civil rights leaders, who immediately recognized the challenge that responses like Pritchett's posed to the movement.[41]

Pritchett's strategy failed to catch on, ensuring that the relationship between segregationists and television cameras remained ambivalent at best. Indeed, shortly after the Albany campaign, more indelible (and accurate) images of the segregationist South were supplied by the likes of

Birmingham, Alabama public safety commissioner Bull Connor. In 1963, Connor loosed attack dogs and firehoses on Black protesters, and photojournalists were there to capture the scene. The widespread amplification of the attacks wasn't a part of the segregationist media kit; they weren't staging the images, and the journalists covering the story weren't there at segregationists' behest. From a segregationist standpoint, the images were a liability.

Even when the journalists *were* there at the segregationists' behest—for example, when they staged cross burnings and bombed Black churches[42]— the resulting images did the Klan few favors, at least with more moderate mainstream white audiences. Those white moderates might have been sympathetic to the gentlemanly segregationist; but explicit violence was something else. During the civil rights movement, the nightly news showed much more of the latter. It's therefore unsurprising that segregationists came to see center-left, and especially Northern, journalists as enemies. A symposium on media and the civil rights movement held at the University of Mississippi in 1987 foregrounded this dynamic. As the panelists—all of whom had covered the South during the civil rights era—explained, members of the Klan actively intimidated, attacked, and sometimes tried to murder reporters.[43]

The antipathy and mistrust white supremacists felt toward center-left reporters was often—and also unsurprisingly—mutual. Phillips's interviews with journalists working in the 1970s and 1980s revealed the efforts some reporters at some newsrooms took to shut white supremacists down. There was no official policy about spiking Klan stories, one reporter explained. But he, and many of the reporters he worked with, lived through the civil rights era and knew what the Klan was capable of. Beyond that, the Holocaust remained omnipresent to many. Fascism wasn't an abstraction to these reporters; it was something they'd seen with their own eyes, or heard told firsthand. So spike the stories they did.

Local papers were especially wary about publishing Klan stories. Their reporters lived in the communities they covered, and they knew that stories about the Klan would set off a powder keg—one that could potentially result in assaults on or murders of the reporters themselves. If they had to file a story about the Klan, local papers would keep the dust kicking to an absolute minimum. Whenever possible, they would run a national wire service story rather than one with a local journalist's name attached.

But all these exceptions help prove the rule. Although some reporters, at some papers, have exercised restraint when covering hate, and although some technological change blunted the spread of some supremacist messaging, for generations in the United States, hate-mongers have been handed microphone after microphone. Sometimes this is because those holding the microphone agree with what the racists are saying. Sometimes it's because the microphone-holders consider what racists do and say to be "just the way things are." Even the extreme violence of post–Civil War lynchings fell into this category, Richard Perloff explains; for white Northern journalists, coverage was "akin to reporting on unpleasant acts of nature such as earthquakes or floods; the events were unfortunate but necessary aspects of the order of things."[44]

The reason most specific to the institution of journalism, however, which is embedded within the very core of the profession, is the knee-jerk impulse to be "fair and balanced." For stories on white supremacy, this means "both sides-ing" bigots. Again, of course, fairness is a good idea in theory. But in the context of hate, this impulse frequently ends up being neither fair nor balanced, as truth and consequence are obscured by pollution and manipulation.

Sociologist Jessie Daniels describes the pervasiveness—and insidiousness—of the "both-sides" approach to hate groups in an exploration of 1990s talk shows featuring white supremacist guests.[45] On these shows, the both-sides-ism was visual; white supremacists would be seated on one side of the stage, civil rights leaders on the other. The white supremacists might have been the hour's buffoons. But, as Daniels argues, the white supremacists' very presence legitimized their bigotries as much as CNN's chyron legitimized Richard Spencer's anti-Semitism. Worse, their bald-faced, even cartoonish, expressions of hate gave more moderate white viewers a pass for those viewers' everyday acts of white supremacy. The real racists are the ones in hoods on daytime talk shows, this logic goes. If you're not in a hood on a daytime talk show, then you've got nothing to worry about.

AS THE DUST BOWL FORMS

In addition to epitomizing both sides reporting, the 1990s talk show hosts who invited white supremacists onto their stage embodied another tenet of center-left journalism and of liberalism more broadly: the pervasive idea that to counter harms, we have to call attention to harms. In other words, that light disinfects. In the case of the Klan, the assumption is that putting Klansmen up on stage and handing them a microphone will expose their racism, which audiences will reject for the backwards ignorance it is. There's some intuitive wisdom to this assumption. That wisdom, however, does not account for the persistence of the white racial frame. Nor does it account for our current climate crisis—beginning with the internet's Dust Bowl conditions.

The actual Dust Bowl resulted from the collision of haphazard and irresponsible farming practices, mechanized equipment, and the strong hot winds of a cataclysmic drought. The 2016 Dust Bowl similarly resulted from the collision of haphazard and irresponsible content-mining, algorithmic amplification, and the strong hot winds of the attention economy. These conditions were exacerbated by the ease of homesteading: that anybody and their mother could go till all the land they wanted and kick up all the dust they wanted—with white supremacists being some of the most active homesteaders on the prairie.[46] This wasn't an informational free-for-all, however. Despite the grassroots affordances ushered in by social media, there remained across the landscape many formidable establishment gates staffed by many competent, eagle-eyed journalistic gatekeepers.[47]

The issue heading into the 2016 election—and this is where the climate crisis looms large—was the hair-trigger on all those institutional gates. To this day, they fling open at the slightest provocation, exposing the landscape to all kinds of pollution. Both-sides-ism is a long-standing reason, as is journalism's "scoop mentality"—which journalism scholar Mike Ananny critiques as "the thrill of being first."[48] Both are worsened by the speed and reach afforded by digital media and the roaring winds of monetization. In such an environment, there must always be new content, and not just any content, but *clickable* content. That's the business model.

By scanning the horizon for the latest dustup then opening the gates to let the story through, journalists in 2016 may have been trying to solve a problem by revealing the problem. Or they may just have been harvesting easy clicks. Either way, mountains of dust blew across whole new fields—dust that couldn't be contained once picked up by the winds. The soil was already taxed, and at many homesteads, already poisoned. But everyone kept planting and planting and panting, and harvesting and harvesting and harvesting. The sky filled with dirt before the gatekeepers knew what happened.

On Being Troll Trained

The pervasive narrative that "alt-right trolls" helped elect Donald Trump is, as already noted, inaccurate; that assertion gives too much credit to the trolls and not enough credit to everyone else who enabled, amplified, and incentivized their behavior. There remains, however, some roundabout truth to the claim. Trolling did indeed play a role in the election, just not the trolling ascribed to right-wing reactionaries. Much more influential, though much less conspicuous, was *subcultural* trolling, the internet culture staple that rose to prominence between 2008 and 2012. The vestiges of subcultural trolling helped shape how online bigotry in 2016 was covered and how audiences responded to it. While the vast majority of journalists at the outset of Trump's campaign were unaware of, or simply indifferent to, the rhetoric and aesthetic of subcultural trolling, reporters who were aware more than made up for their limited numbers. Not only did they amplify this newest iteration of "trolling," they translated it for a mainstream audience.

Essential to both this transmission and translation was fetishized sight and the white racial frame. Standing comfortably behind these frames, white reporters in particular shoveled more and more polluted dirt into the landscape, often without realizing what they were flinging so far and so wide. Pay no attention to the dirt in the air, came the call; it's just internet business as usual.

For years, trolling business had indeed been vast. At the pinnacle of the subculture, trolls' influence wasn't limited to shoddy photoshops and lulzy posts. They also garnered increasing attention from journalists, particularly after 2010, when 4chan became a go-to source for internet culture scoops. Trolls embraced the role and, at every possible opportunity, seeded disinformation to reporters. They did so either by lying during interviews or by posting lies to 4chan, which the reporters were sure to find and report on as fact. Trolls were especially eager to sow confusion after mass shootings; they repeatedly spread the same hoaxes about each new shooter's alleged connections to 4chan, which journalists repeatedly parroted.

During this time, trolls were as likely to target marginalized people and groups as they were to target powerful people and institutions, a point of ambivalence Jessica Beyer, Gabriella Coleman, and Phillips have each explored in their respective studies of early subcultural trolling.[49] Throughout it all, the trolls' pursuit of lulz took precedence; as they constantly crowed, lulz were the only reason to do anything. They may have actually believed that. But whatever they said, however they tried to justify their actions, the trolls' amusement was always predicated on the seriousness of what they were saying for the people they were saying it to. They knew full well what their racist and sexist statements meant historically and politically, and how those statements would be received; that was quite literally why they used the words. So their actions may have been ambivalent, but they were always also full of shit.

The already fuzzy line between lulzy fun and pointed harm grew even fuzzier as 4chan grew increasingly prominent. For many, 4chan's point of no return was 2014's Gamergate hate and harassment campaign. According to feminist scholars Shira Chess and Adrienne Shaw, Gamergate's adherents initially targeted women, with special ire directed at women of color, who spoke out against misogyny in the video game industry. They then began targeting anyone who pushed back against those attacks.[50] The campaign originated and was concentrated on 4chan, with supporting energies emanating from cross-pollinating boards on Reddit, as well as other reactionary corners of the internet. As it generated widespread national news coverage, Gamergate helped shine an even brighter cultural spotlight on 4chan. That visibility, in turn, fueled the network misogyny, to borrow a term from social media researchers Sarah Banet-Weiser and Kate Miltner, at the heart of the campaign.[51]

Gamergate was not the first networked harassment campaign directed at women, particularly women of color. In 2013, Donglegate—in which a Black woman was ruthlessly attacked after highlighting sexism at a Python programming convention—followed a similar script. As Shireen Mitchell, founder of Stop Online Violence against Women, argues, had social platforms taken Donglegate seriously, Gamergate would not have kicked up the dust it did when it did.[52] Donglegate and other concurrent attacks against Black women were only the beginning, Joan Donovan stresses.[53] The utter failure of social media platforms to respond to the emerging threat in 2013 ensured that all those ugly, violent energies had nothing but time and space to fester throughout the information ecosystem.

As Gamergate roared across the internet, 4chan founder Christopher Poole felt compelled to intervene. In an on-site announcement, he explained that he would be deleting Gamergate threads, which were concentrated on the /pol/, or "politics," board, because they violated site policies against posting personal information and organizing raids.[54] Poole's move infuriated the site's free speech absolutists, spurring a mass exodus to 8chan, an unauthorized 4chan spin-off created by a user who thought 4chan had grown too authoritarian. Not everyone left 4chan, however, and over the course of the Gamergate campaign, the site, and especially the /pol/ board, emerged as a safe harbor for self-selecting misogynists and racists. 8chan's /pol/ mirror was another. For these users, bigotries were something to openly embrace; "lol just joking" justifications were no longer needed.

We can't know how many new recruits were attracted to 4chan, 8chan, and other trolling hotbeds because of Gamergate or, before that, how many new recruits were attracted to Gamergate because of Donglegate. We can't know how many existing 4chan users became increasingly amenable to bigoted violence as targeted hate replaced ambivalent lulz. What we do know is that the period between Donglegate in 2013, Gamergate in 2014, and Trump's campaign announcement in 2015 was one of ideological crystallization. By then, the Daily Stormer was actively recruiting on 4chan and 8chan. Posters on both were more than primed to embrace Trump as their xenophobic "God Emperor."[55]

The first instance of physical violence earnestly, rather than trollishly, linked to the chans came shortly thereafter. Less than six months after Trump's announcement speech, two armed, masked white men streamed a LiveLeak video on their way to a Black Lives Matter protest in Minneapolis, Minnesota. They gave /pol/ a shout-out. Later that night, those men, along with two others, opened fire at protesters, injuring five. The next chan-connected terror attack took place in Toronto in 2017. A man referenced 4chan and used site-specific lingo in a Facebook post before ramming his van into a crowd, killing ten and injuring fifteen. Two years later, in 2019, a gunman opened fire on two mosques in Christchurch, New Zealand, killing fifty-one. His manifesto contained numerous references to 4chan and 8chan and included a plethora of trolling memes. The Christchurch attacks were quickly followed by a synagogue attack in Poway, California, complete with its own 8chan white supremacist manifesto. Later that same year, a white nationalist posted yet another manifesto to 8chan before murdering twenty people and injuring twenty-six more—many of whom were Mexican citizens—as they shopped at a Walmart in El Paso, Texas. April Glazer of *Slate* published an article encapsulating the trend: "8chan Is a Normal Part of Mass Shootings Now," the headline read.[56]

The people who had been targeted by the escalating attacks, who had been raising every alarm bell possible for years—with nothing but rejection or retaliation to show for it—predicted this outcome. It was written in the stars. Everyone else was left scratching their heads, staring at the sky, wondering where all the dust had suddenly come from.

TROLLING'S ROTTEN FRUIT

The reactionary turn on 4chan happened right under everyone's noses, in real time. Ironically, the more familiar someone was with internet culture, and even more pointedly, the more familiar someone was with subcultural trolling, the less likely they were to have noticed. The surrounding land may have withered, the soil may have cracked, the wind may have blown in hot and abrasive. But the fruit looked the same and tasted the same to the people who'd internalized the *lol-nothing-matters* ethos of trolling and internet culture.

Growing Up Troll

One of the first reporters Phillips interviewed saw the problem clearly, in hindsight. She admitted that she "grew up" on early 4chan, and explained that her generation—meaning the mostly white, mostly male, mostly privileged people who defined internet culture—"raised all the kids who are Nazis . . . because they saw us, and we were like, 'don't take anything seriously.'"[57]

Other reporters made similar, often sheepish, admissions. The more tech reporters in their late twenties and early thirties Phillips talked to, the more unprompted reflections on internet culture and subcultural trolling she encountered. After several of these conversations, Phillips began asking all the reporters she interviewed about their experiences with trolling. A correlation quickly emerged: a reporter's experience with trolling, and 4chan in particular, strongly influenced how they initially approached stories about the "alt-right."

Not all these experiences were equivalent; some reporters had been closer to the subculture than others, and some had spent years actively mocking trolls as teenagers (even as they often acted like trolls, talked like trolls, and laughed like trolls). Three traits remained consistent, however. The first was reporters' overwhelming whiteness. Indeed, of all the reporters with connections to 4chan whom Phillips interviewed, only one was a person of color. The second shared trait was that these reporters were inclined to approach online aggressions as examples of esoteric internet culture weirdness. The internet wasn't real life; it was the *internet*. So when bigotry and harassment emerged from places like 4chan, it didn't really count; learning that was a basic part of learning how to internet. The final shared trait was that they were, as one reporter put it, "troll trained." They were therefore in a unique position to field the bigotries creeping up from the ground and blowing across the sky as 2016 approached. This was just what the internet looked like, right?

One reporter on the internet culture beat recounted a Facebook meme page he had joined at the outset of the campaign called "Donald Trump's Dank Meme Stash." Because the group so clearly drew from the rhetoric and aesthetics of trolling, and because it featured all the same over-the-top pro-Trump, anti-Clinton content he had seen so many people share ironically, the reporter assumed that the memes and jokes and articles he saw— including a cornucopia of what came to be known as "fake news"—were satirical. Some of the content was satirical, or at least was being shared satirically by other internet culture enthusiasts who encountered the content elsewhere and thought it was funny. Some of it, however, turned out to be the violently racist handiwork of white supremacists and neo-Nazis. Maybe they had crafted those memes with a trollish wink. But what those memes perpetuated was straight-up hate. Speaking to his shock upon discovering where all those funny memes and jokes and articles came from, the reporter could hardly believe how much he had missed. "I didn't see that this was something fundamentally different," he said. "I really should have."[58]

This experience was common among the troll-trained journalists Phillips spoke to. Every day, sometimes every hour, these journalists harvested the fruits of internet culture. Their social lives centered on sharing all that fruit with their friends. Their professional lives centered on making that fruit palatable to a broader audience. Consequently, the lulz, fetishization, and outright bigotry they were seeing on 4chan and Reddit at the outset of the election cycle, which soon blanketed Twitter, Facebook, YouTube, and beyond, were entirely par for the internet culture course. These were the things they had been laughing at, and the people they had been laughing with, for years. They knew what to do.

So out came the listicles, the "lol internet" explainers spotlighting the most outrageous and offensive memes ricocheting across social media. Out came the clickbait slideshows affixing a shruggie-shaped question mark over every racist picture shared. Out came the Twitter snark about how "funny and bizarre" it was, as one reporter explained, that people were "using swastikas, using Nazi language to support Trump."[59] Flinging all that fruit and all that dirt around was fun. The election was fun.

Some coverage was less fun, though the basic outcome was the same. Troll-trained reporters with an existing animus against subcultural trolling wrote "dismissively and crusadingly antagonistic" articles, as one reporter described them, calling attention to that old childhood enemy 4chan.[60] The attempt to mock the site and its users had a serious side effect: advertising the site and its users.

These reporters might not have realized they were sowing catastrophe, but the white nationalists and supremacists whose rotten fruits they were flinging sure did; the leaked style guide for the Daily Stormer lays out that strategy explicitly.[61] In addition to encouraging the disarming use of familiar memes, the guide encourages its writers to lean heavily on humor and to employ the rhetoric of trolling as often as possible. Racist jokes plant the seeds for racist beliefs, the guide explains, and there is no better way to do that than with trolling.

The Daily Stormer wasn't alone. The style guide echoed many of the shitposts cascading across social media at the time, in which participants—taking a page right out of the first Klan's playbook—would forward outrageous statements and images, ironically embrace pejorative labels and stereotypes, and frame racism as high camp. These fruits were so similar, even interchangeable, with what troll-trained reporters themselves had been raised on that many simply could not resist the compulsion to point and laugh.

Deep Memetic Dirt

By responding to what they thought were trollish winks with even more winking, troll-trained reporters inadvertently reinforced their own fetishized sight, as well as the fetishized sight of their audiences. The consequences of bigotry, the people who were at that very moment being targeted and terrorized by that bigotry, were not part of the discussion, not in the listicles, and not in the Twitter snark. Same as it ever was.

Instead, these reporters focused on the irony of the memes and the absurdity of the memes and the comfortably familiar aesthetic of the memes.

There was no reason—at least not that these reporters could see—to stop, so they kept pointing and laughing and rolling their eyes. Other reporters, particularly those who had covered—and certainly those who had been targeted by—Gamergate, Donglegate, or any other coordinated hate and harassment campaign, may have had the sense that something was happening, something was different. And yet too few center-left journalists during the critical early months of the 2016 election cycle called much attention to the eroding soil and bitter fruit piling up at their feet.

One possible reason they didn't, floated by several of the reporters Phillips interviewed, is how unlikely a Trump presidency seemed at the time. Like an enormous number of center-left journalists, critics, and pollsters, troll-trained reporters admitted that they never thought Trump would win. His campaign was, to so many people, for so many months, just a lark, just a publicity stunt, just a media circus. There were no stakes; the whole thing was stupid. Might as well get some good tweets out of it.

Another reason so few reporters were ringing the alarm was the overarching prevalence of the white racial frame within establishment, center-left journalism. Trump employed explicitly racist rhetoric throughout his campaign. He surrounded himself with white nationalist advisers and was giddily embraced by neo-Nazis, the Klan, and other reactionary groups. For people targeted by Trump and his followers, the stakes were always high. For those who could hold embodied harm at arm's length, on the other hand, for those ignorant or dismissive of the threats that others were facing, all the swirling online bigotry got to be just hot air, just internet culture, just trolls being trolls.

The reactionary Right's professional grade media manipulators exactingly exploited this myopia. In particular, reactionary professionals, many of whom had previously worked within center-left media, leaned heavily into the trolling mystique. Far-right microcelebrity Milo Yiannopoulos was especially shameless. Drawing from a cache of leaked emails, *BuzzFeed News'* Joseph Bernstein chronicles the "coy dance" Yiannopoulos performed before and after the election to minimize the white supremacy of right-wing reactionaries and maximize their plausibly deniable trollishness. The endgame was to launder white nationalism into the mainstream.[62] Other reactionary influencers did the same. They were on the same page as the Daily Stormer, at least in terms of communications strategies. They knew how distracting the trollish wink can be. They also knew how many people would recognize that wink, or at least think they recognized the wink, and subsequently interpret their bigotry as, say it with us, just trolling.

And so, throughout the election, and even after Trump's inauguration, people who had the luxury of laughing treated white supremacy like one big joke. Charlottesville was a turning point for many reporters, who at that point looked up from all the fun they'd been having and finally noticed they weren't in Kansas anymore. Certainly by the time fifty-one souls were taken in Christchurch, reporters saw the Nazis for the trolls. Of course, by then it was too late.

An overwhelming percentage of the journalists Phillips interviewed expressed regret over not seeing the signs earlier, for remaining ensconced in what many described as their own liberal bubbles, and for personally and professionally benefiting from such a dark political turn. But no group was more remorseful than the troll-trained reporters who kicked bigotry into the air, half righteous and half ironic, as they continued covering, and continued laughing at, what they thought was internet culture as usual.

Looking back at the information she had at the time, when it seemed like Trump's candidacy was a pipe dream infomercial, one technology reporter admitted feeling torn; she wasn't sure what she could have done differently. And yet, she admitted of the articles she wrote in 2016, "Every once in a while I'll look back and see something that I wrote . . . and the pit of my stomach falls, because either I was joking about these trolls, or making light of the fact, joking about Trump becoming president. It makes me physically sick to read them now."[63]

Another troll-trained reporter experienced a similar emotional reckoning. She noted how, as Trump's campaign was in full swing, she wrote a series of articles that pointed and laughed at all the swastikas plastered across a particular online game. After Charlottesville, she decided to go on the Daily Stormer, which she had heard referenced many times during the election but had never visited. She never had any reason to; as far as she knew, trolling and neo-Nazism were two totally separate worlds. Upon seeing precisely the imagery she'd thought was a joke a few months earlier and, in the process, realizing just how wrong her assumption had been, she felt "a kind of abject horror. . . . Because I feel like I'm part of it, because I've just been writing about the internet like it was no big deal, for years now."[64]

Taken by themselves, the early framings of troll-trained reporters help explain how 2016's alt-right narrative emerged as it did, when it did. But that was only half the story. In addition to reinforcing fetishized sight, early efforts to surface "funny and bizarre" examples of pro-Trump white supremacy also brought more reporters to the story.

And not just troll-trained reporters, either; running just a few steps behind the (typically) younger, troll-trained reporters were more traditional, (typically) older reporters inclined to approach trollish lulz with much more credulity. They might not have been laughing as they did it, but they still publicized all kinds of conspiracy theories and hoaxes— conspiracy theories and hoaxes that were, very often, first surfaced by troll-trained reporters—as they emphatically debunked them. This was the "both sides" impulse at work, as well as the belief that light disinfects— professional norms that they, as the older guard, had been steeped in for much longer.

There were benefits to being troll-untrained. These reporters were able to see the threat clearly. They knew it wasn't funny. At the same time, by ascribing an unwavering, stone-faced sincerity to white supremacist messaging, these reporters were nonetheless vulnerable to manipulation, though in a different direction. Because they were not familiar with the rhetorical tactics of trolling, these reporters were often unable to decode and effectively address the aggressive performativity and head-spinning irony that remained a hallmark of even the most explicitly violent white supremacist content. As a result, they still gave the manipulators exactly what they wanted: lulzy attention, recruiting power, and, perhaps most devastating of all, public legitimacy.

The vulnerabilities of reporters who were not troll trained thus complemented the vulnerabilities of those who were. Together they kicked up more dust from more fields, burying entire swaths of farmland. As everyone else staggered against the winds, gasping for air, the bigots just stood there, grinning, as they surveyed the barren landscape.

EMBODYING FETISHIZED SIGHT

The polluted information that roared, unchecked, across the landscape during the 2016 election cycle didn't appear out of nowhere. Nothing appears out of nowhere, whether it's a dust storm in Kansas or a reactionary on 4chan. As it always does, the spread of polluted information in 2016 stemmed from the choices people made. Those choices stemmed, in turn, from those people's experiences, their assumptions, and their bodies in the world. All influenced the fruit that grew and dust that blew.

Reporters who laughed at the aesthetics and rhetoric of subcultural trolling, even as they might have wagged a that's-so-naughty finger at the people propagating it, had the luxury of laughing and the luxury of disapproving without feeling compelled to do much about it. More than anything else, these reporters had the luxury of approaching violent reactionaries as little more than trolls on little more than the internet. One reporter, a woman of color, reflected on how easily white reporters, and particularly white male reporters, were able to frame persistently racist, misogynist abuse as something so abstract, so whitewashed, so *funny*. "Because the threat isn't at their front door," she explained, "because it isn't going to impact them."[65] That it all got to be an amusing—or at least an interesting—abstraction also helps explain why so many of these reporters ran with bigots' free speech reframes. Never mind that "free speech" only ever meant free speech for the bigots, who would immediately spin around, tell everyone else to shut their goddamned mouths, then start laughing. Apparently unaware of how they were being used—or simply unconcerned because it made for good copy—these reporters helped gaslight their readers into thinking that "free speech" defenses made by white supremacists were legitimate arguments worth considering.

White reporters were not the only people blinded by the one-two punch of fetishized sight and the white racial frame. Election stories in 2016 that focused on the reactionary Right were wildly popular with white audiences, just as stories about white racial terror had been during the Civil War, Jim Crow, and the civil rights movement. Literary scholar Debra Walker King chillingly contextualizes this impulse in her study of Black bodies in pain.[66] Stories about broken, dehumanized, and terrorized Black bodies are popular with white audiences, King explains, because too many white people derive, at best, fascinated befuddlement ("how could anyone be a *racist?*"), and at worst, a dark sort of pleasure, from the stories. A privileged "view from the trees," as King describes it, allows white folks to see violated nonwhite bodies as plot points, object lessons, or abstract stand-ins for the concept of victimhood. Or worst of all, as entertainment.

And that's if those bodies are mentioned at all. Often, stories of non-white bodies in pain are obscured by stories of the white bodies causing that pain; articles about the first Klan, tellingly, recounted the groups' racial terrorism while managing somehow not to talk about the freedpeople the Klan had terrorized. The 2016 election was, once again, no exception to this historical rule. As the reporters Phillips spoke with explained, and many outright lamented, white audiences throughout the election cycle were clamoring to read about white nationalism and supremacy. They couldn't get enough reactionary meme listicles. They couldn't get enough explainers about alt-right trolling (whatever that was). They couldn't get enough colorful portraits of neo-Nazis, as if reactionaries were characters in a Christopher Guest mockumentary. Journalists knew this because journalists measured this. These were the stories their readers clicked on and shared.

And so, just as they did in response to secession and lynchings and the Klan, journalists gave those white audiences what they wanted, either because it meant another paycheck or because the journalists were similarly rapt, or both. In a way, it didn't matter why they did it. By spending the entire election cycle profiling bigots and psychoanalyzing bigots and yelling snark at bigots and huddling in a scrum around bigots outside the Charlottesville General District Court, journalists made the bigots the center of everyone's story. They made the bigots go mainstream.

As it was in chapter 2, this diagnosis is grim. The ecosystem was already strained under generations of racist violence and white obliviousness.

Network climate change deepened that strain and overlaid it with a whole new set of environmental stressors. The result has been devastating. Too many people planted too many of the wrong crops, irresponsibly tilled the land, and ignored warnings from those who have always seen the dangers clearly. And yet, again, it doesn't have to be this way. Kansas after the Great Depression is a case in point. As the US Soil Conservation Service implemented more responsible farming practices, restored native grasslands, and planted hundreds of miles of natural windbreaks, the land began to rebound.[67] We can also begin to rebound by reflecting on what we're harvesting and why, remembering that good intentions can still be messy as hell, and, most important of all, listening to the people who best understand the threats.

The storms on the prairie aren't the only storms to consider, however. Larger, more complex storms gather along the coasts, fueled by overlapping social, technological, and economic forces. These storms spread pollution even further, and in so doing, further complicate its prevention and removal. And so, the next mark to make on our map is up.

4 THE GATHERING STORM

Across the southeastern United States and the Caribbean isles, monsters rise up from the sea. As summer creeps into fall, we wait, warily, for the deluge these monsters will bring. We give them proper names—Hugo, Andrew, Katrina, Maria—and chart their paths as they spin toward our homes, lashing us with rain, blasting us with winds, and raising the sea itself to our front doors. We reverse our highways and evacuate our cities as mayors and governors and people on the news chronicle the damage.

We're afraid of these monsters, yet we keep making them stronger. We're warming our oceans, so when the monsters form off the coast, they have that much more energy to grow that much larger and stay that much longer. We're filling in marshes for condos and laundromats, so when the monsters reach land, their natural barriers are gone. What they have instead is a playground, extra blocks to flood, extra buildings to smash. We furrow our brows and batten our hatches as these monsters, these menacing blobs on the radar, lumber toward our shores in greater numbers each year, giving us more chances to look back and say, "Now *that* was a big one."

Yet "one" isn't quite right. Hurricanes might be big, but they aren't really *one* thing. They are, instead, the sum of many parts. They're the temperature of the water. They're the descending and ascending air. They're the spin of the earth's axis. They're how all these things interact. As their causes aren't singular, neither are their effects. If the winds miss you, the storm surge might not. If you dodge the storm surge, you still have to worry about flooding rivers. Exactly what happens, exactly what's destroyed, is the result, of course, of the hurricane itself. But it's also the result of a whole host of other less obvious factors, like coastal development, population density, and details like whether metric tons of manure from your friendly neighborhood hog farm spill out into the tributary. No matter how singular and self-contained the angry red blob looks on the radar screen, hurricanes are not singular and they're certainly not self-contained. They're a process, more verb than noun.

That people still refer to hurricanes as singular, self-contained things makes perfect sense. Singular, self-contained things are the things you can see. Singular, self-contained things are the things you can evacuate from. It's simply easier to warn people about nouns, not verbs. Even so, locking a hurricane into singularity and self-containment, as if the hurricane begins and ends with the angry red radar blob, undercuts the ability to tell more holistic, more revealing, and more instructive stories about what the storm is, where it came from, and how we should respond.

By actively *verbing* the nouns being studied, hurricane analysis tells exactly these kinds of stories.[1] This approach is especially helpful when trying to make sense of conspiracy theories, which number among the most menacing storms on the internet. Because they loom so large, have traveled so far, and have lingered so long after making landfall, this chapter focuses on Deep State conspiracy theories: the reactionary pro-Trump narratives purporting that Democrats are, among other horrors, engaged in a secret plot to destroy the Trump administration from within. Prominent Deep State theories include Pizzagate, which maintains that Hillary Clinton ran a satanic child-sex-trafficking ring out of the back of a Washington, DC, pizza shop, as well as the Seth Rich assassination theory, which asserts that a Democratic National Committee staffer was killed for attempting to expose the shadow government's schemes. One Deep State theory, however, towers above all the rest. Launched by a self-proclaimed whistleblower within the Trump administration known as Q, the QAnon conspiracy theory claims that Trump and his allies are quietly planning a counteroffensive against the globalists, Satanists, and child molesters embedded within the government.

Each of these theories emerged as a storm unto itself. Over time, however, they began to replicate a rare meteorological phenomenon known as the Fujiwhara effect, in which multiple storms churning in the same region impact each other. When these storms are equivalent in size and strength, one storm will alter the course of another. When one of the storms is much stronger, it will lasso the smaller storm into its orbit. The latter is what happened with Deep State theories. Pizzagate and the Seth Rich assassination theory, both destructive in their own right, were ultimately absorbed by QAnon, creating a Deep State bomb cyclone so enormous and all-encompassing that it roared to the center of Donald Trump's impeachment. To even greater and more deadly effect, Deep State theories whipped up the winds around another kind of storm altogether: the COVID-19 pandemic, which many in the MAGA orbit denied as another media hoax, even as the gale was bearing down on their own homes.

To explain how Fujiwhara-fueled hurricanes engulfed US politics, it's not enough to chronicle when each storm emerged. Nor is it enough to lay out their conspiratorial claims and debunk them one by one. To understand Deep State superstorms, we must analyze how overlapping historical, technological, and economic forces have strengthened the winds; how asymmetric polarization has warmed the informational waters; and how efforts to contain the storms have instead pushed them into whole new areas on the map. Conducting such an analysis doesn't just assess the causes, effects, and risks of conspiratorial storms. It gives the people on shore time to prepare and preempt the worst impacts when the next storm arrives. The long-term goal, however, is much more ambitious than that: it's to prevent these storms from forming in the first place.

CONSPIRATORIAL FRAMES

Conspiracy theories postulate how and why some hidden, usually under-handed, group is working toward some hidden, usually nefarious, agenda. These theories take many different forms and emerge from many different communities for many different reasons. The term *conspiracy theory* doesn't hinge on truth or falsehood; an objectively false conspiracy theory and one that turns out to be fact are both conspiracy theories while they're being theorized.[2] In terms of demographics, white communities advance conspiracy theories at extremely high rates, but so do communities of color.[3] No one single characteristic makes someone more inclined toward belief in conspiracy.

The pervasiveness of conspiracy theories undercuts the widespread assumption that such theories are fringe phenomena. It also undercuts the stereotype of the isolated, wide-eyed true believer wearing a tinfoil hat and rummaging around what looks like a set from season 3 of the *X-Files*. Conspiracy theories can thrive on the margins, but they also thrive within the highest seats of power.[4] They emerge during times of extreme strife and during times of relative stability.[5] Some have understandable, even outright rational, origins, while some do not. For example, many of the theories that spread through Black communities have verified historical precedent, stemming from the persistent, structural, all-too-real efforts by those in power to poison, experiment on, and murder Black people.[6] Other theories, like white nationalist fears that people of color are conspiring to eliminate the white race, are irrational and the opposite of precedented. In short, conspiracy theories come in as many flavors as the people who amplify them. The world of conspiracy theories is large and contains multitudes.

This isn't to say that conspiracy theories have nothing in common. American Studies scholar Peter Knight argues that conspiratorial thinking demonstrates a "pervading sense of uncontrollable forces taking over our lives, our minds, and even our bodies."[7] Richard Hofstadter, one of the most oft-cited commentators on American conspiracy theory, made a similar point in 1964, arguing that, across the political spectrum, true believers are marked by a distinctly paranoid rhetorical pattern and overall "style of mind."[8]

This style underscores another commonality between conspiracy theories: their abiding preoccupation with some subversive *them*, the personification of everything *we* hate.[9] Chapter 1 outlined the evil *them* of the Satanic Panics. As is the case with all subversion myths, the thing the Satanic Panics was about—Satan, of course—wasn't the only thing it was about. Fear of the devil incarnate reflected a generations-old deep memetic frame that maintained who the *us* was, who the *them* was, and what hung in the balance if *they* successfully destroyed *our* way of life.

Similar kinds of subversion myths, and all the deep memetic baggage they carry, are central to many conspiracy theories. As historian Kathryn Olmsted explains, alien subversion myths—which zero in on nonwhite or non-Christian immigrants deemed threatening to "real" Americans—are especially common within the United States; they were, according to Olmsted, the dominant conspiratorial frame in the US throughout the nineteenth century.[10] Hofstadter devotes particular energy, and particular ire, to myths of this ilk, which remained prominent within right-wing circles through the twentieth century. The animating premise of these theories, Hofstadter argues, is the fear that "America has been largely taken away" from the so-called real Americans.[11] Even if nothing had, in fact, been robbed from this *us*, the belief was that *we* have been victimized by *them*, and further, that America had been great—until all these different others came along and ruined it.

A second conspiratorial frame emerged in the US during the 1960s: deep suspicion about the federal government. Olmsted argues that this suspicion developed with good reason; it was a response to the United States' growing surveillance apparatus and willingness to use that apparatus to stick its nose, and of course its weaponry, where it didn't belong.[12] Conspiratorial side-eyes were also cast for the very simple reason that the government engaged in actual conspiracies, at times floating disinformation to deflect attention away from damaging truths. When these plots came to light—about the FBI slandering and spying on Black activists, about the Kennedy assassination, about Vietnam, about Watergate, about the Iran-Contra arms deal—people had ample reason to doubt official explanations of later events. As a result, government credibility plummeted. That establishment news media tended to repeat official talking points verbatim, often while denigrating alternative explanations, similarly damaged trust in journalism and, more broadly, trust in institutions—including the very notion of professional expertise.[13]

Although public trust in the government took an across-the-board nosedive during the second half of the twentieth century, the nature of that mistrust could vary greatly depending on one's experience and one's frames. For progressives, particularly those who had been caught up in the

Red Scare, or civil rights activists who had been targeted by the FBI, or any number of people who objected to the United States' bloody colonialist interventions, the government was run by right-wing fascists. For conservatives, particularly in the South, the federal government's desegregation efforts during the 1960s, along with other pushes for equality, were the offensive encroachments.[14] In their minds, those white southerners were the real victims of an oppressive state; their reaction, as historian Jason Sokol explains, was to cast the government as the far-left fascist *them*.[15]

Looking for Enemies

Add one part alien subversion myth to one part antigovernment suspicion, filter through Hofstadter's paranoid style, and you've brewed yourself a Deep State storm.[16] The continuity between Deep State narratives and midcentury antigovernment frames is as straightforward as it is clichéd (certainly by *X-Files* standards): there exists, these theories go, a villainous bureaucratic shadow government that sets the nation's foreign and domestic agenda based on its own self-interested globalist whims, "real" Americans be damned. Trump, running as a Washington DC outsider, rode precisely those antigovernment, antiglobalist suspicions into office.

But antigovernment suspicion is complicated when your party runs the government. The Deep State theory is essentially a work-around, allowing Trump and his supporters to keep their cake and eat it too; the federal government can be full of nefarious shadow agents, *and* the head of that government can be the hero. That contortion satisfies antigovernment frames, but it creates consequential tensions. While it may be the case that the US government has long disseminated conspiracy theories, or merely created the conditions for conspiracy theories to thrive, the conspiracy theories now disseminated (or merely tolerated) by the government *are directed at that same government*. Every time Trump phones into Fox News, the antigovernment call is coming from inside the White House.

Alien subversion is just as integral to Deep State narratives. In the 1960s, when Hofstadter was writing, the un-American alien *them* were the communists (often synonymous with Jews, even if not stated outright) and any progressive social causes that could be tethered to Communism, including civil rights and feminism. By the time Arlie Russell Hochschild was studying Tea Party conservatives in the 2010s, the alien subversion dog whistle had redirected to the "line cutters" absconding with the opportunities and benefits that conservatives believed "traditional" (as always, "white") Americans should be receiving.[17]

In Trump's America, the valiant *us* beset by alien subversion follows a similar pattern, uniting white, patriarchal, Christian Americans behind a Reagan-era campaign slogan with deep memetic roots: Make America Great Again. Carol Anderson, an African American Studies scholar, zeros in on the white rage at Trump's MAGA core.[18] What Trump warned throughout his campaign, Anderson explains, was that people of color would continue getting more than what they deserved, while "real" Americans would continue getting less (a statement itself implying that people of color were already getting all they needed and more). Trump pulled from and fed into these concerns, implicitly and explicitly promising to return America to the halcyon days of the 1950s, an era when white dominance remained firmly entrenched, when white folks didn't need to share resources, and when beleaguered white men didn't have to worry about "political correctness."

It should go without saying: the 1950s were a brutal, violent era for the tens of millions of Americans who happened to be any color other than white, and especially brutal and violent for those who also happened to be any gender other than male. And yet this idea is what Trump publicly and unrepentantly stood for: the government should be serving the interests of those "traditional" Americans, not the invading horde of immigrants that the leftists were trying to coax across the border. The enemy—*them*—included anyone who stood on the other side of that potent, xenophobic frame.

The demonization of the anti-MAGA *them* was on full, and indeed literal, display on June 19, 2019, at Donald Trump's 2020 reelection kick-off rally. The event opened with a prayer from televangelist Paula White, Trump's spiritual adviser. Midprayer, White pivoted to the anti-Trump *them*. "Right now," she declared, "let every demonic network who has aligned itself against the purpose, against the calling of President Trump, let it be broken, let it be torn down in the name of Jesus!"[19] Later she promised the rapt crowd that "President Trump will overcome every strategy from hell and every strategy from the enemy—every strategy—and he will fulfill his calling and his destiny."

A white nationalist America is the America Trump champions. That is the "calling" and "destiny" Paula White asked Trump's supporters to pray for, and that is the vision that conspiracy theorists endorse when they rail against the Deep State getting in Trump's way.

"I Don't Like to Use It, Because It Sounds So Conspiratorial"

Deep State conspiracy theories are, in other words, highly precedented. At the same time, when they emerged in 2016, they were the unique products of the contemporary weather system. That historical specificity is key to understanding how the theories emerged, how they became central to Trump's impeachment, and how they endangered millions of lives during the COVID-19 crisis.

One of the first Deep State catalysts was Trump's incessant calls during the 2016 election to "lock up" democratic candidate Hillary Clinton for her involvement in a laundry list of alleged criminal activities. Another was Trump's declaration that, as president, he would drain Washington's "swamp" of corrupt bureaucrats. Trump's bellowings fired up his base, which emboldened Trump, which fired up his base, which emboldened Trump—a cycle supercharged by the news media at every turn.

Conservative media played a crucial role in this process, epitomizing the asymmetric polarization Yochai Benkler, Robert Faris, and Hal Roberts mapped during the 2016 election cycle.[20] This polarization is asymmetric because, while media on the Right have grown increasingly insular and reactionary, center-left mainstream media have remained traditionalist and entrenched in norms from previous media eras.

On the Right, these shifts are often attributed to the rise of Fox News, which was founded in 1996 just as the network climate crisis was gaining strength. As Anne Nelson's history of the American right-wing influence network shows, however, asymmetric polarization began long before that.[21] Indeed, the Right's baked-in ideological resistance to the Left was a central message of 1970s Evangelical media networks. The reach of these networks grew throughout the 1980s and 1990s, with vast right-wing radio empires playing an especially pivotal role. By the time local journalism began collapsing under the weight of technological and policy shifts in the 1990s and 2000s, far-right media were perfectly poised to swoop into the resulting "media deserts" devoid of local media coverage, filling them with reactionary, verging on extremist, content.[22]

Meanwhile, center-left publications remained loyal to the Fairness Doctrine, or at least the spirit behind it, as the actual policy was abolished by Ronald Reagan's FCC in 1987. Good faith commitment to both-sides fairness is easily gamed by propagandists who have no interest in the truth, yet still want to see their lies given equal billing. Or, more simply, who want to "win"—measured through ratings or getting out the vote or waging a holy war. Or all three at once. This is a fight the center-left has always been set up to lose, as the both-sides impulse simply doesn't fit within a right-wing, holy *us* vs. demonic *them* worldview.

Enter 2016. The swirling collision of asymmetric polarization on the Right and knee-jerk both-sides-ism on the center-left ensured that Trump's claims would be widely amplified across the political spectrum. Even mainstream coverage that condemned Trump, called out his lies, and countered them with facts spread his claims. And that's not all it did. Coverage critical of Trump—and of Trump supporters—also played into long-standing hostilities on the Right toward center-left media. For Evangelicals in particular, the assertion that the mainstream news media were in cahoots with the same criminal incompetents inhabiting "the swamp" was an easy sell; they'd been hearing how fake and terrible and downright satanic the liberal establishment was for decades. The more the establishment tried to counter Trump's accusations with facts, the more it triggered reactionary pushback against the perceived elitist *them* trying to tell *us* what to think.

Trump carried this antiestablishment grievance into the first moments of his presidency. The theme of his inauguration speech was "American carnage," and the newly sworn-in president spent the occasion decrying how low the country had fallen ("That was some weird shit," former president George W. Bush reportedly said after Trump's remarks).[23] It's no surprise that even as Trump and his party took power in January 2017, he and his supporters were still searching for enemies within the government.

Deep State theories didn't emerge solely from what Trump said, of course. As the Fujiwhara effect would predict, each new theory drew considerable energy from existing theories. One of the earliest centered on the July 2016 murder of Democratic National Committee staffer Seth Rich. Proponents of the theory claimed that Rich had been killed by some combination of Clinton goons and the Democratic National Committee after he allegedly leaked the DNC's stolen emails to WikiLeaks (a claim WikiLeaks' Julian Assange himself strongly suggested). Rich had done no such thing; police concluded that his death was the result of a botched robbery.

In 2019, Michael Isikoff of *Yahoo! News* chronicled how the Seth Rich assassination theory was in fact seeded as part of the Russian government's sweeping 2016 election interference efforts.[24] These efforts paid off handsomely, as Rich's already traumatized family was incessantly retraumatized by the onslaught of increasingly bizarre accusations, which, after bubbling up through Russian propaganda channels, filtered through forums like 4chan and Reddit before spreading into the right-wing media ecosystem.

The Seth Rich story laid the groundwork for another prominent pro-Trump conspiracy theory known as Pizzagate. This theory emerged in October 2016 and amassed enormous social media visibility thanks to the same DNC email leak that falsely placed John Podesta at the not actually demonic spirit-cooking dinner discussed in chapter 1. This theory, cobbled together from stolen DNC emails, held that Hillary Clinton and other prominent Democrats were running a satanic child sex ring out of the back of a Washington DC pizza shop. The Far Right—and without doubt the Russian government—was enthralled.

The 2016 election marked a turning point for both theories. Suddenly Trump's own administration became the hidey-hole for enemies within the government. The FBI, which had for months been investigating Russia's election interference, along with its possible ties to the Trump campaign, was at the top of Trump's conspiratorial shit list. Within months of his inauguration, Trump publicly accused the agency of wiretapping his phones as part of its inquiry, which by that point Trump was already calling a "ruse," a "hoax," and "non-sense."[25]

These suspicions went thermonuclear in May 2017. First, Trump fired FBI director James Comey. His reason, Trump explained in a taped interview with NBC's Lester Holt, was that "this Russia thing, with Trump and Russia, is a made-up story" (Trump later denied having made this admission). Days later, in response to Comey's firing, the Department of Justice appointed Robert Mueller to oversee a special counsel investigation into possible ties between Russian disinformation efforts and the Trump campaign—in essence, to continue the FBI's work. Not coincidentally, Anna Merlan notes, May 2017 was when the term *Deep State* experienced its first uptick on Google Trends.[26]

The Mueller investigation first elevated the Deep State enemy to national prominence; the accusation within far-right circles was that "Obama holdovers" were conspiring to undermine Trump from within the Justice Department. Deep State conspiracy theories were, in turn, supercharged by the narrative energies already fueling the Seth Rich and Pizzagate theories. Though both theories emerged before the 2016 election, they were each retroactively absorbed into the Deep State storm after May 2017. The ever-present influence of Fox News all but ensured this outcome. In the same week that the DOJ opened its special counsel investigation, Fox News published an article pushing the Seth Rich conspiracy theory. Ultimately the network was forced to retract the story, because it was nonsense. That didn't stop prime-time host Sean Hannity from doubling down; he continued doing nightly backflips to publicize the connections between the Deep State, Clinton, and the DNC.[27]

From May 2017 onward, a steady stream of reactionary videos, memes, and manifestos dedicated to the Deep State pinged back and forth across pro-Trump media. The chans, MAGA corners of Reddit, and other far-right forums served the younger demographic, while Fox News breathlessly covered a variety of Deep State plots for its older viewers. High-profile figures within the Trump orbit also pushed the theory, including two—former national security adviser Michael Flynn and longtime Trump adviser Rodger Stone—who used the Deep State as a legal defense after being indicted as part of Robert Mueller's special counsel investigation.[28] Twitter played a crucial role in linking each of these networks, ensuring that the energies of one would feed into all the others.

The frenetic cross-posting between right-wing networks was not restricted to the MAGAsphere. Center-left news media covered the Deep State story with equivalent energy, often as more of a Trump circus sideshow. Progressives on social media also joined in to fling their own hot takes, ensuring that Deep State theories traveled well beyond the *us* pushing the narrative. These reactions, in turn, helped the conspiracy entrepreneurs who built an entire brand on top of the Deep State parlay all that free publicity into merch sales and monetized YouTube channels.[29]

And then there was the president, who professed to dislike the term *Deep State*—because, as he explained in an interview, it "sounds so conspiratorial"[30]—yet spent years decrying the Mueller investigation as a "phony witch hunt" invented by the Democrats and their allies within the "fake news" media. The latter, Trump argued, were, first, enemies of the people and, second, just mad because Hillary Clinton lost the election—a default line of attack wielded by people defending the Deep State theory and denouncing anyone who challenged Trump. Through his incessant protestations and invectives and tweeted obstructions of justice, Trump thus posited a false conspiracy theory to obscure a true conspiracy undertaken by the Russian government, which, as Mueller's report revealed, did in fact interfere with the election to benefit Trump—help that the Trump campaign may not have initiated, but was certainly aware of and more than happy to accept.[31]

YOU CAN'T SPELL *GREAT AWAKENING* WITHOUT THE LETTER Q

Fueled by Seth Rich's murder and Pizzagate, the Deep State conspiracy theory roared forward, absorbing as much energy as it generated. The bombshell arrest in July 2019 of Jeffrey Epstein, a wealthy financier indicted for an *actual* underage sex-trafficking conspiracy, churned the waters even more. The fact that Epstein had links to Bill Clinton and other high-profile liberals, coupled with the troubling detail that Epstein had been cut an unusually generous plea deal for similar charges in 2008 by US Attorney Alex Acosta, spun off a slew of Deep State accusations. Same with accusations of Satanism. As anthropologist Jessica A. Johnson highlights, when YouTube conspiracy theorists first got wind of Epstein's sweetheart plea deal, they zeroed in on his Clinton connections and in their videos included fictionalized "ritual sacrifice montages" featuring masked perpetrators.[32]

As Pizzagate's falsehoods collided with Epstein's very real crimes, right-wing conspiracy theorists were inundated with what, to them, provided the ultimate proof of their claims—proof that remained unshaken by Trump's own ties to Epstein, like Trump making Alex Acosta his Secretary of Labor, Trump praising Epstein's exploits with women "on the younger side," and 1992 news footage of Trump and Epstein leering at women together during a party.[33] Inconvenient truths aside, the Epstein-Pizzagate connection became even more compelling for believers in August 2019, when Epstein died by suicide in his jail cell. Almost immediately, *Epstein didn't kill himself* became a meme, as did accusations that the Clintons were the real killers.[34]

The arrest and death of Jeffrey Epstein strengthened the Deep State surge; it was a powerful force. But it wasn't the most powerful. The Epstein story was so easily roped into the Deep State superstorm because that storm was already a monster, having recently absorbed a bomb cyclone known as the QAnon conspiracy theory. QAnon marked the mainstream tipping point; it powered the Deep State superstorm out of the Fox News orbit, through the Epstein scandal, into the eye of impeachment, and forward to the COVID-19 crisis. It was a perfect conspiracy storm.

A Sitcom Star and Her President

It all began, as it so often does, with a tweet. On March 27, 2018, actor Roseanne Barr accused David Hogg, a student at Marjory Stoneman Douglas High School, of giving a Nazi salute at a gun control rally. This was false. Hogg, who had emerged as a prominent gun control activist after a mass shooting at his school, was raising his fist in protest.

As out of left field as the claim seemed, Barr wasn't posting a random attack. Nazi David Hogg was already a meme, at least in some reactionary circles. This was the profound insult added to the indescribable injury of the shootings themselves, which claimed the lives of seventeen Stoneman Douglas students and staff members. The false Nazi connection wasn't the only accusation, either. In the wake of the tragedy, many Stoneman Douglas students were subjected to a series of harmful, patently false conspiracy theories. Most prominent were assertions that they were paid crisis actors, a term reactionaries use to suggest that mass shootings are hoaxes and survivors are only pretending to be victims. Fox News dutifully helped publicize this indignity.[35]

For her part, Barr had been pushing a laundry list of right-wing conspiracy theories for years. Not only was she a proponent of the Seth Rich assassination theory, she also claimed in February 2017 that Democrats were blocking Jeff Sessions's Attorney General nomination because he promised to start making arrests over Pizzagate (which she called #PedoGate).

After her Nazi David Hogg tweet, however, Barr recanted and quickly deleted the post. But not quickly enough; the tweet lived on through screen grabs shared widely by outlets like *BuzzFeed News*, *Business Insider*, and *Newsweek*.[36] The day after deleting her tweet, Barr responded to the controversy. She claimed that she had reacted to a photoshopped image and only later realized her error. Many weren't convinced, noting that the apparent source image she was responding to was in fact *not* photoshopped; it was Hogg raising his fist in protest, plain as day. More damningly, Barr's critics noted that the highly anticipated reboot of her show *Roseanne* had premiered that same night on ABC; they speculated that the network had forced her to remove the tweet.

Despite—or maybe aided by—this controversy, the sitcom enjoyed massive first-night ratings, even prompting Trump to call and congratulate Barr. The show also, unsurprisingly, precipitated a great deal of news coverage. Stories focused, first, on the politics of the show itself, as *Roseanne* was one of the few network programs to sympathetically portray Trump voters. Stories also focused on the politics of *Roseanne*'s star, specifically the extent to which Roseanne Barr, the offscreen woman, could or should be separated from Roseanne Conner, the onscreen character. These stories often addressed growing calls to boycott the show based on Barr's conspiratorial and often explicitly racist tweets. Barr was a media storm in and of herself. Those conspiratorial energies were primed to collide with the clouds already gathered on the horizon.

Hurricane Q

Such was the backdrop for Barr's maelstrom of tweets on March 30, 2018, posted the week after she'd called David Hogg a Nazi. Her tweets on March 30 covered a favorite subject: the QAnon conspiracy theory. QAnon maintains that Donald Trump is waging—and winning—a war against the Deep State. Conspiracy theorists know this because an individual, or group of individuals, called Q knows this. Q knows this because they claim to be embedded within the Trump administration and have "Q-level" security clearance. In addition to the overarching assertion that Trump is valiantly fighting the Deep State, Q maintained (at least initially) that Robert Mueller was actually in secret league with Trump and was using the Russia investigation as a ruse to take down the Deep State and expose its satanic child sex ring.

Q first appeared in late October 2017, when they posted a series of cryptic messages to 4chan's /pol/ board. Q's initial flurry included several vague prognostications, some of which appeared to come true, or at least could be contorted toward confirmation. Perhaps because participants sincerely believed, or wanted to believe, Q's story, perhaps because they recognized its potential for media manipulation and conspiracy entrepreneurship, perhaps because they simply thought the meme was funny, Q's posts catalyzed ceaseless storytelling, speculation, and play on 4chan. Technology researcher Benjamin Decker followed the story as it traveled.[37] First, participation spread from 4chan to 8chan in early December 2017. Then it jumped to the Calm before the Storm subreddit several weeks later, and a Discord server after that, in January 2018. The Great Awakening, another subreddit devoted to QAnon, became a hotbed in early summer 2018. By this time, QAnon had evolved into its own distinct conspiracy brand, complete with the slogan "Where We Go One, We Go All," or, more economically, WWG1WGA.

Barr was tracking QAnon's evolution from the very start. All the way back in November 2017, she expressed interest in the theory and asked if it would be possible to meet the individual or individuals posting as Q. She was also caught up in her own microconspiracy about QAnon: soon after she sent those November tweets, her account was briefly suspended. As Kelly Weill of the *Daily Beast* chronicles, conspiracy-inclined followers speculated that Barr had somehow been replaced or otherwise "taken care of" by the Deep State.[38] Barr wasn't gone for long, and upon her return to Twitter, she continued pursuing her interest in Q. In her round of tweets on March 30, 2018, she zeroed in on the Pizzagate-inflected elements of the theory, praising Trump for having broken up pedophile rings "in high places everywhere" and freeing children from sexual bondage, Barr claimed, at a rate of hundreds per month.[39]

Harnessing the attention generated by Barr's David Hogg tweet, the premiere of her show, and her long-standing interest in QAnon, journalists dove headfirst into the MAGA Roseanne story. "Roseanne Keeps Promoting QAnon, the Pro-Trump Conspiracy Theory That Makes Pizzagate Look Tame," the *Daily Beast* proclaimed; "Roseanne Tweets Support of Trump Conspiracy Theory, Confuses Twitter," echoed CNN; "The Conspiracy Theory behind a Curious Roseanne Barr Tweet, Explained," wrote the *Washington Post*.[40] Reporters covering Barr's March tweets summarized the QAnon theory and linked out to existing coverage of the saga—explanations that often took half an article just to lay out the basics. Many also addressed Barr's November 2017 tweets and her fondness for conspiracy theories more broadly.

These news articles, to be sure, chronicled things that were actually happening in the world. Countless proponents, detractors, and onlookers besides Barr clamored for information about QAnon. For many of them, "The Storm," as the theory came to be called, was all too real; allegedly just around the corner, as reporter Paris Martineau explained, were "arrests, political turmoil, and Republican vindication."[41] At the very least, the story was something fun to speculate about on the chans. As active as these participants might have been, however, QAnon didn't become international news solely because of its social media presence. Like so many far-right activities, QAnon was supercharged by center-left journalists.

Roseanne Barr was, unwittingly, vital to this process. As had been the case in 2017, but much more prominently in 2018, the gravitational pull of Barr's celebrity directed a great deal of interest, and therefore a great deal of energy, to the story. These energies were compounded by *Roseanne*'s Trump connections. All those stories about Barr's QAnon tweets, in turn, propelled the theory well beyond Barr's personal reach—indeed, beyond any proponents' personal reach. Same with stories designed to explain or debunk QAnon. All of it furthered the QAnon narrative and its associated claims about satanic Deep State pedophiles.

Consequently, people who had no knowledge of or interest in QAnon but did have knowledge of or interest in Barr or Trump were exposed to the theory. Not because they spent any time on 4chan, or because they followed Barr on Twitter, or because they followed anyone on Twitter. They didn't have to go to the conspiracy theory to encounter the conspiracy theory. The conspiracy theory came to them. It then filtered back into the information landscape when the same people responded with social media likes or commentary or simply clicked through to an article, feeding ever more data into the mouths of waiting algorithms. The end result was to grant widespread, often deeply serious, cultural traction to a theory that may very well have started as what Know Your Meme calls "a live action roleplaying game."[42]

News coverage helped amplify QAnon even when it wasn't the direct focus of an article. For example, on May 29, 2018—two months after her QAnon-meets-Pizzagate tweet—Barr tweeted a racist epithet about Valerie Jarrett, a Black woman who served as senior adviser to President Obama. Almost as quickly as the tweet was posted, *Roseanne* was canceled. A great deal of the subsequent coverage tethered Barr's hateful comment to her historically outlandish social media presence. To provide readers with context, fresh articles about Barr hyperlinked to the compendium of Barr-focused conspiracy explainers and debunkers already in existence—in the process, adding a whole new gust of wind to the storm. For example, in the postcancelation article "Roseanne Barr's Tweets Didn't Come from Nowhere," *New York Times* author Sopan Deb begins discussing QAnon by the third paragraph.[43] *Roseanne* may have been canceled, but Barr wasn't deterred: "we r the army of truth," she tweeted on June 20, 2018, "wwg1wga."[44]

Where They Go One, We Go All

The feedback loop between news coverage and cultural visibility wasn't lost on QAnon's most active proponents. Regardless of their specific motives—Phillips notes the difficulty of determining who was participating sincerely, who was in it for the media manipulation, who was a live-action role player, and who was some combination of all three[45]—all worked to amplify the theory. Indeed, attention was the goal from the very beginning of the QAnon saga, when two 4chan moderators and a YouTube vlogger came across Q's initial posts on /pol/, saw potential in the story, and decided to spread it across social media.[46]

Benjamin Decker's research provides even more insight into proponents' highly coordinated propaganda efforts, which were firmly in place by November 2017.[47] Armed with cheat sheets full of time-tested manipulation strategies—including ironic humor, zippy memes, and canned talking points—QAnon proponents began working across platforms to push the story as far as possible. They also discussed how to maximize Q exposure at Trump rallies; in one June 2018 thread on the Great Awakening subreddit, posters compared notes on how to make Q shirts and signs for an upcoming rally in South Carolina. One poster said they would pass out Q business cards.

All this work paid off at a rally in Tampa, Florida, on July 31, 2018. Members of the Great Awakening subreddit had coordinated in advance to wear matching Q shirts and brandish Q signs—all the better to bait reporters with.[48] The paraphernalia was an immediate news sensation, thanks in part to the wall-to-wall coverage of Trump's recent policy of separating immigrant families at the US-Mexico border. Whether or not QAnon proponents knew it, the backlash against Trump's inhumane order meant more cameras trained on the Florida State Fairgrounds Expo Hall. Trump might say something new, or something worse, about the policy. Instead, journalists saw a whole lot of Q signs, and *there* was something novel to cover. Decker chronicles how proponents reacted to the resulting panic. "You are now mainstream," one 8chan poster declared. "Handle w/ care."

For the next several days—indeed, for the next several weeks—more and more news outlets published more and more articles detailing the ins and outs of the theory, many of which referred back to Barr's initial involvement and subsequent unemployment. Articles from *Vox*, the *New York Times*, *GQ*, and the *Guardian*, among many others, included the words "explained," "explaining," or "guide to" in the headlines.[49] Other articles focused on how the online conspiracy had gained traction offline, evidenced by headlines like NBC's "What Is QAnon? A Guide to the Conspiracy Theory Taking Hold among Trump Supporters," NPR's "What Is QAnon? The Conspiracy Theory Tiptoeing into Trump World," and *Rolling Stone*'s "As QAnon Goes Mainstream, Trump's Rallies Are Turning Darker."[50]

Still others took aim at the nature of the conspiracy itself, headlining QAnon stories with terms like the *Independent*'s "bizarre," PBS's "false, fringe," and the *Washington Post*'s "bonkers" and "deranged conspiracy cult."[51] No matter how condescending and snarky the headlines, no matter how negative the coverage, QAnon proponents basked in the attention. This was perfect; this was exactly what they wanted for their "great awakening."[52] As noted by the *Washington Post*'s Abby Ohlheiser, one YouTuber who streams conspiratorial musings to his forty-five thousand subscribers perfectly captured this giddiness.[53] "I haven't been this happy in a very long time," he said. "CNN, NBC News, MSNBC, PBS NewsHour, *Washington Post*, MSNBC, those are our new QAnon reporters!" The man paused, then burst out laughing.

The Tampa Trump rally did not mark the end of the QAnon story. Not by a long shot. Articles about the conspiracy spiked in the coming months following additional Q-specific developments. For example, in December 2018, Vice President Mike Pence retweeted (and later deleted) a picture of himself standing with several Broward County, Florida, SWAT team officers, one of whom had affixed a Q patch onto his uniform. In the same month, a city councilperson in California, stepping down after losing an election, proclaimed "God bless Q" in her farewell address. This was, as *Daily Beast* reporter Will Sommer notes, the first known case of an elected official referencing the conspiracy theory during official business.[54] Reporters also continued covering the QAnon contingent at Trump rallies. "Write off the sheer prevalence of the QAnon cult at your own risk," NBC reporter Ben Collins tweeted in March 2019, responding to a YouTube video of Trump rally attendees brandishing Q paraphernalia.[55]

And then, again, there was the president. In late July 2019, Trump retweeted a QAnon promoter who had previously claimed, among other conspiratorial musings, that Democrats murder children so they can harvest their "pineal glands," and that the Clintons torture children in order to extract a drug from inside their skulls.[56] The retweet capped off twenty other instances in which Trump had retweeted QAnon supporters.[57] Then, in early August 2019, one of the opening speakers at a Trump rally in Cincinnati declared onstage, "We are all in this together. Where we go one, we go all."[58] After the 2019 jailhouse suicide of Jeffrey Epstein, Trump pushed the limits of the Deep State myth even further by retweeting the accusation that Epstein was actually murdered by the Clintons.[59] The hashtag #ClintonBodyCount immediately trended.

A Tale of Two Impeachments

As the president's tweets illustrate, the QAnon story is much bigger than QAnon. The story is predicated, instead, on all the overlapping storms, and all the overlapping energies, that fuel its metanarrative. Pizzagate. Seth Rich. The Satanic Panics. Older energies than even that. These energies, in turn, helped fuel entirely new storms. As 2019 concluded, the most politically consequential was the category 5 hurricane known as impeachment—which, unsurprisingly, Evangelical leaders immediately began describing as "a Satanic scheme to upend God's plan for America."[60]

It was not the actual Deep State, but rather a conspiracy theory about the Deep State, that triggered impeachment. During a July 2019 call with Ukrainian president Volodymyr Zelensky, Trump dangled the promise of foreign aid in exchange for two sets of investigations: one of Democratic rival Joe Biden and his son Hunter and another of the conspiratorial fever dream known as CrowdsStrike, which claims that the Deep State had secretly been working with Ukraine since 2016 to frame Russia for US election interference.

Trump didn't explicitly say the words "Deep State" in his call with Zelensky (though he did refer to CrowdStrike by name), opting instead for his usual euphemistic hints. By then, Trump wouldn't have *needed* to say the actual words to transmit the Deep State wink to his supporters. Vast swaths of the population were already convinced—by the president, by Fox News, by social media, by figures like Trump's lawyer, bagman, and constant cable surrogate Rudy Giuliani, who right up to impeachment worked with reactionary conspiracy theorists to boost Trump's defense—that the Democrats were trying to stage a secret coup.[61] Their first attempt was the Mueller investigation, this widely accepted argument went, and next was the sham impeachment—all because Hillary Clinton lost the election in 2016.

As evidenced by Giuliani's dubious on-air defenses, the disconnect between the Left and the Right during impeachment was immense. The millions of Americans not standing behind reactionary frames, whose worldviews had not been shaped by wraparound right-wing narratives, had no earthly idea what Republican congresspeople were talking about (Ukraine framing Russia? The server? *What?*). Conversely, the millions of Americans who *were* standing behind reactionary frames, whose worldviews were confirmed by everything they saw and read, had no earthly idea what Democratic congresspeople were talking about (Quid pro quo? Unconstitutional overreach? *What?*). The proceedings, Ryan Broderick of *BuzzFeed News* explains, were thus cleaved into two separate impeachments, one focused on the facts of the Ukraine scandal, and one raining down from a Deep State superstorm energized for decades by far-right influence networks.[62] Representative Paul Gosar, a Republican from Arizona, perfectly embodied the collision of these energies. In response to the House Intelligence Committee's impeachment hearings, Gosar wrote a series of twenty-two tweets whose first letters spelled out "Epstein didn't kill himself."[63]

Here things become meta. When we submitted the first draft of this book to the MIT Press production team in January 2020, we ended this section on the above Epstein line. Then, as it goes with books, time passed. As the weeks clicked by, the global COVID-19 crisis intensified. By the time we received copyedits back in March 2020, there was an entirely new chapter of the QAnon story to tell, and somehow, astonishingly, an even larger storm than impeachment to track.

The first connection between QAnon and COVID-19 is straightforward. Starting in January 2020, QAnon proponents teamed up with anti-vaccination activists to claim that former Microsoft CEO Bill Gates had, in consort with the usual Deep State suspects, created COVID-19 to profit from its eventual vaccine. During this window, Trump continued retweeting QAnon boosters and even a QAnon catchphrase ("Nothing can stop what's coming") captioned over a Photoshopped image of himself fiddling ("As Rome burned?" many critics asked).[64]

The second connection between QAnon and the pandemic is much less straightforward. It's also much more insidious. Months and months, even years and years, of drum beating within far-right circles about the evils of the Deep State and their efforts to destroy Trump's presidency all but ensured that, when the COVID-19 winds began picking up in the US, the virus would be dismissed as another Deep State plot. And that's exactly what happened. More extreme narratives outright blamed the Deep State for the COVID-19 outbreak. Other narratives, particularly those amplified by Fox News, claimed that the fake news media, working in lockstep with the Democrats, was overhyping COVID-19 to hurt the economy and thereby Trump's reelection chances.

Trump fixated on this narrative, and for weeks tweeted bitterly about the effect COVID-19 was having on the stock market. At one of his final campaign rallies before he too was forced to respect social distancing guidelines, Trump even claimed that the virus was a hoax. Trump's defenders insisted that he wasn't saying the virus itself was a hoax, but rather that the panic was a hoax the way that impeachment had been a hoax. This defense may have been semantically true, but conveniently sidestepped the fact that when Trump said impeachment was a hoax, he meant that everything about it was made up by the Democrats.

We finalize this latest round of edits—our last chance to add new content to the book—in mid April 2020. The Trump administration had months to prepare the country for COVID-19, yet chose instead to dismiss and downplay the threats, ensuring an utterly bungled federal response that threatened the health of hundreds of millions. Eventually, Trump acknowledged that COVID-19—which, true to xenophobic form, he'd taken to calling the "Chinese virus"—was in fact a public health emergency. With a gaslighting blitz that was breathtaking even by 2020 standards, Fox News likewise pivoted to emphasizing the seriousness of the virus, praising Trump's amazing response, and raining down hellfire on anyone who dared criticize him during a national crisis.[65] We're at war with this virus, Fox News insisted; and that makes Trump a wartime president—a designation that Trump tweeted about with great masculine vigor.

Trump kept tweeting, of course, but it wasn't long before the narrative shifted back to conspiratorial rumbling; soon Fox News was again questioning the wisdom of the quarantine, and Trump was bellowing in all caps about how people needed to be "LIBERATED" from states with Democratic governors who insisted on not reopening the economy before it was safe to do so.

The US death toll just hit thirty-five thousand. It's unclear how many more will die because so many, for so long, refused—and in many cases, are still refusing—to take the appropriate protective measures on the grounds that the Deep State, the fake news media, and the wily Democratic establishment (it's all the same evil internal enemy) was at it again. Trump broke with his tradition of conspiratorial euphemism to emphasize this point during a March 20, 2020 press briefing. At the briefing, he stood on stage flanked by Secretary of State Mike Pompeo and Anthony Fauci, director of the National Institute of Allergy and Infectious Diseases. A rarity within the Trump administration, Fauci was known for giving straight answers and actual facts to the press. Reporters asked Pompeo a question, but Trump interjected. "I'd like him to go back to the State Department,"

Trump said. "Or as they call it, the Deep State Department." Fauci blinked and tried not to laugh. After a moment, he covered his face with his hand.

NETWORK CLIMATE CHANGE AND EVERYTHING AFTER

None of this happened by accident. Yes, some of the energies fueling Deep State conspiracy theories are generations old. But such extreme media events, and such suffused, out-of-control pollution, are only possible in *this* specific climate at *this* specific moment in time. Analyzing how the network crisis helped manifest the Deep State superstorm is the first step toward preventing future hurricanes. And, very possibly, saving lives. As the COVID-19 catastrophe illustrates, conspiracy theories can kill.

Portrait of a Changing Ecosystem

Three points of divergence between contemporary conspiracy theories and theories of generations past highlight how and why our networks have been pushed into crisis.

First, while conspiracy theories have spread through all kinds of everyday networks since the 1960s—from Kennedy assassination truthers trading self-published speculations to the paranoid separatists that Oklahoma City bomber Timothy McVeigh hobnobbed with at gun shows[66]—conspiratorial frames can now cascade into the feeds of millions of nonbelievers in a matter of seconds. As a result, being a believer in a particular theory is no longer the primary precondition for learning more about it—or for helping propagate it. Deep State theories provide a striking case in point, but they're hardly anomalous. People can encounter all kinds of theories without even trying, and can send someone else scurrying down the rabbit hole to find more information with a single retweet. Even if they're sharing with an eye roll, because the story is just too bizarre.

Second, although the United States has incubated a robust, increasingly polarized right-wing media apparatus since the 1950s, this apparatus has been turbocharged by network climate change. One of the contributing factors is what computer scientist Kate Starbird and her team call an "echo-system."[67] When people ensconced within their echo-system see information, they have good reason to trust that it is correct; it has been corroborated here and there and everywhere they look. This corroboration, however, is an illusion of source diversity, not actual source diversity. As Anna Merlan argues, right-wing media, encompassing everything from 8chan to reactionary YouTube channels to Fox News to fundamentalist radio to Donald Trump and back again, is nothing if not an echo-system.[68]

The Left, of course, has its own ideological silos—but not with the same insularity, and not emerging from decades of ideological intensification. Ironically, the powerful signal boosting afforded by the center-left is a major catalyst *for* far-right intensification. Recall, for instance, how little attention mainstream journalists paid to the extraordinary popularity of televangelists in the 1970s and 1980s. Tens of millions of Americans' lives were shaped by televangelism. For mainstream journalists, though, fundamentalist stalwarts like Pat Robertson and Jerry Falwell were a passing joke, if they had heard the names at all.[69] Over time, slowly and steadily, network climate change rendered the barriers between the Left and the Right increasingly permeable. The Left is now well aware of far-right goings-on. What they do isn't just newsworthy. It's *clickbait*.

The most immediate consequence is that far-right messages—conspiracy theories very much included—that never would have traveled beyond reactionary circles are catapulted across the ecosystem. This creates new audiences for reactionary claims. Some are taken in. Others have their perspectives muddied by how incompatible far-right claims are with center-left accounts of the same events—to the delight of media manipulators, who succeed when people take in all the noise, throw up their hands because "nobody really knows the truth," and stop paying attention entirely.[70]

A less obvious but just as consequential effect of center-left signal boosting is to trigger a full-on Galapagos response. People further to the left, who have long been separated from those further to the right, are for the first time seeing what to them feels like a whole new species. And they don't like it—because what in the hell kind of alternative-fact bullshit are they talking about? People on the far right have long harbored, and indeed have long publicized, similar antipathies—unbeknownst to the liberals they've been railing against for decades. Back then, the Right was fighting a holy war only they knew was happening. Now, center-left media comment on the far right's every maneuver, mocking them, approaching them like malformed birds—only reinforcing right-wing beliefs about the elitist, biased, fake-news mainstream.

This disconnect is devastating for democracy. It's bad enough that folks on the Left and Right see each other as actual monsters; that makes consensus-building, not to mention policymaking, next to impossible. It's worse that one side has evolved to mistrust facts, science, and institutional knowledge, including the boring but crucial role establishment bureaucracy plays in keeping the world running; the COVID-19 pandemic illustrates the sweeping public health consequences of the impulse to trust no leftie, a designation equated with anyone who can claim expertise based on training and experience. The disconnect between the Left and Right has also ratcheted up the heat in an already-warming informational climate, ensuring that the most outrageous reactionary claims can spool up into raging storms very quickly with very little coordinated effort.

These informational consequences speak to the final historical divergence between conspiracy theories past and present. Ever since the 1960s, when trust in government began to plummet and antigovernment conspiracy theories became something of a national pastime, everyday citizens have clamored to "get to the bottom of things."[71] The same impulse has, for just as long, inspired conspiracy entrepreneurs to cash in on America's increasingly paranoid style. Social media certainly didn't create either impulse, but they have changed the alchemy of both. Everyday people—and, increasingly, politicians—looking to "get to the bottom of things" have more access to more information, more opportunities to mine more networks, and more incentive to parlay those investigations into a personal brand. Donald Trump is a classic example. He launched his political career in 2011 by propagating the racist Birther conspiracy theory, which maintains that President Barack Obama wasn't *really* born in the United States. In speech after speech and interview after interview, Trump wouldn't let questions about Obama's birth certificate go. As they would continue doing for years about lie after lie, reality TV spectacle after reality TV spectacle, the center-left news media rewarded him for his efforts.

As Trump's political genesis demonstrates, citizen sleuthing and conspiracy entrepreneurship have fundamentally fused. More than that, conspiracy theories have become for many a full-time job. And not just any job; the kind of job that can get you invited to the White House. On July 11, 2019, for example, Trump hosted a who's who of far-right conspiracy entrepreneurs at a "social media summit." During the event, Trump praised attendees for their ability to spread reactionary pollution. "The crap you think of is unbelievable," Trump fawned. "I mean it's genius—but it's bad."[72]

Peddling conspiracy theories and courting conspiracy theorists have become, in short, good business and good politics.[73] The extent of these financial and political benefits isn't just supported but often outright encouraged by the contemporary media climate. Enter the new normal of extreme weather events. After all, peddling conspiracies creates visibility, and visibility creates votes, or money, or both. So that's what politicians, particularly on the Right, do—because they benefit. That's also what everyday citizens, particularly on the Right, do—because they benefit. In many cases, it's all just a presidential retweet away.

Extreme Weather Events and You

Just as it's tempting to cordon a particular conspiracy theory off as a singular, self-contained narrative, it's tempting to presume that we somehow stand outside the information storms we observe. Both impulses are a mistake, but the second is particularly dangerous. As hurricane analysis insists, a storm isn't some singular "out there" thing. Instead it comprises everything we use, read, and interact with—our own social media accounts very much included. Increasingly extreme and increasingly frequent, informational superstorms draw their energy from the technological, the social, and all their points of connection.

Technological Actors

A major—if easy to overlook—energy source for emerging storms is platform design, and the powerful but subtle ways that design decisions influence user behavior. Online platforms guide their users through algorithmic docenting, which steers users via trending topics, search rankings, and other suggested content. These influences and the design decisions behind them do not unfold in a vacuum; they emerge, instead, from the collision of the liberal assumption that information should be free from censorship and the neoliberal assumption that markets should be free from regulation. Polluted information is the consequence of both.

In her study of Google search results, Safia Noble highlights this confluence, arguing that the hate, abuse, and conspiracy theories floating to the top of the search page aren't a surprise; they're baked into the company's business model.[74] Google's results are far from straightforward, of course; they're influenced by a number of factors, including page rankings,[75] search histories, and search engine optimization purchased from third-party companies or Google itself. No matter the specific algorithmic formula, when pollution spreads, Google benefits. As an advertising platform first and foremost, Google makes money when citizen sleuths use the internet to "get to the bottom of things" and when conspiracy entrepreneurs produce content for alternative media echo-systems. The company has every financial incentive to serve up as much of that pollution as possible.

Similarly, Tarleton Gillespie attributes the roar of polluted information—particularly hate and harassment—across social media to the corporate monetization of views, likes, clicks, and shares.[76] Like the hate and harassment Gillespie chronicles, like anything that generates interest online, conspiracy theories are, very simply, *valuable* to social media companies. And when content—whatever that content might be—is valuable to a platform, it's further promoted through recommendations, trending topics, and algorithmically weighted feeds. The content might be damaging. It might be harmful. It might be outright false. But it's good for business—which is precisely why, Gillespie notes, social media companies enforce the weakest possible moderation policies with the weakest possible consequences for abusers. The result might be devastating for the people who are abused, but for platforms it makes financial sense not to intervene; Danielle Citron highlights that, within their own corporate ethos, these platforms act rationally—even responsibly to their shareholders—when they stand idly by as their most vulnerable users are subjected to relentless attacks.[77]

Relatedly, Becca Lewis zeros in on how YouTube's algorithms reward, and in the process spread, bigoted conspiracy theories.[78] Not only do YouTube's algorithms initially expose users to pollution through video recommendations, they ensure that once users click a recommended video, they are continually fed videos that are more and more extreme. Lewis's argument is corroborated by a large-scale data analysis conducted by Manoel Horta Ribeiro's research team; they found that users who started clicking and commenting on more moderate right-leaning content were soon clicking and commenting on outright extremist content.[79] It's not that YouTube—or its parent company Google—actively loves and supports conspiracy theories. It's that these videos keep people on-site, clicking their hours away.

The *Atlantic*'s Taylor Lorenz chronicles a similar problem on Instagram.[80] Despite its reputation for inspirational quotes and stylized images of well-lit millennials, Instagram serves a more exploratory and informational function for Gen-Z users. Just following a few conspiracy-focused accounts, Lorenz explains, sends users "spiraling down a path toward even more extremist views and conspiracies." After following a single reactionary account, Lorenz herself was inundated with suggestions to follow other reactionary meme pages and far-right media figures. Once she followed these pages, she received even more recommendations for conspiracy accounts. Most leaned heavily on conspiracy theory hashtags, making it even easier for users to find related content with a single click.

Given all this, when the falsehoods at the core of QAnon swirl across social media, when "evidence" of conspiracy creeps into search results, when increasingly unhinged Deep State videos are served up with each new click, it's not because the system is broken. It's because the system was designed to maximize speed, spread, and profits.

Human Actors

Platforms are not our only problem, however, and are far from the only energy sources for our most destructive storms. Everyday people do just as much damage. During the 2016 presidential election, for instance, journalists filed an enormous number of stories about reactionary chaos agents and bigots and conspiracy theorists. They did this, in large part, because audiences *read* an enormous number of stories about reactionary chaos agents and bigots and conspiracy theorists. People loved those stories; they wanted to read them.

Similarly, stories about QAnon or Pizzagate or Seth Rich didn't spread solely because algorithms pushed readers to the stories. QAnon, Pizzagate, and Seth Rich made for good clickbait because the stories themselves compelled people to click. These narratives resonated with audiences. The *why* of this resonance could vary: maybe it was true belief, furrowed skepticism, or an ironic chuckle. Whatever the reason, even in a sea of algorithmic recommendations, people make choices. The attention economy might lead people to content, but it can't make them click.

Audience affinities, and the choices fueled by these affinities, broaden the blame for radicalization well beyond algorithms. Algorithms are certainly a concern. They splash pollution into corners of the internet that would never have been tainted by it otherwise. They reflect deep memetic frames that privilege unchecked spread over thoughtful restraint. They reinforce ignorance, bigotry, and paranoia, often making those impulses worse, more concentrated, more actionable. Algorithms do not, however, create any of those problems. Polluted information is a social problem, not a strictly algorithmic one.

Becca Lewis charts the complex interplay of the social and the algorithmic.[81] YouTube audiences, she argues, are exposed to reactionary views—and at times are outright radicalized—by conspiracy entrepreneurs. Algorithms, which direct audiences to increasingly fringe content, play a clear role in this process. But that relationship goes both ways. Conspiracy entrepreneurs *are also radicalized by their audiences*, whose appetites for all that increasingly reactionary content are both whetted and sated by algorithms. Content that meets the audience's growing need for conspiracy theories is rewarded by clicks and likes and comments and shares and subscriptions, generating revenue for the content creator. Like the platforms themselves, conspiracy entrepreneurs have every economic reason to keep ratcheting up the pollution.

As danah boyd chronicles, media manipulators have mastered the art of weaponizing these audience-algorithm feedback loops.[82] First, manipulators use social media to trigger news coverage, typically through some outrageous, destructive, or over-the-top behavior that journalists can't *not* report on—like wearing match-to-match QAnon shirts to a Trump rally. Second, manipulators frame the resulting controversy with terms that are unfamiliar to new audiences, prompting them to search for those terms online—terms like "the great awakening," "the storm," or "where we go one, we go all" ("WWG1WGA" is even *less* scrutable and therefore even *more* provocative). Ideally, for the manipulators anyway, these searches will send audiences down precisely the reactionary rabbit holes that social media economics incentivize. Third, manipulators either pretend to cry hot, indignant tears in response to the coverage, laugh so hard they actually *do* start crying, or simply lash about in the spotlight, giving reporters even more to write about. The QAnon boosters who took to their YouTube channels and subreddits to crow about how much they love all the QAnon news coverage, hoping reporters would see this and write stories about that too (they did), provide textbook examples. The goal is to keep the story alive, ensuring that audiences will keep asking the algorithms to feed them poison. Journalists, audiences, and algorithms unwittingly work together in destructive harmony.

And so, stories about QAnon or Pizzagate or Seth Rich, stories about any pollution on any subject, must be understood—indeed, can only be understood—as an entire hurricane, top to bottom, front to back, land to sky. The storm isn't a single news report, or a single influencer, or a single tweet, not even from the president of the United States. The storm is, instead, all those things all at once. Journalists write articles about a thing because algorithms surface the thing because audiences are interested in the thing because the thing reinforces deep memetic frames because journalists write articles about the thing because algorithms surface the thing because audiences are interested in the thing because the thing reinforces deep memetic frames. Around and around, until the storm fills the sky.

ON FUTURE STORM CHASING

Other people do a lot of environmental damage. We, ourselves, do too. The center-left journalists who covered and covered and covered the QAnon story illustrate how we all, every single one of us, fit within the storms we track. This is the final lesson of the Deep State.

To be clear: center-left QAnon reporting wasn't *bad*. Many of these articles—whether explainers, debunks, or denunciations—were quite good, or at least interesting in a rubbernecky sort of way. They provided critical contextualizing information about QAnon, its proponents, and its relationship to the paranoid style of Donald Trump's presidency. However, on the whole, these articles missed as much as they illuminated. Notably, with very few exceptions, they sidestepped the role the articles themselves played in amplifying QAnon. Reporters instead presented the conspiracy theory as a wholly organic phenomenon gurgling up from the Trumpian swamp. The theory certainly gurgled up from somewhere. But the QAnon ooze was flung into the clouds and entered the water cycle thanks to a considerable assist from the howling winds of journalism.

First and foremost, journalistic winds spread the Deep State superstorm far outside the right-wing echo-system—a basic hallmark of network climate change. This happened even when articles debunked the theory point by point, illustrating one of the most vexing consequences of the debunking impulse itself. Indeed, for all the explainers and fact checks published between 2017 and 2019, the QAnon theory didn't just fail to dissipate; its surge grew stronger, until the Deep State became a common talking point for members of Congress and served as the backbone for Republican impeachment defenses of Trump. It also became grounds to reject medical expertise about a global pandemic on the grounds that *I'll never let the Deep State tell me what to do.*

Reflecting another hallmark of network climate change, journalistic attention drove an even deeper ideological wedge between the Left and the Right, particularly via eye-rolled declarations that *of course* Trump supporters would believe in QAnon, because they're stupid. Even if people on the Right weren't Deep State truthers, condemnation and mockery from establishment journalists further justified (for people standing behind that frame, anyway) the Right's visceral disgust for progressives. Relatedly, the deluge of hot takes and tweets and articles on the Left gave right-wing chaos agents, professional propagandists, and lest anyone forget, Russian disinformation agents all the more reason to keep pushing the Deep State story. It was *working*. It was working for audiences on the Right and for critics on the Left, who couldn't stop talking about the Deep State, allowing cynics and state agents and Deep State believers alike to play up that discord to maximum personal benefit.

By not considering how they themselves were helping spread the story, by not considering how they themselves were making the story worse, or at least making the jobs of far-right agitators and manipulators that much easier, center-left reporters were unable to tell the biggest and most important truths about the gathering storm. More than that, they helped feed it. Journalists weren't the only storm chargers, of course; this is the fate we all tempt, particularly when we position ourselves outside the story we're writing about or commenting on or laughing at.

And that, right there, is the consequence of a fully realized network crisis. None of us are ever outside anything. The inability—or outright unwillingness—to see how or why all but ensures that we will ourselves become part of the problem, even if we're desperate to help. As we generate more and more extreme weather events, we churn up more and more pollution, obscuring our shared land and our shared purpose. All we can do is grope for something steady while the winds whip and debris flies. There can be no functioning democracy or civil society or individual vibrancy when we can't see three feet in front of our faces. We're certainly not equipped to navigate a public health catastrophe when information about a threat is as dangerous as the threat itself.

It is here that the network map transforms from discussion aid to navigational tool, from "you are here" to "now how do we make our way through?" The question is not an idle one. Understanding how polluted information seeps through our networks, how our everyday decisions help spread that pollution, and how overlapping energies fuel media storms forward, allows us to better protect the online environment from those who seek to contaminate it. It also allows us to better protect the health and safety of the communities who inhabit it. As we venture into uncharted territory, network maps in hand, we must keep our eyes on those guiding stars—stars that remain as bright as ever, even as the storms howl overhead.

5 CULTIVATING ECOLOGICAL LITERACY

(Milner)

It was a sunny morning on Aunt Lynda's porch in Kennesaw, Georgia, as the birds serenaded me and the breeze dropped September's yellowing leaves. Lynda's rosy-cheeked ceramic frog flowerpot stared into the middle distance, serene behind a placid painted smile. A quiet companion as my kids ran through the yard, counting the fluorescent butterflies landing on the grass.

The reports from back home in Charleston, South Carolina, on the other hand, were less idyllic. A few hundred miles away from Aunt Lynda's porch, Hurricane Dorian roared along the coast. It sent a tree through some kid's bedroom up by the airport, dropped a sparking power line into the flooded City Market downtown, and ripped the roof clean off a church about a mile from my house. And those were just the last three tweets. There were countless other disasters to take in and hours to go before the storm drifted north to darken the doorsteps of Myrtle Beach, Wilmington, and the Outer Banks. All the while, my commander in chief was vigorously altering five-day-old forecasts with sharpies instead of admitting that he misspoke when he said the storm was headed toward Alabama—a real encouraging fixation when more than a million of my fellow coastal Carolinians had been told to vacate their homes and brace for the destruction. I put down my phone and sighed, the gentle wind rustling as I looked at Aunt Lynda's ceramic frog mirroring my glass-eyed stare.

I don't know if the frog knew what I knew. That it was all too much. After all, this was the fourth time in as many years that I had to drag my family up a lane-reversed highway to the North Georgia hills (thanks, climate change).

Each time meant new worries. Matthew flooded my study. Irma wrecked up the yard. Florence just sat in the ocean for an extra week before turning north (Charleston got a half inch of rain but lost a lot of tourism dollars). With each, I couldn't do anything but watch and wait and wonder as sky and sea and ground interacted in all their mysterious ways. High winds plus wet soil might unmoor roots that might topple trees and the power grid with them; a strong surge at high tide might flood out a neighborhood, especially one built on marshland never meant to hold condos; a heavy flow of evacuees returning to Florida might make the drive home a gnarled nightmare.

No matter what, the cleanup wouldn't be simple; it never was. I'd do my part on my own little lot, hoping that just meant moving mulch, instead of an amateur attempt at sawing up a downed live oak or killing mold inside my walls. The city, county, and state would have bigger pollutants to contend with. The streets don't flood with spring water; they flood with raw sewage that splashes disease over any surface or person it comes in contact with. And eroded beaches aren't rebuilt without consequence; rebuilding means more coastal development, and more coastal development means even more to rebuild the next time a storm rolls through. Year after year, the cleanup was becoming more and more daunting, and all the answers kept feeling too small.

Or at least all the answers I could come up with. From the heavens themselves to the president on down, I had little power to fix any of it. So there I sat, yet another September day on Aunt Lynda's porch, contemplating a crisis that was always bigger than me, was only getting worse, and felt like it was on the verge of swallowing us whole.

The frog just stared.

ECOLOGICAL LITERACY

The media hurricanes that cloud our horizons are just as unpredictable, just as disruptive, and just as difficult to clean up as their meteorological counterparts. Like real hurricanes, they put bodies and livelihoods at risk. They're complicated by wide-scale human activities. And they have a long history of interventions hurled their way, with a long history of mixed results.

Media literacy education scholars Renee Hobbs and Sandra McGee explain that efforts to track, warn about, and respond to information storms coalesced after World War I.[1] The chief concern for researchers and educators was political propaganda, which became all the more pressing with Adolph Hitler's rise to power. Following World War II, the focus on propaganda broadened to include the study of mass persuasion in advertising and other media. The goal of these efforts—which were often framed as ways to resist the tricks played by manipulators—included calls to closely analyze media messages, identify rhetorical techniques, and assess creators' underlying motives.[2] Modern media literacy education emerges from this lineage.

As with any field of study, media literacy is large and contains multitudes. Most basically, educators often disagree about what exactly they mean by the term, immediately complicating efforts to assess the effectiveness of media literacy curriculum.[3] The field has also generated a wide range of sometimes-conflicting strategies. For example, a number of postwar educators resisted framing propaganda as a trick, since that had the tendency to make students cynical and mistrustful of everything, including teachers—a perspective ultimately drowned out by a louder and larger chorus insisting that propaganda is absolutely a trick, one for which close rhetorical analysis is the only solution.[4] The emergence of digital media has inspired even more changes to how media literacy is taught and understood.[5]

Despite these shifts and disagreements, contemporary media literacy efforts remain broadly consistent with the goals of postwar propaganda analysis: to equip citizens with the necessary skills to make sense of the messages they read, see, and hear. For the National Association for Media Literacy Education, this means learning to effectively "access, analyze, evaluate, create, and act" on information.[6] *Media Essentials*, the textbook Milner assigns in his introductory media studies class, similarly identifies "description, analysis, interpretation, evaluation, and engagement" as the five steps necessary for a "media-literate critical perspective."[7]

A fact-checking guide published in 2019 by the Poynter Institute for Media Studies, collated from several other guides published around the world, exemplifies how this approach tends to be framed for everyday citizens.[8] The guide's basic argument is baked into its title, which references a mass shooting in El Paso, Texas, in August 2019: "Don't be the one spreading false news about mass shootings." Its tips include checking to make sure that the information you're sharing comes from a trusted source, with preference given to official sources, and even more preference given to sources whose reporting is corroborated by other sources. The guide also explains how to spot and avoid sharing fake images. These strategies reflect the kinds of good-sense skills offered up—by journalists, by third-party fact checkers, by public media literacy programs—as a cure for what ails us. And why not? Who would argue against verifying sources and analyzing texts for accuracy? Isn't that how we should be cultivating the land, with facts?

Although these strategies seem well suited to the task, verifying sources, checking claims, and even critical thinking aren't clear-cut remedies for the problem of polluted information. For one thing, they aren't consistently effective. Particularly online, these strategies often outright backfire, sending more and worse pollution zooming across overlapping networks. This happens, in part, because of the affordances of social media, which influence how quickly, and to what effects, information spreads. It also happens because these strategies draw their energy from the old-growth grove of Enlightenment liberalism, the very same one that, as we've seen throughout the book, so easily pumps polluted information into the soil, into the rivers, and into the atmosphere.

Liberalism is a deep memetic frame. It aggrandizes autonomy and self-sufficiency, recasts communities as markets, and privileges individual *freedoms from* outside restriction over communitarian *freedoms for* the collective to enjoy equally.[9] Liberalism trains us to be alone and think alone. But we exist ecologically, not atomistically. Our fundamental interconnection is only deepened by network climate change, by the twists and tangles linking one grove to another to the entire globe. When liberalistic literacy strategies sidestep these connections and focus instead on individual autonomy, they have exactly zero chance of enacting meaningful change— because autonomy over connection is part of the overall problem.

Our proposed alternate to liberalistic literacy is *ecological literacy*. In advocating for this shift, our goal isn't to reject facts or throw critical thinking into the river. It's not even to challenge the value of media literacy. It's to argue that liberalistic literacy is an ecological liability. It obscures the full contours of the landscape, fails to consider how deep memetic frames affect the information ecosystem, and allows pollution to rush in without detection. Chapter 6 presents recommendations for cultivating ecological literacy in everyday life. For now, in this chapter, we must think big. We must set aside the systems that have, at best, failed to protect our shores, and at worst, have invited more widespread destruction. What we've tried isn't working. It's time to start doing something else.

INFORMATIONAL BOOTSTRAPS

The liberal ideals at the heart of modern media literacy can be traced back to political philosophers like John Milton, writing in the seventeenth century, and John Stuart Mill, writing in the nineteenth century.[10] Channeling the spirit of the Enlightenment, each argues that the overall health of a society is determined by how free its citizens are to express a diversity of opinions—even when those opinions are unpopular or harmful. We might not like the speech, the well-worn argument goes. We might hate it. But we must not censor it. We might learn something, for one thing. For another, if we start censoring bad speech, it's only a matter of time before good speech is also silenced—our own very much included.

These ideas are woven into the political fabric of the United States. They underscore US Supreme Court justice Louis Brandeis's assertion in 1927, now enshrined in contemporary free speech debates, that "fallacies and falsehoods" are best remedied by "more speech, not enforced silence."[11] The complicating factor is that a public square blessed with the freest possible speech is also cursed by a deluge of conflicting, misleading, and ugly information threatening to drown out what's helpful and true. People therefore need to learn to parse fact from fiction, and good arguments from bad arguments—something Milton argued hundreds of years ago.[12] Media literacy is the only way to cut through that noise.

Within this tradition—particularly in the US, where commitment to free speech echoes religious fundamentalism[13]—the goal of media literacy isn't just to counter harmful perspectives. The goal is also to bolster helpful ones. The presumption is that as people weigh their options, separate the good arguments from the bad, and passionately defend their positions, the most truthful ideas will win out. This rhetorical survival of the fittest is the "marketplace of ideas" at work. Liberalistic literacy is itself a winner within the marketplace; it's been embraced by so many across so many generations that it's often treated as a self-evident truth.

In addition to its replication of free speech fundamentalism, liberalistic literacy reflects a ruggedly individualistic, ripped-from-the-Enlightenment ethos of self-sufficiency and autonomy. Within this frame, Clifford C. Christians, John Ferré, and P. Mark Fackler explain, society is no more than "an aggregate of the self-seeking automatons that compose it."[14] Its sole purpose is to protect the negative freedoms of all those automatons, so that they are free *from* undue restriction. Media literacy, here, is mission critical. If people can't figure out for themselves how to properly navigate the marketplace of ideas—if they can't do their own homework, follow their own evidence, and arrive at their own conclusions—the government or some other oppressive authority would need to step in to help. Media literacy is what saves us from an informational nanny state.

Most public media literacy programs in the United States, media scholars Monica Bulger and Patrick Davison note, foreground this individualistic focus, including its baked-in assumptions about the dangers of censorship. These programs, in turn, pay much more attention to the person interpreting specific media than to the broader social and technological networks the media emerge from, or the regulatory reasons those networks look the way they do.[15] Danah boyd likewise explains that online literacy efforts tend to be framed through the liberal lens of individual agency and choice.[16] The implication is that media *illiteracy* represents a failure to pull yourself up by your informational bootstraps—rather than a failure of the broader policies that allowed so much bad information to flood the marketplace to begin with. Platforms replicate these logics, particularly social media companies that, as Siva Vaidhyanathan argues, underfilter polluted information in the name of maximizing free speech.[17] Happily for these platforms, maximized free speech leads to maximized profits, so they have twice the incentive to leave moderation to the marketplace of ideas.

THE LIMITS OF LIBERALISTIC LITERACY

The most conspicuous sources of pollution online are the coordinated hoaxes, bullshit claims, and manipulated media that cascade across social media. These are the things we need the most help cleaning up.

At least that's the assumption. But as example after example in this book has shown, falsehood is not the only source of pollution. Entirely true, well-sourced, well-vetted accounts of coordinated hoaxes, bullshit claims, and manipulated media can do just as much damage. So can empirically verifiable facts about the world. The problem isn't necessarily the facts themselves or the stories themselves, but the environmental consequences they trigger—consequences that are obscured when the focus is on whether a story is true, whether it's been confirmed by multiple outlets, and whether it's been analyzed thoughtfully. These strategies make good sense. The problem is, giving people permission—even encouraging them—to share things that are safe from a liberal perspective discourages broader self-reflection about the unpredictable ecological impacts of that sharing.

Donald Trump's 2019 summer of racist tweets illustrates the limitations of liberalistic literacy, particularly through gold-star strategies like fact checking, critical thinking, and holding falsehood up to the light of reason. Whether you're a reporter trying to determine what about a story to cover or a citizen trying to determine what about a story to share, doing everything right by liberalism doesn't guarantee that you won't spread pollution. Our best intentions might make the problem worse, as efforts to flush out pollution *now* can open the floodgates for more pollution *later*.

Everyday Presidential Racism

On July 14, 2019, Donald Trump fired off a round of tweets before heading out to play golf. These microblog blusterings followed a week of public infighting between congressional House leadership and its progressive caucus. At the center of the controversy were four high-profile congresswomen of color: Ayanna Pressley of Massachusetts, Rashida Tlaib of Michigan, Alexandria Ocasio-Cortez of New York, and Ilhan Omar of Minnesota. The president, apparently, wanted to add his two cents.

In his first tweet on the topic, Trump sneered that the progressive representatives came from "countries whose governments are a complete and total catastrophe,"[18] echoing his reported assertion from 2016 that African, Middle Eastern, and Latin American nations are "shitholes." Because their home countries were such messes, Trump asserted, the congresswomen had no right to criticize how the US was run. In his second tweet, Trump added that those representatives should go back to where they came from, so they could fix their own broken countries first. He rounded out the trilogy by quipping that he was sure Speaker of the House Nancy Pelosi would be happy to make travel arrangements.

Trump's tweets resulted, of course, in an uproar. Pelosi quickly responded, pointing to the tweets as proof that when Trump talks about Making America Great Again, he actually means Making America White Again. The four congresswomen responded just as quickly, taking the occasion to denounce Trump's racist policies and his general disdain for women like them. Trump responded by calling them racist.

A cascade of Democratic politicians, and a pallid smattering of Republicans, also expressed disgust; some even called Trump a racist outright, despite a long-standing reluctance among elected officials to say such a thing about the president in public. Other candidates described the tweets, but not Trump himself, as racist. Likewise, the mainstream press was almost uniform in its condemnation, though many center-left outlets struggled with how to employ "racist" as a presidential descriptor. Some publications used the term immediately (typically referring to the tweets, not the man), but others took their time. Still others chose to perform a well-worn euphemistic dance, claiming that the tweets "replicated well-known racist tropes" or that they were "racially charged," an oft-used phrase that, taken literally, doesn't mean anything.

The factual accuracy of Trump's tweets, on the other hand, and Trump's claim that the four congresswomen were the ones who were racist, were much easier nuts to crack. Reporters wasted no time. Katie Rogers and Nicholas Fandos of the *New York Times*, for instance, noted in an article titled "Trump Tells Congresswomen to 'Go Back' to the Countries They Came From" that Pressley, Tlaib, and Ocasio-Cortez were all born in the United States, and Omar was a naturalized citizen.[19] This *was* their country.

Unsurprisingly, Trump didn't back off; over the next few days, he doubled down, then tripled down, on his attacks. When asked by a reporter if it bothered him that white supremacists were rallying around his rhetoric, Trump shrugged. "It doesn't concern me because many people agree with me," he said.[20] In subsequent follow-ups on the controversy, he singled out Representatives Tlaib and Omar in particular, denouncing both women, who have been critical of the Israeli government, as anti-Semites. At a July 17 rally in North Carolina, Trump continued his attacks on Omar, prompting his elated crowd to chant "Send her back! Send her back!" For thirteen seconds, Trump just stood there, basking in the vitriol.

Clips of the chant went thermonuclear as soon as they hit social media. Cable networks looped it on repeat; news outlets embedded it in articles; reporters, along with countless everyday citizens, tweeted and retweeted the video. Journalists at publications small and large, in print and on television, again assailed Trump's comments, with more journalists and more politicians (especially Democrats running for president) willing to actually use the word "racist," at least regarding the content of the tweets. Just as they had in response to the initial "go back" tweets, reporters also highlighted the fundamental flaw in the crowd's logic: Omar *is* a US citizen. She's *already* home—a fact check embodied by a viral video recorded on July 19 of Omar arriving in her home district. Shared as a much-needed salve to Trump's racism, the video shows a gathered crowd cheering and chanting "Welcome! Home! Ilhan!" as the congresswoman exits the airport.

Meanwhile, White House aides told the *New York Times* that Trump was pleased by the dustup; it was all part of his 2020 reelection strategy.[21]

Another wave of stories, in turn, pondered the broader question: just how smart was Trump being? Reporters and pundits clamored to answer, with particular focus on how the story might play in the Rust Belt. A representative CNN segment interviewed two white Wisconsinites who had voted for Trump in 2016. One declared that he would not vote for Trump in 2020 because of the "embarrassment going on" ever since Trump's "go back" proclamation. The voter said he didn't think the tweet was racist, but still, it was hateful. The other voter didn't see a problem with any of it. "How is that racist?" she asked. "If you don't like this country, get out!" The title of the segment, posted to CNN's website, read "Trump Voter: How Is That Racist?"[22]

And then Trump decided to comment on the majority-Black city of Baltimore, Maryland. This attack, which came a week after the "send her back" chants, followed a racist Mad Libs template similar to what Trump had said about the presumed "home countries" of Pressley, Tlaib, Ocasio-Cortez, and Omar: that Baltimore is dirty, worse than the US-Mexico border, filled with rats, and that no human being would want to live there. Trump directed these tweets at another congressperson of color, Representative Elijah Cummings of Maryland. Cummings, who represented most of the Black folks in Baltimore before his death in October 2019, was chair of the House Oversight and Reform Committee. Perhaps not coincidentally, the committee had recently ratcheted up its investigations of Trump on a host of potentially impeachable offenses.

The lingering energies of Trump's "go back" tweets and his crowd's "send her back!" chants collided with the Baltimore story. Many journalists were again confronted with the choice of whether and how to call the president's racist tweets racist. After all, the hand-wringing went, Trump didn't come right out and *say* that the residents of Baltimore are subhuman. He just implied it, giving many reporters, or at least their editors, pause—ambiguity further stoked by Trump's many apologists, who insisted that Trump wasn't even *talking* about race, Baltimore really does have rats. The result was a roaring superstorm of news coverage, social media commentary, and anonymous White House sources whispering to reporters about how this was all part of Trump's plan, he's playing four-dimensional chess, trust us.

Trump's racist tweets, reflecting a long public life of racist action, were not a story that could have been ignored. The tweets were not a story that *should* have been ignored. And yet much of the resulting news coverage, particularly coverage that insisted on fact-checking the president, completely missed the point. Adam Serwer of the *Atlantic* was especially pointed in his critique of people who responded to Trump's "go back" tweet by rattling off its targets' true national origins.[23] Trump wasn't making a fact-based claim to begin with, Serwer observed; he was asserting a moral conviction about the conditional citizenship of people of color. They will never be real Americans, Trump was implicitly arguing, because they aren't white.

Put another way, the factual *truth* of their citizenship mattered less than what was *real* to Trump and his chanting supporters: the fundamental belief that black and brown skin equals foreignness, and more fundamentally, that America is a country for white people. People of color are here, this logic goes, solely because *we* allow them to be. Reporters' efforts to jump in and fact-check citizenship status overlooked this deeper, and much uglier, part of the story. These efforts also inadvertently replicated the racist frame they were trying to counter: that people of color need justifying and, when challenged, need to show receipts. Even the most heartwarming "Welcome! Home! Ilhan!" chants implicitly affirmed the charge that "home" is an open question if your skin isn't the right color; white congresspeople, even those who are the children of immigrants, even those who have naturalized from another country, don't need a cheering airport crowd to remind everyone that they're American.

All the Media Literacy That's Fit to Print

The liberalistic literacy strategies employed by people responding to 2019's summer of presidential racism were great ideas on paper. Sometimes these strategies—in this case and others—are great ideas in practice as well, at least for certain audiences. The benefits for those audiences, however, are often counterbalanced by the harm caused to others. Fact checking, critical thinking, and shining a righteous light on our problems might clean up a beach here and there—but that's not the same thing as having a pristine coastline, especially when one beach's gain is another's loss.

Online Affordances and the Tools of Liberalism

Many will resist the assertion that liberalistic literacy efforts are unreliable at best and counterproductive at worst; it's a big assertion to make. In the context of networked media, however, it's actually a second-order conversation. Digital affordances—the tools digital media provide to users—complicate liberalistic literacy efforts before those efforts can even be deployed.

The opaque curation of algorithms is an especially powerful affordance complicating liberalistic literacy efforts. Algorithms direct our eyes to *this* at the expense of *that*, without telling us what we're not seeing as a result. They are instrumental in reinforcing partisan echo-systems, encouraging asymmetric polarization, and delivering increasingly radicalized content to audiences increasingly eager to consume it. They also feed into and are fed by social behavior; whether or not anyone realizes it, journalists, audiences, and algorithms work together symbiotically to drive the attention economy, often to very disturbing places.

That attention economy is propped up by an even more pervasive digital affordance: the quick and easy spread of information. Trump's Twitter feed epitomizes this spread. It also epitomizes how algorithms amplify messages far and wide. Within minutes of declaring something, Trump can generate a global hashtag that captures the attention of hundreds of millions. The message might begin on Twitter, a relatively niche platform in terms of actual active users, but through extensive news coverage and social sharing on other platforms—again amplified by trending-topic algorithms—it's able to filter into the networks of countless additional audiences. Some audiences spread the message as a cheering MAGA endorsement; others do the same as a disgusted psychic scream; still others exhibit every shade of affect in between. No matter the motive, the outcome remains the same: the message pings across more and more networks, prompting more and more responses from more and more participants along the way.

This ceaseless, cascading network spread has two effects. First is context collapse, the unpredictable commingling of audiences online, and the related unpredictability of the people you might be talking to at any given moment.[24] Trump's Twitter feed epitomizes context collapse, particularly when he retweets a random conspiracy theorist, white supremacist, or chaos agent, whose audience suddenly spans the entire globe. The second effect of out-of-control-spread is Poe's Law. Poe's Law is an axiom emphasizing how difficult it is to parse sincerity from satire online. By highlighting this difficulty, Poe's Law speaks to a much deeper problem inherent to the internet ecosystem: knowing what something is supposed to mean, simply by observing.[25]

Trump's presidency is a Poe's Law presidency; it's often dizzyingly unclear whether any given Trump statement is an actual policy proposal, a strategic provocation meant to rile up his base, a deflection from the latest disaster of his own making, or merely rambled words about a cable news show he just watched.[26] Poe's Law also complicates efforts to assess the motives of the conspiracy theorists, white nationalists, and chaos agents breaststroking in Trump's wake. Whether these hangers-on are spreading coordinated propaganda, sincere hate, entrepreneurial clickbait, or some mix of god knows what else, is often unclear.

The question of intent—and related question of how someone can or should respond to content—becomes proportionally more vexing the less is known about the content-sharers. In many cases, the only thing knowable is the impact a message has—a particularly critical point when considering messages that, trolling or not, cynical brand-building or not, are dehumanizing and violent. But even then, the impacts of a message can be uneven, depending on who intercepts the message, the deep memetic frames they're standing behind, and what they end up doing as a result. Under such conditions, merely identifying what something *is* can be enormously challenging.

Critiquing the Critical

Online, streamlined spread and all its Poe's Law complications is no accident. Designing platforms to maximize speech is a liberal impulse.

Assuming that the best and brightest content will win out is a liberal impulse. Looking around and feeling pretty good about the systems rich white men have built is a liberal impulse. When profound informational dysfunction emerges from these impulses, liberal responses are highly unlikely to do much to solve the problem—because they emerge from the same taproot as the problem that needs solving.

The seemingly unassailable pursuit of critical thinking exemplifies how insufficient liberal solutions can be when applied to problems caused by liberalism. Of course, within education scholarship, critical thinking, like media literacy more broadly, is large and contains multitudes; how exactly educators can or should implement critical thinking in the classroom remains hotly debated.[27] In more common usage, particularly in the context of news literacy and other public media literacy efforts, critical thinking tends to refer, broadly, to an analytic way of being in the world. A critical thinker doesn't just accept claims without question. A critical thinker does their homework. A critical thinker is an active, informed liberal citizen.

Francesca Tripodi illustrates the limitations of informational bootstraps-style critical thinking in her research on how conservative Christian Republicans search for truth in the contemporary media landscape.[28] Tripodi's work upends the common argument that Trump won in 2016 because so many Republicans were the unwitting victims of "fake news" criticizing Clinton and celebrating Trump. Rather than being duped by anybody, Tripodi maintains, these Republicans arrived at their conclusions by doing everything that liberalistic literacy advocates ask for. They methodically read multiple news outlets across the political spectrum. They meticulously analyzed the specific word-for-word transcriptions of Trump's speeches and compared those words to subsequent mainstream news narratives. They carefully pored over exact phrases in documents like the Constitution. They did everything right.[29]

The issue is what they ended up believing as a result. In many cases, these were not objective truths, as the Christian Republicans assumed and their research seemed to corroborate. Rather, they were realities filtered through a series of deep memetic frames. For the Christian Republicans

Tripodi interviewed, the most relevant of these frames was the secular media subversion myth that animates so much far-right conspiratorial thinking, from the Satanic Panics to the Deep State superstorm. In each of these cases, critical thinking efforts launch from the premise that left-leaning media are morally bankrupt, biased against conservatives (particularly Christians), and a threat to "real" American values. You couldn't trust CNN or the *New York Times* to tell you the truth. You had to find out for yourself.

Subsequent efforts to "Google for truth" sent these Christian Republicans down increasingly biased, reactionary, and asymmetrically polarized rabbit holes—rabbit holes that Democrats weren't ushered down nearly as frequently, because they weren't standing behind those same frames and therefore didn't feel as compelled to look outside the mainstream for answers. The result wasn't just to reinforce far-right messaging within Christian Republican circles. It was to further entrench the epistemic gulf between the Right and the Left, since the information circulating through the right-wing echo-system was shockingly discordant from what outlets like CNN and the *Times* were saying. To these Christian Republicans, it must have seemed like the center-left media was living on a totally different planet; just look at all the trash in their networks! The only reasonable response from their frame was to continue searching for the *real* truth though alternative channels.

Citing Tripodi's study and other examples of people doing their homework but arriving at problematic, false, or otherwise harmful conclusions, danah boyd similarly challenges the idea that critical thinking is a universal fail-safe—particularly when algorithms push searchers toward gamed information sources.[30] Boyd bases her argument on two primary concerns. The first is the deeply ambivalent paradox that emerges when people are encouraged to be critical. Questioning authority, challenging our long-held assumptions, and remaining skeptical of capitalist motives all make for good, informed citizenship. Up to a point. Taken to the extreme, however, the warning "trust no one" easily snakes back to those who are worth trusting—a paradox that educators teaching propaganda analysis realized almost a century ago. For example, yes, we have very good reasons to question and critique journalists, boyd maintains. But too much of that cynicism, and establishment journalism becomes the enemy of the people.

Boyd's second concern with critical thinking is its tendency to, ironically, prevent critical self-reflection. People who have arrived at conclusions based on facts—at least what look and feel like facts to them—would only ever describe their efforts in terms of critical thinking. They *earned* those conclusions, all too easily collapsing critical thinking into assertions of personal authority. And personal authority isn't something you can easily argue a person out of—just ask someone convinced that Trump's "go back" tweets weren't racist, on the grounds that they don't think they were. In these cases, algorithmically supercharged critical thinking does not bring people to the truth. It entrenches existing deep memetic frames, foreclosing the possibility that other frames, and other realities, might be worth consideration.

The Light of Liberalism

Critical thinking isn't the only facet of liberalistic literacy that can backfire. Another is the knee-jerk instinct to find, chronicle, and rebuke as many malignant falsehoods as possible. Once again, this impulse is rooted in the marketplace of ideas. You have to keep feeding the marketplace good information to counter all the bad, the argument goes; once you expose a lie or dehumanizing attack, individual citizens will weigh the evidence and arrive at the correct conclusion.

The summation of this long-standing ideal is often credited to Supreme Court Justice Louis Brandeis, of "more speech, not enforced silence" fame, who in 1913 declared that "sunlight is said to be the best of disinfectants."[31] This was not a modern insight. Brandeis was instead channeling the Enlightenment's centuries-old call to shine the light of reason on human ignorance and superstition. That was the whole point of the Enlightenment: to enlighten people. The Enlightenment's focus—even obsession—with the curative powers of light reflected an even older religious history, particularly the extreme dualism of Catholicism, which framed the light of God in apocalyptic opposition to the forces of darkness.[32] The assumption that shining a light on falsehood will usher in facts is so pervasive in the

West that it serves as a kind of creation myth. In the beginning, there was Light; and the Light was Truth.

While this underlying theme is ever present, Phillips argues that there are in fact two parallel tracks of the light disinfects model: the light of liberalism and the light of social justice.[33] The light of liberalism tends to shine its spotlight on those doing the harming, with the assumption that if people can see the bad actors for what they are, they'll reject them. It also tends to align with center-left journalism, which is a product of liberalism through and through. Negative freedoms, fierce autonomy, and the imperative to report as many truths as possible from the most impartial "view from nowhere" possible[34]—all are woven into what it means to be a mainstream journalist.[35]

The light of social justice, in contrast, tends to shine its spotlight on those who have been harmed, with the assumption that if citizens can see the embodied effects of bigotry and injustice, those citizens will embrace the structural changes necessary to fight back. The light of social justice isn't totally absent from center-left journalism (the *New York Times*' 1619 project, helmed by Nikole Hannah-Jones, is one example), but is comparatively rare within establishment, legacy, majority white newsrooms more geared towards liberalistic *freedoms from* than communitarian *freedoms for*.[36]

Journalism isn't an anomaly; the light of liberalism suffuses capitalist institutions—certainly in the United States, a nation born of liberalism. The result isn't, as we might expect or hope, steady beams with predictably just outcomes. Instead, the light of liberalism can be ineffective at best and outright destructive at worst. This happens, most basically, because the marketplace of ideas—that great clearing house for all that's been illuminated—isn't itself all that steady or just. As free speech lawyer Nabiha Syed argues, certain kinds of speech, speakers, and experiences have always been elevated within the liberal marketplace, while others have been silenced or pathologized.[37] Rather than reliably defaulting to the truest, most rational ideas, the marketplace reliably defaults to what resonates most with the people whose voices carry loudest. It's a power-replication machine, in other words, not a truth-telling one.

Those power differentials can send the light of liberalism scattering to all kinds of strange places, ensuring that even the most well-intentioned illuminations can backfire. A historical case in point is Northern news coverage of the Klan discussed in chapter 3. As both Elaine Parsons and Felix Harcourt show, Northern papers may have intended to stymie the Klan's influence by spotlighting its dangers and self-aware absurdities.[38] What that coverage managed to do, instead, was amplify the Klan's propaganda and bolster its recruitment efforts. The light of liberalism didn't solve the problem of the Klan. The light of liberalism helped the Klan. This was a known risk to the Klan's targets. That's why so many Black newspapers in the 1920s defiantly refused to run stories about the Klan. That's also why Jewish groups in the 1960s implored journalists not to publicize the rise of the American Nazi party, even in order to condemn it. The light of liberalism has a funny way of empowering perpetrators from dominant groups while disempowering their marginalized victims.

Online, the light of liberalism is an even less reliable ally—evidenced by what a boon it was to the nationalist publicity blitz known as the alt-right. Because of Poe's Law, because of context collapse, because of rampant information spread, it's extremely difficult to know where even the most righteous light might travel online, how its beams might refract, and what the consequences might be for the people spotlighted. This is true of the light of social justice as well; even when the lights shine on victims, they can still bend unpredictably. But, as the light of liberalism actively ushers the ugliest, most misleading, and most harmful speech into the funhouse mirror that is the marketplace of ideas, it's the most likely to do the most damage.[39] The consequences can be dire. However sincere a person's intentions, however illuminating the light might be for some audiences, that light can have the opposite effect on others. It can grow something just as toxic as the thing it disinfects.

"Go Back"

In the case of Trump's racist tweets about Pressley, Tlaib, Ocasio-Cortez, Omar, and Cummings, weeks' worth of wall-to-wall coverage of the who, what, where, and when of the tweets only made those messages multiply. More than that, the coverage generated whole new waves of pollution.

Most basically, light-of-liberalism coverage kept whiteness central to the "Go back!" narrative—not just because most of the establishment journalists reporting the story were white. Throughout the controversy, the cameras, both metaphorical and literal, lingered on Trump's face, repeating and repeating every hateful word he spoke. They lingered on the overwhelmingly white faces at his North Carolina rally. They lingered on white Trump voters in the Rust Belt, giving them sympathetic chyrons that framed white nationalist musings about who gets to be American as an abstract thought exercise with two morally equivalent sides.

It's true that people of color were part of the story, most obviously the representatives Trump singled out, who received almost universally sympathetic coverage after Trump's outbursts. It's also true that center-left coverage had improved since 2016. As Joan Donovan quipped in an interview with *Wired*, had the case unfolded two years earlier, she would have been on the phone begging reporters not to ask white nationalist influencers for comment.[40] Still, a great deal of even the most anti-Trump coverage privileged white people's experiences, reactions, and frames over the experiences, reactions, and frames of people targeted by bigotry.

These experiences, reactions, and frames included the ability to have, as *Washington Post* reporter Wes Lowery explained in an interview with *Politico*, "high minded" conversations about the traumas people of color confront every day.[41] White journalists and pundits got to play "fruitless, if earnest, pedantic games" with questions like whether or not a racist statement was *technically* racist.[42] A similar game was made out of assessing the alleged brilliance of Trump's reelection strategy. The very existence of these stories implied that there was a world in which Trump's statements could be considered good politics, divorced from the impact those politics have on millions. Such stories pushed journalistic impartiality to its most grotesque extremes, as the fundamentally unequal statements "the president is being racist" and "the president is being smart" were both-sidesed into just another political discussion between talking TV heads.

Some mainstream journalists whose light arced toward social justice avoided the worst of these traps. In the wake of Trump's "go back" tweets, for example, many reporters and influencers of color described how frequently they're told to "go back" to some other country, and what a toll that psychological violence takes on them. Similarly, after Trump's Baltimore comments, a number of prominent Black folks—including writer Ta-Nehisi Coates and CNN anchor Victor Blackwell, both of whom are from Baltimore—foregrounded their own bodies and affirmed the value of the other Black bodies who populate their city.[43] The El Paso mass shooting that followed Trump's tweets also generated some light of social justice coverage. Rather than focusing exclusively on the shooter or other white supremacists, these stories explored how violent white supremacy impacts Latinx communities. "It feels like being hunted," one *New York Times* headline read.[44]

That said, even in stories that explicitly and unflinchingly addressed how Trump's rhetoric puts people of color in the literal crosshairs of racist violence, center-left coverage broadly omitted a critical point: that the amplification of Trump's words was, fundamentally, part of the problem. Trump's racist statements persist as national earworms because they're repeated—and, of course, retweeted—hundreds of thousands, even millions, of times. All those amplifications ensure that the citizens lucky enough to have missed his comments the first time will have to hear them again and again and again.

Repeating Trump's racism doesn't just amplify that racism. Amplifying racism normalizes racist ideology. Normalizing racist ideology, in turn, emboldens and validates bigots. When bigots are emboldened and validated, they feel freer to lash out. The result is a public square that is less hospitable and less safe for people of color, particularly for those who are immigrants. Lights may have been beamed on Trump's ugliness in the name of both liberalism and social justice. For some, those lights disinfected. For others, the lights incubated, illuminated, and nurtured their very worst impulses.

Those impulses don't stop at racist rally chants. Research teams at the University of North Texas and California State University, San Bernardino, both found a correlation between Trump's racist rhetoric and white supremacist violence.[45] The El Paso shooting, which took place two weeks after Trump's racist tweetstorms, evidences this correlation. In his manifesto, the shooter offered the same justification for murdering twenty-two people, many of whom were Mexican citizens, that Fox News gives its viewers for fearing "white replacement," and Trump gives his followers for fearing the immigrant "invasion."

El Paso native and Democratic presidential candidate Beto O'Rourke had little patience for the reporters dancing around the underlying cause of all this violence and naively asking why any of it was happening. "Members of the press, what the fuck?" he snapped during one interview, having just been asked what possible cause there could be. "It's these questions that you know the answers to. . . . He's inciting racism and violence in this country. I just—I don't know what kind of question that is."[46]

This question, and the problem of amplification it reflects, certainly didn't begin with any individual presidential tweetstorm. The pattern was established on the very first day Trump announced his candidacy in 2015, when he described Mexicans as criminals and rapists and the American press corps responded by laughing. By summer 2019 there was no way to ignore Trump's public statements, tweeted or otherwise, certainly not under the current rubric of newsworthiness; when the president does anything, it's by definition news. When the president does something racist, it's doubly so. To turn away from the individuals and communities that Trump dehumanized would have signaled complicity in that dehumanization. And yet turning toward Trump with yet another camera, to chronicle yet another attack against people of color—regardless of what kind of light a person might have been shining—only incentivized Trump to do the same thing again, with increasingly grim stakes for the people threatened by his statements.[47]

The Fact Check Fallacy

As the "Go Back" case illustrates, the insistence that light disinfects is often accompanied by efforts to check facts and debunk falsehoods. These efforts are enshrined within the profession of journalism, and have long been regarded as foundational to liberalistic literacy. So much so, Alice Marwick explains, that fact checks are often considered a "magic bullet" in the fight against falsehood online—understandable, when the diagnosis is a terminal case of not having all the facts.[48]

But online, fact checking efforts face immediate, logistic challenges. In an environment governed by Poe's Law and context collapse, it's difficult to know what even needs to be fact checked—and even more difficult to know what the consequences will be. A fact check might, for example, direct sympathy and support to a targeted person or group. Or it might subject the targeted person or group to additional attention and therefore additional attacks. It might do both things at once. The difficulty, in essence, is that information traveling across collapsed audiences does so unevenly and unpredictably. Liberalistic fact checking, which treats falsehoods as static objects to pin content warnings on, simply isn't calibrated for all the zooming and chaos that, ironically, is engendered by liberalism itself.

There are, however, deeper problems with fact checking than the logistics of where to pin the content warnings. First, people don't always post things because of facts to begin with. In a 2016 Pew Research Center study, for example, 14 percent of Americans reported sharing a story they knew to be false when they shared it.[49] Similarly, danah boyd notes that "If you talk with someone who has posted clear, unquestionable misinformation, more often than not, they know it's bullshit. Or they don't care whether or not it's true. Why do they post it then? Because they're making a statement."[50] That was the entire problem with fact checking Trump's claim about the nationalities of Pressley, Tlaib, Ocasio-Cortez, and Omar. Fact checks are definitionally useless when directed at people whose reaction is a snorted "lol we know."

These kinds of bad-faith arguments are vexing. But the principle is straightforward enough: if the truth doesn't matter to the person speaking, then facts won't work as counterarguments. The effectiveness of fact-checking good-faith misperceptions, on the other hand, is even more vexing and even less straightforward. When people truly believe what they're saying, do fact checks even work?

The existing research on the subject is, to put it lightly, mixed. Some studies show that efforts to correct false information actually reinforce that information, a process known as the *backlash effect*.[51] Some studies show that support for the backlash effect is tenuous, and that facts do indeed correct misperceptions.[52] Some studies show how little consensus there is across multiple studies.[53] Others show how little consensus there can be within the same study.[54]

There may not be any clear, incontrovertible evidence proving once and for all that fact checks backfire. But neither is there any clear, incontrovertible evidence proving once and for all that they *don't*. On the contrary; outside the confines of research studies, backlash abounds. Nonstop fact-checking of QAnon, for example, didn't decrease its size, influence, or follower count. QAnon only got bigger as time wore on, particularly as it collided with the COVID-19 crisis in January 2020.[55] QAnon's take on COVID-19, that Bill Gates created the virus in a lab, itself then collided with what passed in 2020 as a mainstream Republican talking point: that COVID-19 was a plot by the "fake news" media and the Democrats to destroy Donald Trump. Eventually, the tragic reality of the pandemic tamped down many (but certainly not all) of the conspiratorial claims about the virus. Weeks and weeks of relentless mainstream corrections, on the other hand, did nothing—other than convince even more conservatives that they didn't need to take COVID-19 seriously, precisely because center-left journalists said that they should.[56]

The rejoinder here might be that, okay sure, fact checking clearly wasn't effective in these cases. But that's because of ideological siloing between the Right and the Left; thanks to asymmetric polarization, facts proffered by the center-left simply don't *count* as facts to the far-right. To which we say, yes, that disconnect is precisely the problem. If facts truly were corrective, then they would be equally so for everyone. They aren't. So, the question remains: if fact checking works so well, then why is there so much evidence to the contrary?

Social psychology offers some possible explanations. None uniformly explain why certain debunks fail so abysmally with certain audiences. Instead, these explanations help contextualize the failures when they do occur.

One possibility is the *illusory truth effect*. This effect was first identified by Lynn Hasher, David Goldstein, and Thomas Toppino in 1977.[57] It reveals a strange contour of human cognition: that repeated claims seem more true than new claims. In the context of media manipulation, the implication is stark. Say a lie enough times, and even the most airtight fact check will seem false in comparison. The illusory truth effect can occur even when a person already knows that the repeated claim is false.[58] It can also occur after corrective information is issued, believed by research subjects, but then misremembered over time.[59]

A second reason some fact checks might fail is the *continued influence effect*, which states that belief in misinformation can persist even when countered with clear corrections. According to Brendan Nyhan and Jason Reifler, the strength of this effect derives from the causal inferences people make between events.[60] Once someone establishes a coherent causal explanation for a particular outcome—*this* happened, therefore *that* happened—it's extremely difficult to dislodge the misinformed conclusion; people who hear the fact check have an odd tendency to integrate the new information, yet continue to believe that *this* caused *that*.

A third, related reason that fact checks might fail is how tightly people cling to consistency in the stories they tell themselves about the world. As multiple fields of study have long emphasized, the human brain seeks out narrative coherence.[61] When the integration of a new fact would dismantle a person's psychic curio cabinet of coherent narratives, those efforts face cognitive resistance—because people don't like dissonance. Applying facts to false (if coherent) narratives might, Stephan Lewandowsky and his research team suggest, even trigger new misinformation to take hold when the fact check transforms a previously coherent narrative into nonsense. Irritated by the sudden gap in the story, a person's brain casts about for something, anything, to fill that spot in its curio cabinet.[62]

Which loops back to deep memetic frames. Our frames exert enormous reciprocal influence over the stories we tell ourselves and others. It therefore stands to reason that they would also exert enormous influence over when and why certain fact checks succeed and others implode. Research conducted by Lewandowsky and his team supports this connection.[63] As they show, when people are presented with a claim, they tend to evaluate it based on "knowledge consistency," that is to say, how well the claim lines up with their accepted frames. Knowledge-consistent information *feels* right, feels *real*, and therefore is easily believed. Knowledge-inconsistent information feels wrong and, beyond that, would make too much of a mental mess to investigate further. So that information is sent to the cutting-room floor.

For people who already know the information being fact-checked, or who don't know the information exactly but whose deep memetic frames give them no reason to resist it, the fact check isn't *un*helpful. It's probably interesting. But it's the cognitive equivalent of golf claps. On the other hand, when a fact check misaligns with a person's frames, that fact check can have a very different effect.

One of the most vexing is a type of backlash known as the *boomerang effect*. This effect occurs, danah boyd explains, when a person mistrusts the source of a fact check, and as a result, comes away from the correction more convinced of the falsehood than before.[64] This effect is essentially an inverse of source credibility bias, in which people are more likely to believe falsehoods from a trusted source than the truth from an untrusted source.[65] Secular professors dismissing the satanic threat, Democratic officials defending representative Omar, the "liberal media" sounding the alarm about COVID-19—all can cause audiences that mistrust professors, Democrats, and center-left journalists to dig in their heels. Of course these groups would try to mislead, the boomerang logic goes; they're known liars and are always up to something. Whatever they say, the opposite must be true.

D.J. Flynn, Brendan Nyhan, and Jason Reifler help contextualize the boomerang effect.[66] In the process, they also help contextualize why it's so difficult to fact-check information positioned behind a deep memetic frame. As they argue, when people search for and evaluate information, they demonstrate either *accuracy* or *directional* motivations. Accuracy motivations are straightforward; they occur when someone is looking for correct information without an existing investment in the outcome. They just want to know, for example, how cold it is outside. Directional motivations, on the other hand, reflect the pursuit of a conscious or unconscious goal, like confirming an existing belief or communicating partisan identity. Backlash effects correlate most strongly with directional motivations, particularly when the issue in question is contentious.[67] As they help cohere a person's basic sense of self, deep memetic frames are the ultimate directional motivation. Therefore, deep memetic frames are a likely source of backlash when it occurs.

Of course, just by observing, it's difficult to know exactly why a particular fact check fails, or exactly why it results in even stauncher false belief. What *is* observable is how often these things happen. If the answer was as simple as fact-checking believers out of their satanic panics or white racial terrorism or far-right conspiracy theories, then those problems would have been solved as soon as they were held up to the light of reason. That is, most decidedly, not what has happened.

It hasn't because of a basic liberalistic miscalculation: the belief that people are rational subjects who arrive at conclusions after dispassionately weighing all the evidence. Much more often than we might like to admit, that's simply not how we think. That doesn't mean we're unintelligent or unsophisticated; it means that we're guided by frames as much as facts. And yet the inherent power of facts, and more broadly, the inherent effectiveness of liberalistic literacy, persists as a deeply resonant frame—one that, appropriately enough, just isn't supported by the facts.

The answer isn't merely to adopt better media literacy tools; we need to adopt a better media literacy frame. And we need to do it fast. Disaster is already upon us, and will only intensify, because our most prominent tactics don't work very well. They can't handle the hyper-networked spread of information; they can't handle the compounding complications of Poe's Law and context collapse; they can't handle the symbiotic relationship between audiences and algorithms. All of that is bad enough. What's worse is that liberalism tricks people into thinking that liberalistic literacy is enough. Just throw facts at falsehoods, just trust the marketplace of ideas, just pull yourself up by the informational bootstraps, and everything will be fine. We've been doing that for centuries, and things are not fine. We don't have the luxury of continuing to get the same things wrong, over and over.

FROM FACTS TO ECOLOGY

The problems we face are structural. To cultivate enduring solutions, we need legislative action, economic restructuring, and educational reform. We're not going to get any of that overnight. We can, however, begin cultivating a different, more robust, and yes, more rational way of situating ourselves within the networked world.

Enter ecological literacy. Unlike liberalistic literacy, ecological literacy doesn't fight against the affordances of the information ecosystem. It doesn't assume that falsehoods are easily decontaminated by the application of facts, or indeed, that falsehoods are the only pollutants to worry about. It doesn't cast people as atomistic islands unto themselves. Instead, ecological literacy emerges from network complications. It foregrounds the downstream, communitarian consequences of falsehoods and facts alike. And it takes people's frames seriously. These frames might not be true, but they are real; they shape how people navigate the world. Understanding these frames—indeed, approaching them as basic features of the information ecosystem—is key to protecting our public lands. To get us there, ecological literacy zooms out, way out, to survey the entire landscape.

Interdependence in the Biomass Pyramid

Just as they are in the natural environment, all our problems, and all our pollutants, are fundamentally connected online. No clear division exists between the biggest, most harmful pollutants and the smaller, seemingly less harmful pollutants; efforts to mitigate one must also consider the other. The same holds true for the polluters themselves. Those who spread pollution deliberately and those who spread it unwittingly feed into each other, always. Biomass pyramids provide an ecological framework for understanding the energetic exchange between the worst, most abusive, most toxic actors and the rest of the ecosystem. Approaching harms from such a frame helps illustrate the interdependence of people, their tools, and the broader media environment.

In biology, biomass pyramids visualize the relative weight and number of one class of organism compared to other organisms within the same ecosystem. The top level represents the apex predators: the lions and tigers and bears. Each descending level grows larger, reflecting that there are more foxes in the ecosystem, and beneath them more rabbits, and beneath them more insects, and beneath them more fungi. Each level is distinct and, at the same time, intertwined with all the others. Apex predators succeed because their prey succeeds, and their prey's prey succeeds. Moreover, the fate of each creature depends on its surroundings: how much it rains, the health of the soil, the strength of the trees. Robin Wall Kimmerer emphasizes just how dependent everything is on everything else. "All flourishing," she explains, "is mutual."[68]

The biomass pyramid of online harm exhibits similar interdependence. At the top of the pyramid are the propagandists, violent bigots, and chaos agents—the most obvious sources of abuse and pollution. These actors make a choice to harm; it's in their emotional, social, and financial interests to harm. Just below the apex predators are the secondary predators who don't quite reach the top tier and likely harm with less intention, but whose behaviors still wound; fetishized laughter and arm's-length irony fit within this category. Beneath them are the lowest and widest rungs of the pyramid, which represent the everyday actions of everyday people: folks posting news stories, commenting on what others post, and chatting idly with friends. These everyday behaviors tend to be neutral or even positive in intent.

When considering their varying impacts on the digital environment, it makes good sense to separate levels. What the apex predators do is, simply, worse and more damaging than what the secondary predators do, which is simply worse and more damaging than what broadly well-intentioned everyday people do. As distinct as these harms might be, however, each level can't—and shouldn't—be approached as a closed system. Our fates are connected, both to one another and to the environment: how much is tweeted, the health of the platforms, the strength of our networks. We can talk about specific predators on their own, like we would talk about specific species and specific animals. But we can't understand any group or any individual without placing them in their full ecological context.

For example, the people at the base of the biomass pyramid—which includes, we suspect, the majority of our readers—might, individually, be massively overshadowed by the apex predators. Collectively, however, well-intentioned everyday people have massive power within the ecosystem, so much so that the apex predators' very lives depend on them. Predators rely on the rest of the pyramid for their signal boosting. They rely on the rest of the pyramid to determine that, yup, this is safe to share because it's true and unbiased and corroborated by multiple trusted sources. They rely on the rest of the pyramid to carry out all the deeds they cannot do themselves.

The biomass pyramid thus illustrates how everyday actions like posting articles and telling the truth can still do what is ultimately very dirty work. The end goal might be to denounce racism. The means to that end might meet a whole host of liberalistic literacy criteria. But spreading bigoted messages, even to denounce them, exposes others to coordinated manipulation, risks poisoning the very bodies it seeks to protect, and directly enriches the worst actors. These actors might be big. They might be dangerous. But they're also the ecosystem's most needy inhabitants.

On Feeding the President

Donald Trump is an apex predator. When approaching the harmful things he says and does, it makes sense that people want to focus on the factual truth of his statements, to critically analyze his words, and to consider the motives behind his messages. It makes less ecological sense to start with those points. Not because those things don't matter, but because those questions divert attention from the unintended consequences of responding to a person like Trump: who might be standing downstream from the fact check, what other networks could be activated by amplifying his latest lie, and the broader environmental impact of clogging the landscape, yet again, with his antidemocratic poison.

Focusing solely on Trump himself—or any other predator of his caliber—has another unintended consequence. It perpetuates the myth of the lone wolf. From this view, predators are atomistic; they're the beginning and the end of the conversation. But apex predators, presidential or otherwise, have *always* been raised by other apex predators, either directly, within an existing community, or indirectly, within the echo-system of a given ideology.

Sarah Banet-Weiser and Kate Miltner make a similar point in their analysis of the social, technological, and legal structures that cultivate misogynist expression online.[69] Sociologist Jessie Daniels likewise foregrounds the interconnections between white supremacists and mainstream culture. Racism emerges *from* these structures, Daniels argues, not outside of them.[70] These scholars avoid the pitfall—common in analyses of apex predators—of treating harmful action as singular, or worse, anomalous. The truth is much more complex. All misogyny is networked misogyny. All bigotry is networked bigotry. All pollution is networked pollution. It might be tempting, even intuitive, to paint someone—from the president to a mass shooter—as the sole perpetrator of an attack. Especially if, technically, the perpetrator acted alone. But focusing on the individual tells a much smaller, much less revealing story. What needs telling, instead, is a story about how these predators are created and continually reinforced. Not just by other predators, but by expansive cultural systems that, on their face, might not seem related—or even remotely harmful.

Applied to Trump, sensitivity to these interconnections inspires whole new lines of questioning. Rather than asking, "what fresh hell did Trump stir up today?" an ecologically literate approach to the president would begin by asking, "what conditions have made this fresh hell possible?"— with an eye, always, toward the intended and unintended consequences of what Trump said, what the people reacting to him said, and what you're about to say. The resulting stories would, obviously, have to do with Trump. But they wouldn't be *about* him—certainly not separated from everything else.

AN ETHICS OF RECIPROCITY

The question is, how do we translate ecological literacy into everyday action, particularly for those of us just sitting there, yet again, in our metaphorical aunt's metaphorical backyard following the latest informational shitstorm, not sure what to do next?

Our proposal is network ethics, which foregrounds reciprocity, interdependence, and a shared responsibility for the whole digital ecosystem. Network ethics is fundamentally oriented toward justice and demands full-throated, strategic pushback against people who harm and dehumanize. That word "strategic" is key; network ethics is keenly attuned to how everyday actions impact others, particularly those already under siege—whether those effects are caused deliberately or inadvertently.

Needless to say, network ethics is not the norm online, where liberalism reigns. Negative freedoms animate everything from platform design to moderation policies to user contributions. The liberalistic frame is epitomized by what danah boyd labels the "right to be amplified": the assumption that I deserve to be heard, not just to speak, regardless of the impact that speech might have on others.[71] Network ethics trades these negative freedoms for the positive freedoms of communitarian thinking: action designed to secure freedoms *for* everyone in the collective.[72] Freedom that is equally distributed and enjoyed by all. Freedom that emerges from an acute understanding that all our freedoms are connected.

Feminist scholars long ago diagnosed the need for such an inversion. Writing in 1982, psychologist Carol Gilligan underscored the behavioral gulf between a "morality of rights," predicated on independence, and a "morality of responsibility," predicated on *inter*dependence.[73] We're in the mess we're in because the individual has, in so many ways, from so many different directions, been privileged over the collective. Because a morality of rights is more interested in *me* than in *we*.

A morality of responsibility draws from a different taproot. It can, as a consequence, bear different fruit. Writing about ecological climate change, Robin Wall Kimmerer considers this possibility.[74] What would happen, she asks, if we shifted our culture of rights, whose narratives center on what's *mine*, to a culture of responsibilities, whose narratives center on what's *ours*? We could nurture relationships of gratitude and reciprocity. We could nurture appreciation for shared abundance. The gentleness of Kimmerer's question and the poetry of her answer aren't some floaty, idyllic, tree-hugging daydream. They speak bluntly to the existential threat that all living beings face. What is ultimately at issue, Kimmerer explains, is "the evolutionary fitness of both plant and animal."[75] Not to redirect our perspective from one frame to the other—or at least to try to move the needle away from individual rights and toward communitarian responsibility—is to court catastrophe. It is to keep doing what will, quite literally, destroy the world.

This is the steel at the core of the softness—or what might seem like softness to those who have internalized the misconception that softness is opposed to strength. Feminist philosopher Virginia Held presents a similar steeliness in her exploration of feminist ethics of care. "There is nothing soft-headed about care," she writes, emphasizing that caring for others doesn't mean retreating into a receptive, permissive, or weak place.[76] To care for others is to fight like hell so we all can survive. Otherwise the storms will keep coming, the marshes will keep flooding, and the most dangerous actors will keep roaring forward.

Bigger storms loom on the horizon. And yet our living rooms are still grimy from the ones we're weathering right now. The final chapter ends our journey—and begins our journey—with a network ethics guide designed to help with the immediate cleanup. By thinking ecologically about the problem, we can begin acting ecologically. And by acting ecologically, we can begin shifting the paradigm, bit by bit, whether we're average citizens or high-profile journalists or anything in between. These everyday cleanups might seem small and disconnected from systemic solutions. But in our networked ecosystem, there is no small or disconnected anything. More effectively, and of course more ethically, responding to today's pollution is the first and most critical step in cultivating what we need more than anything: foundational, systematic, top-to-bottom change.

6 CHOOSE YOUR OWN ETHICS ADVENTURE

Our network climate is in crisis. It's inundated with pollution not just old, and not just new, but new as a catalyst to old, and old as a catalyst to new. It pulses without end underfoot. It blights the land we harvest. It swells and swirls in the clouds above. And it overlaps. Storm runoff filters into forest beds. Cyclones suck up slowly pooled poisons and dump them far afield. Fruits emerge from toxic soil. Just recognizing a pollutant's source can be vexing enough. Trying to quarantine that source when it's coming in from everywhere, when half the time it's invisible, when efforts to help so easily backfire, is Sisyphean. As the filth piles up and we gasp for air, the question looms: why even try?

The answer is simple: because there's hope. By embracing a communitarian approach to information—achieved through ecological literacy and network ethics—citizens of good faith can help clean up the pollution already present, minimize the new pollution produced, and, most profoundly, cultivate a different way of being in the world—one that can, if enough seeds are planted by enough people, grow into industry, education, and government. In some networks, those seeds have already begun sprouting. As the COVID-19 pandemic exploded, journalist April Glaser chronicled how everyday citizens created mutual aid groups by using text threads, Google Docs, and Facebook pages to assist community members in need.[1] In the most dire moments, these neighbors recognized the value of communitarian care: that when the people around you are healthier and safer, everyone is healthier and safer. The energies we need to cultivate already exist; they just need nurturing. That's our collective job moving forward.

The work ahead isn't restricted to any one profession or political affiliation; nor is it dictated by the size of our platforms. The information ecosystem is such that whatever we do for a living, whatever we believe, however many people might be listening to us, what we do and say can have sweeping effects. We might not all be journalists, but we all sow content across and between networks. We might not all be influencers, but we all hold sway over someone. We might not all be educators, but we all can teach by example. We might not all be students, but we all have something to learn. We all have a part to play in what the world is like. It's time to start working together to ensure the healthiest possible future for all. Here, we offer some first steps on that journey.

ONE: PULL OUT THE NETWORK ECOLOGY MAP

The first task is to triangulate our respective "you are here" stickers on the network map. Offline, we benefit greatly from knowing where we're standing. When we can assess what's happening around us, we're able to make the best possible choices about what we can or should do next—which turns to take more slowly or avoid completely, where we need to watch our footing, what we need to bring. The same holds true for our online roamings. When we know where we are in relation to everything else, we're in a better position to consider the consequences of what we do and say (or don't). Offline, we do this by looking up, looking down, and looking side to side. Online we can do the same thing, just with a more poetic eye: by charting the roots below, the land around, and the storms above.

Looking down at the roots beneath our feet helps us trace where polluted information came from and how it got there. What networks has the information traveled through, and what forces have pinged it from tree to tree, grove to grove? This pollution might be economically rooted, grown from profit-driven corporate institutions. It might be interpersonally rooted, grown from long-held assumptions about what's acceptable to share, or funny to share, or necessary to share. It might be ideologically rooted, grown from the deep memetic frames that support people's worldviews. The trick is to remember that polluted information never just appears. Pollution filters in, driven by countless catalysts. When trees start dying, when they fail to flower, when their leaves go brittle—that's the symptom. The cause is how and why that pollution spreads. Neither symptom nor cause makes any sense without the other.

Looking around at our vast tracts of farmland helps us pinpoint the impact people have on their networks. Some of these impacts are the result of deliberate choices. Some are the result of simply existing. The trick is to remember that motives have very little to do with outcomes. Like Kansas farmers in the 1920s, people with the best intentions and the worst intentions can harm the land in equal measure. The environmental damage inflicted by the people setting out to sow chaos and confusion is obvious. Much less obvious, but just as sweeping, are the cumulative effects of all the pollution everyday people kick up without trying. Searching for the source of this pollution doesn't necessarily mean searching for villains. It means highlighting effects and identifying causes—most critically when that cause is you.

Looking up at the storms raging overhead helps us identify the holistic, evolving forces driving a story forward. Pizzagate, QAnon, and the Seth Rich assassination theory didn't spread solely because some people believed—or at least promoted—those particular theories. They spread because social media monetized, incentivized, and surfaced harmful content. They spread because journalists reported incessantly on far-right narratives during and after the 2016 election. They spread because audiences read and responded to what journalists published. They spread because these things, and so many others, influenced and were influenced by everything else. The trick is to remember, first, that no hurricane can be reduced to any of its parts, and second, that hurricanes are verbs. They absorb everything that caused them to form, and all the responses they generate. Each moment, each thing, becomes yet another source of energy. None of us exist outside the storms we track. So all of us must be careful about what we feed them.

TWO: TAKE WHAT YOU DON'T KNOW AS SERIOUSLY AS WHAT YOU DO

Triangulating your position on the network map is as much about identifying what you don't know as it is about establishing what you do. Critical yet frequently missing information can include where exactly a claim, attack, or campaign originated, or who exactly has joined in since. Additionally, why a particular poster or group is doing what they're doing is often difficult if not impossible to verify; this is the consequence of a media landscape governed by Poe's Law. Something might look a certain way online, but that doesn't mean you can know what's fueling a claim, attack, or campaign. It could be organic, driven by actual, embodied people sincerely participating. It could be artificial, driven by sock puppet manipulators, cynical propagandists, or automated bots. It could be the result of some dizzying combination of both. All that missing information leads to the most vexing unknown of all: who or what might benefit from a story.

Not knowing the answers to these questions means not knowing the underlying ethical stakes. Not knowing the underlying ethical stakes means not knowing the best course of action. Not knowing the best course of action almost guarantees that any amplification, of any kind, will send pollution flying in unpredictable directions. Assessing what we don't know is therefore a critical first step before publicizing anything.

Mainstream news coverage of the QAnon-infested Trump rally, discussed in chapter 4, exemplifies how faulty premises and limited observations can warp a story—and how warping a story can help supercharge that story as it roars up the coast. In this case, reporters made sweeping pronouncements about how widespread the QAnon conspiracy theory had become among Trump supporters, conclusions based on how many people showed up to the rally wearing Q shirts and holding Q signs. The result was a deluge of QAnon coverage. The small detail that the people brandishing QAnon paraphernalia had coordinated beforehand—indeed, that they had been coordinating for weeks at other rallies as well, with the specific intention of tricking reporters into declaring QAnon the zombie that ate the Trump campaign—wasn't included in the stories. This omission allowed disinformation to masquerade as fact, much to the delight of the people seeding the pollution.

Of course, it's not always possible to know what isn't known, especially given that manipulation strategies—like those of QAnon proponents—are almost always developed outside the public spotlight. Not having access to those secluded corners, or even knowing for sure that there are secluded corners to look for, makes anticipating traps all the more difficult. That said, tracing the network map helps, at the least, to block out what areas *are* known. Based on that information, it's easier to identify what's missing.

Surveying the known landscape also helps pinpoint the areas on the map that are ripe for manipulation. The most common targets are unfolding news stories about human suffering, from acts of extreme violence like mass shootings to pandemics like the COVID-19 outbreak. In these cases especially, you can be certain that any media manipulation strategies you can identify, the manipulators have identified too. As you try and head the bad actors off at the pass, keep your eyes glued to the network map, and do what you can to learn what you can from what the map can't tell you.

THREE: REMEMBER THAT AFFORDANCES HAVE CONSEQUENCES

The information ecosystem is not a natural environment. It was developed by people, none of whom stood outside their creations as objective, neutral observers.[2] They created certain things for certain purposes, encoded with certain assumptions about who their users would be and what those users would do. So while digital media allow a great deal of freedom, they're also limited by a curated set of tools for navigation and play. The affordances of these tools direct what we are able to do—indeed, what even occurs to us to try to do—as we traverse the landscape. Understanding the affordances that surround us online and what impact those affordances have on our behavior allows us to move with greater care and self-awareness. That digital media are often designed to *preclude* care and self-awareness only underscores the need for a manual override.

The most foundational affordances are the ones we employ without thinking. These include the ability to edit digital content, to use a segment of the content without destroying the larger whole, to store and index content, and to access content quickly and easily. Separately and together, these affordances work to sever individual texts—words, images, audio, GIFs, and video—from their broader personal, political, and historical contexts.[3] The result, gesturing back to why we need to take what we don't know seriously, is to obscure crucial information like the text's origins, the circumstances of its collection, and the impact it had on the people who created it or were featured in it—essentially, everything that would help a person assess the consequences of sharing. With so much information missing, people tend not to make ethical choices. Not because they're *un*ethical, but because they don't realize there's anything to be ethical about. This is a trap; there's always something to be ethical about.

Platform-specific affordances further shape our behavior online. The most basic functions of social platforms, namely, the ability to post, like, comment on, and share, and to see what others post, like, comment on, and share, might not seem worthy of much reflection. That's just social media. However, those basic platform affordances—coupled with how all that content is moderated, or not, and how algorithms promote it, or don't—lay an even more treacherous set of ethical traps.

Most pressingly, design choices predicated on the liberal assumption that information wants to be free prime the landscape for context collapse and its messy commingling of audiences. Different users might encounter the same words or image or audio or GIF or video, but what that content means for—or does to—each of those users can vary wildly. A single post can occupy the entire emotional gamut, from obvious joke to obvious attack to just about anything in between, all depending on whose eyes are seeing it. Context collapse further exacerbates and is exacerbated by Poe's Law. The original intended audience for any given post might—and this is a big *might*—know what something "really" means. Outside the intended audience, however, meaning is in the eye of the beholder; for every deep memetic frame a person might be standing behind, and for every embodied reality that shapes a person's understanding of the world, there are different ways of seeing.

As the unfettered-speech, share-at-all-costs ethos baked into social media sends content screaming across different audiences with different assumptions, the very notion of *meaning* is jumbled beyond recognition. And when meaning is jumbled, so too is any clear sense of how best to respond to questionable content. Jokes are especially fraught online; they require a clearly carved-out play frame to function as a joke—one that signals to all involved, "Hey don't take what I'm about to say seriously; I don't really mean it."[4] That signal is the first thing chucked out the window by context collapse and Poe's Law.

The effect doesn't just ruin someone's good joke. If it's not clear whether a message—whatever form it might take—is meant to be a joke or a threat or an earnest observation, that message can be adopted, reframed, and potentially weaponized by others. These second- and third- (and forth-, and fifth-) order sharers can then import their own meanings to the message, spinning it off into increasingly far-flung corners of their networks. When that message contains even the slightest trace of falsehood or dehumanization, it's almost guaranteed to leave a trail of pollution in its wake. Because new audiences don't know to look for it, they are unlikely to notice this trail and therefore are unlikely to be wary of the message being shared. All they see is the content in front of them—not where it came from, not what it has done, and certainly not what it started out as.

The ethical pitfalls inherent to context collapse and Poe's Law are epitomized by the "Donald Trump's Dank Meme Stash" Facebook group discussed in chapter 3. The young reporter who joined the group for laughs assumed that the racist and sexist anti-Clinton, pro-Trump memes posted there were satirical, just another bit of lulzy fun. What the reporter didn't know, what Facebook's platform affordances obscured, was where the memes came from, who made them, and why. Had the reporter known that many of those memes were created and spread by white supremacists, conspiracy entrepreneurs, and hostile state actors, he would have been less inclined to laugh. He would certainly have been less inclined to pass them on.

This young reporter, like so many of the other young reporters who covered the internet culture beat during the 2016 election, like so many reading now who have likely had similar experiences, didn't share or laugh at harmful and dehumanizing content with the specific intent to harm and dehumanize. Some people did, of course. But most people simply didn't see what they were doing, because the platforms they were navigating didn't allow them to—or want them to. The result was a windfall for the social media companies who hosted and monetized all that pollution.

The underlying problem is that there was not then, and is not now, much incentive for these companies to foreground network ethics or build protective guardrails into site design—because ethics and guardrails aren't good for business.[5] What's good for business is people not thinking very hard about the content they share, and sharing as much of that content as possible. As users of these sites, and conversely, as people being used by these sites, we must understand that we don't own the land we traverse. Just being there comes at a very high, if largely unseen, price. Namely, we have been set up to pollute, because corporations and their shareholders benefit when we do. We must therefore work that much harder to navigate our landscapes carefully, to not allow the tools we use to restrict our sight, and, when we encounter particular texts, to actively, doggedly, seek out context. The alternative is to stand there, smiling and oblivious, as we kick over our own personal holding tank of accidental toxins.

FOUR: ADJUST YOUR UNDERSTANDING OF HARM

Typically, conversations about harm online focus on people who relentlessly taunt, harass, and dehumanize others. These are the lions and tigers and bears at the top of the biomass pyramid: smaller in relative weight and number than other animals in the ecosystem, but outsized in the dangers they pose. Assessing harm based on their predatory intent makes perfect sense. Logistically, it's difficult to imagine how ongoing hatred and harassment would even be possible unless someone was actively trying to hate and harass.

What makes perfect sense for apex predators, however, makes increasingly less sense as you move down the pyramid. In fact, positing intent *to* harm as a fundamental criterion *of* harm can inadvertently encourage damaging behavior by stifling ethical self-reflection. If harm is defined as something an abuser or manipulator or bigot does on purpose, and people don't consider themselves abusers or manipulators or bigots and certainly aren't *trying* to harm anyone, then they're almost guaranteed to give their behavior a pass. Harm is something that bad people choose to do. I'm not a bad person, and I'm not making that choice. So everything's good.

Of course, just because people believe they're in the ethical clear doesn't mean they actually are. They can spend all day justifying what they did. They were just trolling. They were just joking. They were just playing devil's advocate, no offense, you're being so sensitive. Fine; that's what they believe. But the second those actions harm another person, the wide-eyed insistence that, but-but-but, I didn't *mean* anything bad by it, doesn't change, can't change, and shouldn't be expected to change the impact of what that person said or did. If that impact was harmful, then by definition, they caused harm.

Patrick Davison, reflecting on the legacy of the MemeFactory performance trio discussed in chapter 2, epitomizes this tension. Looking back, Davison explains, he has regrets about the fetishized memes and jokes MemeFactory set their audiences up to laugh at—memes and jokes Davison also helped publicize through other venues like Know Your Meme. But, he says, "It's not that I look back and regret having attempted to cause harm; I look back and regret that my attempts to contribute (whatever it was) likely ended up contributing to lots of different kinds of harm."[6] You can't regret making a choice you never actually made, and Davison didn't choose to hurt anyone. Still, the jokey antagonisms MemeFactory helped normalize, the jokey antagonisms internet culture helped normalize, the jokey antagonisms the two of us as young researchers helped normalize, together shifted the media ecosystem. All this seemingly harmless play allowed, even encouraged, bigotry and falsehood to climb into the sheep-skin of trolling.[7] The result was to flatten unwilling people into fetishized memes, spread lies far and wide, and reinforce lulz as an aspirational register. It may have been unintended, but the damage was still sweeping. It still herded prey of all shapes and sizes into the mouths of all those lions and tigers and bears.

These are the harms we miss when we train our eyes on the top of the biomass pyramid. To reduce the pollution we spread, to reduce the pollution we create, we must lower our eyes to the bottom of the pyramid, to the rabbits and worms and fungi. In other words, to *us*. There the harms aren't just larger in number and weight. There the harms have something the top layers will never have: our ability to intervene, right now, with our own fingertips.

FIVE: SPREAD INFORMATION STRATEGICALLY

As we think carefully about whether and how to respond to information, particularly when that information is already polluted or has the potential to mutate into pollution once it leaves our feeds, the call is not for people to keep their mouths shut. It certainly isn't for people to "remain civil," an all-too-frequent gaslighting tactic deployed by those whose behaviors are blaringly immoral but who don't like being criticized for it. Indeed, as the journalists interviewed in chapter 3 explained, there can be as many arguments *for* responding to polluted information as there are for *not* responding. Not responding prevents people from telling the truth, educating those around them, showing the embodied effects of online harms, and pushing back against bigots, manipulators, and chaos agents. Not responding can signal complicity. Not responding doesn't make the problem go away.

Given these risks, silence isn't always possible. Silence isn't always advisable. The challenge is to be strategic about the messages we amplify.[8] More than that, the challenge is to approach amplification with ecological literacy. The question isn't just "to amplify or not to amplify?" The question—to be asked anew case after case, click after click—is: What are the environmental impacts of my choices? What pollution might my actions generate, for whom? What pollution might my actions mitigate, for whom? Most important, whose bodies might my actions nourish, at the expense of whom and what else? As ethical precepts, the following guidelines are far from a list of "thou shalt nots." Not every case poses the same risks. Not every case will have a clean outcome, particularly when the information storms loom especially large. Sometimes the best we can strive for is *less* pollution, not *no* pollution. These guidelines reflect that underlying ambivalence. So, rather than offering false comfort ("when *x* happens, just do *y*"), they emphasize the deep reciprocities between audiences and institutions and affordances. To the extent that there are solutions, they live within those connections.

Give Yourself Some Credit

First and foremost, whatever our professions or ideologies, we are all part of the amplification chain. This is obvious for people with large platforms, who are well aware, even painfully aware, that their words can travel across the globe in an instant. Everyday folks, on the other hand, with everyday follower counts, can feel like their words don't matter. That simply isn't true; everyday folks have enormous power. Everyday folks might get handed a menu of options by algorithms, but that's because algorithms are trained by the patterned actions of social media users. Everyday folks might get media narratives shoved in their faces, but that's because journalists are trained by the habits of their readers. Everyday folks might get products and ideas peddled to them by influencers, but what those influencers peddle is shaped by the support, needs, and preferences of their audiences. Recognizing that what we do has consequences across networks and even entire industries is the first step in making more strategic choices—because it reminds us that people are watching, often in ways we can't confirm or predict.

Everyday people play an especially crucial role within the biomass pyramid. In the natural world, the lions and tigers and bears wouldn't last a season without the bunnies and worms and fungi. Likewise, the apex predators of the online world, whose actions are most toxic, are able to do what they do thanks to the energies provided by everybody else. From our retweets to our comments to our laughter, what the rest of us do helps keep bad actors well fed. Understanding just how much they depend on our resources is the first step toward minimizing their harms. They need us, which is one power we have that they don't.

This is not a set up to the command, "don't feed the trolls," often presented as the only viable defense against the dark arts online. "Don't feed the trolls" implies that if you, as an individual, feed the trolls, then what happens to you, as an individual, is your fault. For one thing, that's victim blaming. The perpetrator is the harmful one and shouldn't be doing what they're doing (so cut it out, you assholes). For another thing, framing hate or harassment or dehumanization as an isolated problem obscures the structures that support and even incentivize those actions. Simultaneously, framing the *target* of hate or harassment or dehumanization as isolated, as a singular receptacle for harm, obscures the interconnections between biomass strata—and, most important, the collective power of people at the bottom of the pyramid to reshape their networks.

In other words, the call—unlike the highly individualistic "don't feed the trolls"—isn't to more effectively fend for ourselves when someone harms us. The call is to protect the people around us from harm and, more broadly, to make the landscape less amenable to those who are harmful. By making life harder for the apex predators, we ensure, together, that more people can be more free, more safe, and more empowered within our shared spaces.

Understand the PR Goals of Bigots, Abusers, and Manipulators, and Do Not Help Them Do Anything

Asking people to protect one another from apex predators is one thing. Explaining exactly how to do that it is another.

Those who work for social media platforms have a unique opportunity, and from a communitarian perspective, a unique responsibility to affect these kinds of changes. Efforts to cultivate healthy community norms are especially crucial to ensuring the safety of users and signaling to abusers, "you are not welcome here." As computer scientist J. Nathan Matias shows, steps as straightforward as clearly and consistently reinforcing community guidelines can reduce harmful behaviors and allow more people to participate more meaningfully online.[9]

But of course, relatively few of us work for social media platforms. For everyone else—even those with the smallest social media following—one of the most effective strategies is to reconsider where we're pointing our cameras (metaphorically and sometimes literally). In particular, we should avoid focusing too intently on the motives of bigots, abusers, and manipulators, or too intently on the community they originated from, or too intently on anything that frames them as the protagonists of the story. The bad actors are part of the story, certainly, but they're not the whole story.

The risk isn't just that we'll tell a worse and smaller story by highlighting bad actors. Treating them as inherently interesting and deserving of our undivided attention incentivizes future bad actions and, by extension, future harms to others. Because from the perspective of those bad actors, it makes sense to use the same weapon again; it worked so well the last time. Intense focus on what bad actors think and do and feel also risks replicating their marginalizations by implicitly saying, you know what, this terrible bigot or abuser or manipulator is right; it *is* their world, and we really are just living in it. You, targeted person—who are statistically more likely to be a woman or a person of color or both—are little more than a bit player in their drama. Please stand aside while we take their picture. Don't give bad actors that satisfaction, and don't provide them tools for future abuse. Most important, don't be complicit in their harms. If a response seems warranted—and sometimes it is—whip that camera around to the rest of the landscape, making sure to train your lens on the people targeted.

That said, don't merely to show the effects of those harms and then stop filming—particularly when the person holding the camera is white and the person they're documenting is not. Debra Walker King warns of the unintended consequences of reducing marginalized people to abstract representations of pain.[10] A person who has been harmed is so much more than the violence they've been forced to endure. Narratives about their experiences should strive to foreground the agency, resilience, and unique subjective experiences that allow them to navigate a systemically hostile environment. That's where the counternarratives are, including the subtly powerful reminder that people who choose to set the world on fire, who don't care about the lives of others, who are violent and hateful and inhumane, are not the only people on the internet. Their targets also exist; the rest of us also exist. And not just exist, but are foundational to the ecosystem. How can we reframe the story so that the overwhelming number of citizens of good faith, and more pressingly, the overwhelming number of community organizers, activists, and heroes who selflessly work for the benefit of others, are the ones in the spotlight?

Consider What Light Might Do Besides Disinfect

When confronted by violence, bigotry, and lies, many people ascribe to the maxim that "light disinfects." As explained in chapter 5, this assertion can be made while standing behind two different frames. The first is the light of liberalism, which maintains that we must show what the bad actors are doing so that rational observers can recognize, analyze, and reject their harms. The second is the light of social justice, which maintains that we must show what impact the bad actors have on their targets so that public opinion can shift and usher in needed social change.

This is an important distinction. *And,* the difference between the light of liberalism and the light of social justice online can crumble under the weight of platform affordances designed to maximize sharing, scramble audiences, and generally affix question marks over what anything really means. As a result, both kinds of light can be quite volatile. The light of liberalism, which trains its spotlight on the worst actors, is most obviously so; for one thing, many of the people illuminated have perfected the art of weaponizing light. But the light of social justice can pose similar challenges. For instance, while social justice interventions might elevate a target's experiences for some audiences, other audiences might simultaneously flatten those experiences into a series of consumable agonies, even entertaining agonies. They might also single that target out for more and worse abuse.

Online, we can't escape this ambivalence. All the light shining on one side of the network might disinfect a particular toxin admirably—or at least serve as a beacon of solidarity for those who already know the toxin is hazardous. But in the corners infested with bigots and abusers and manipulators, where disinfectant is most desperately needed, the same light can grow something worse. It can serve as proof of concept for even more egregious behavior. It can unify otherwise disorganized groups. It can make bigots, abusers, and manipulators feel good about themselves and excited to see what else they can ruin.

That's not the only thing light can do. In addition to helping cultivate poisoned gardens, light can also fix things in place. Dentists use these kinds of lights—typically high-powered halogen or LED bulbs—to set composite fillings. In the context of polluted information, spotlights can serve a similar function. Whether we're shining the light of liberalism or the light of social justice, when we point at something online through our comments, retweets, or hot takes, we help amplify that thing. Maybe we have no other alternative; maybe the benefits of amplification outweigh the risks of silence. At least, maybe they do as far as we can tell in that moment. Regardless, our amplification makes that thing stable and searchable, particularly if other participants join in and pile on.

The bigger your audience, the brighter your light, the stronger your stabilizations. But as above, so below: even people who have very few followers can generate a chain reaction of illumination, especially when coupled with the power surge provided by hashtags, curated feeds, and other bits of algorithmic docenting. Unfortunately there are no simple, universal answers for questions about when to illuminate and when to leave something in the shadows. Whether we're the first or the thousandth person to encounter that thing, there are no guarantees about what our light might do. But there are questions we can ask ourselves as we weigh our options. What audiences might the post or comment or hot take reach, both intended and unintended? Is clarifying or condemning a point for one audience worth emboldening, validating, or otherwise delighting another? Whose interests might I ultimately be serving by what I share? There may not be perfect answers to these questions; there may be no way to avoid spreading some pollution. Still, the takeaway is simple: shine your high beams wisely.

Remember That Facts Are Not Cure-Alls

Like many assumptions about how best to respond to polluted information, the "light disinfects" maxim is premised on the old-growth liberal presumption that when people are exposed to lies and dehumanizing attacks, they will reject them. All we need to do is present those harms unvarnished, and critical thinking will do the rest.

Unfortunately, as case after case throughout the book has shown, facts and facts alone are not why people believe in and do things. It's not that we *never* believe things because of facts. That happens too. But very often, when we commit ourselves to something strongly enough to act with gusto, we have arrived at that point not because of facts but because the belief or action lines up with our deep memetic frames. If facts aren't how we got there, then facts won't change our minds.

So while the impulse might be noble, throwing a fistful of facts at someone who is wrong about an empirical truth is highly unlikely to solve the problem. The best-case scenario is that the person will reject our evidence out of hand, because from their vantage point, seeing through their frame, we are unintelligent, misinformed, or downright disturbed. The worst-case scenario is that our fact checks inadvertently reinforce their false beliefs, particularly when the person hearing the fact check already believes that we are biased, hostile, or a representative of a vilified *them*.

That doesn't mean we should look the other way when someone says that a pandemic is a hoax, any more than we should look the other way when confronted by violent bigotry. It means we should intentionally craft thoughtful responses that minimize unintended consequences while remaining conscientious, always, of the complexities of human psychology. The question is, how do we do that? If facts aren't enough, if facts might even make things worse, how can any of us hope to clean up all this pollution? How can we stop the pollution from flowing in the first place? There are no simple, one-size-fits-all answers to these questions either. But there is one basic place to start, and it returns us to the declaration: "you are here."

SIX: KNOW THY POLITICALLY SITUATED SELVES

Determining where someone stands on the network map begins with assessing their deep memetic frames. This can be tricky, as deep memetic frames are often difficult to detect, especially for the people standing behind them. For these people—indeed, for everyone—the frames we see the world through aren't frames. They're just how the world is. In some ways, that's right: deep memetic frames are both constructed realities *and* how the world is, at least for the person whose frames they are. The frames might not be true, but they are certainly *real* to the person peering through them.

This is not to fall back on slippery, noncommittal, beige-tinged relativism, the moral equivalent of shrugging and saying, "people are different" as someone commits a crime against humanity. Not all deep memetic frames are created equal. Some are explicitly damaging and false. The point of identifying a person's frame is not to make excuses for the person or their frame. It's to better contextualize what that person believes and how they came to believe it. It's to get the lay of that person's land.

Doing so helps us better target our responses to false beliefs, most critically when the beliefs pose a threat to public health. Stephan Lewandowsky's research team, as well as studies by Brendan Nyhan and Jason Reifler, lay out how this can work.[11] As highlighted in chapter five, both sets of researchers emphasize how essential narrative coherence is to our worldviews. Fact checks that merely pull the narrative rug out from under someone are unlikely to be successful. And so, when a corrective is issued, it must not merely reject a certain detail. It must instead present an alternative coherent story that explains why something is the way it is.

The trick is figuring out what alternative coherent story would be needed. That requires assessing the stories that people are already telling themselves, which in turn requires assessing how those stories connect within the person's deep memetic frames. These stories and their supporting frames reveal contextualizing information like who the *them* of that person's conspiracy theories are, and where that person sees the most pressing dangers. Merely yelling at someone about how wrong they are—about COVID-19, about the Deep State, about climate change—isn't going to tell the sort of alternative story that might, just might, get them to start seeing, or at least start being open to the possibility of seeing, things differently.

This approach has two immediate benefits. First, presenting a frame-appropriate alternate narrative minimizes the polluted splashback that our most well-intentioned fact checks, along with our less well-intended insults, can generate when they collide with someone else's beliefs about the world. Instead, it zeros in on the coherency gaps that people don't realize are there, which emerge from internal contradictions within their own stories or because some element of those stories doesn't line up with the norms the person otherwise accepts. In other words, these interventions are like a water gun pointed at a hole in a fence. As long as your aim is steady, the water goes one place and one place only. This is a much more exacting approach than broadly fact checking, which is like throwing a bucket of water against the fence; some of the water might go where you need it, but a lot will splash all over everything else.

Second, the very act of acknowledging someone else's frame and aligning the discussion with where that person is standing offers a basic affirmation of their identity, an approach that, as Lewandowsky and his team highlight, helps increase a person's receptivity to factual counterpoints.[12] Relatedly, starting with the logics and vocabulary of a frame, even when pushing back against it, guides the conversation toward meta-reflection.

The satanic conspiracy theorists discussed in chapter 1 show how this might work. These theorists alleged that the similarities between satanic abuse narratives proved the truth of those narratives and therefore justified efforts to out Satanists within local communities. How could so many people tell the same basic story if there weren't an extensive network of Satanists committing the same kinds of ritualized crimes in the same kinds of ways? An eye-rolled "Oh Jesus, there are no child-sacrificing Satanists" wouldn't just *not* convince a conspiracy theorist. It would likely serve as proof that they were onto something. In contrast, a discussion about the echo-systems that push information across networks—with each network seeming to corroborate the others but actually just reflecting back the same sources, details, and atrocity stories—would help guide believers to the gaps in their frame, because, in less loaded circumstances, with a subject matter they're less invested in, they would likely be able to understand how echo-systems work and what impact such systems would have across networks. The focus of the discussion, then, wouldn't merely be the facts being checked. It would be the coherence and explanatory power of the alternative explanation.

Such a discussion is certainly not guaranteed to dislodge false beliefs about Satanism or whatever the conspiracy theory might be. We are, all of us, strange and stubborn creatures. But if we guide someone's attention to the coherency gaps they've never needed to notice, while at the same time offering an alternative story explaining not just *that* something is the case but *why*, that person may begin to see the deep memetic frames they experience the world through.

This is, of course, slow and subtle work, infuriatingly so when responding to harmful or dehumanizing frames. It can be outright cruel to tell habitually targeted people to wait patiently while someone holds their attackers' hands and tries to get them to see the world a little differently ("you need to be more gracious; the person who hates that you exist is *learning*"). It would be better if we had a switch to flip, and better still if marginalized people were not always asked to bear such disproportionate burdens. But encouraging people who cause harm to think about *how* they think and *why* they think is at least somewhere to start. Ideally, efforts to access deeper shared truths will arc toward justice—even while those efforts themselves highlight how much injustice there is.

Such outward effort requires inward reflection as well. As we stand there, considering what frames another person is seeing through, we too are seeing through frames. Those frames might correspond to objective reality. They might be ethically robust. But they're still filters that shape our experience of the world. At the least, what we see and know about the world can directly influence—and directly interfere with—what we're able to see and know about another person's experiences. Before we turn our attention to others, we must therefore ask ourselves: What frames am *I* seeing through? What cultivates *my* sense of reality, of goodness, of justice? What do *I* feel in my bones to be true about the world and my place within it? What do I think about how I think?

For white people, particularly white people who are middle-class, able-bodied, cisgender, and straight, this requires a careful look at the deep memetic frame that guides every aspect of life. Our own two lives very much included. This is, of course, the white racial frame, which directs sight to certain people, places, and things while muting or outright pathologizing other people, places, and things. Because this frame is so normalized and so central to mainstream life in the US—and life in the Western world more broadly—it's a particularly difficult frame for people seeing through it to detect. This is no accident. The more invisible the white racial frame is, the less questioned it is, and the less questioned it is, the more successful it can be. As sociologist George Lipsitz says, whiteness is nothing if not possessively invested in preserving itself.[13] It doesn't want to be seen. Otherwise it would be dismantled.

Of course, the invisibility of whiteness only works in one direction. Those who aren't seeing through the frame have a much easier time detecting it—largely because they are harmed by it. This is an uncomfortable truth that many white people haven't fully contended with. It's easier to keep telling yourself the story that if you're not a cross-burning bigot, if you've never targeted or harassed anyone because of their skin color or religion, you're one of the good ones. It's easier to see racism as an ugly relic of the past, one that *you've* gotten over, so why can't everybody else?

You might not see your whiteness; you might not feel its effects. But whether you personally see it or not, the white racial frame harms people of color, and has for centuries. And not just people of color: the white racial frame harms everyone. The oceans of pollution that roared across the landscape because of the unexamined whiteness of early internet culture, and later because of the perfect confluence of white abstraction and white irony when faced with white supremacist violence, are a testament to what the white racial frame can do to the landscape. It must be seen. And it must be dismantled.

The act—and clearly it can be a distressing act—of exploring our own deep memetic frames is the final, most critical step in "you are here" network mapping. Triangulating our personal relationship to the technologies we use, the people we interact with, and the networks we navigate is critical. But the map will only ever be static and one-dimensional if it doesn't address our own ideologies and experiences. To truly steward the land, we must understand how we shape the land—and how that land has shaped us.

YOU ARE HERE

The dense networks connecting everything to everything else online can be a source of profound destruction. They can also be a source of profound resilience. In her reflections on the natural world, Robin Wall Kimmerer reminds us what resilience looks like. In so doing, she reminds us that we already have the answers we need. All plants and all animals are linked within an intricate, interconnected gift economy. Humans often refuse and exploit these gifts. And yet, still, the natural world is guided by giving—between families, across species, throughout the entire ecosystem. "Such communal generosity might seem incompatible with the process of evolution," Kimmerer observes, "which invokes the imperative of individual survival. But we make a grave error if we try to separate individual well-being from the health of the whole."[14]

Our information ecosystem is no different, and the stakes are just as high. Too many people exploit and refuse the gifts of connection, instead embracing the bundles of rights that jealously guard what's theirs. Too many people fixate on their own freedoms *from*, burying their responsibility to cultivate freedoms *for*.

This is certainly a grave error. How we tend our own soil affects the soil of those around us, and those around them, as the camera zooms out, revealing glowing connections across neighborhoods, counties, states, nations, and the entire globe. From such heights, there are no individual parcels of land to carve out, no property lines to defend, no untouched acres from which to bellow *not in my backyard*. This, in the end, is what the "you are here" map reveals. The networks of networks comprising our intertwined lives, the speed with which information travels, the effect of that information on so many unseen others, beats with reciprocity, and therefore with responsibility. If we choose instead only to see the rights we have, rather than the space we share, then the forest will die, and we will die with it.

It doesn't have to be that way. We can choose, instead, to tend the land wisely, acknowledging always that our fates are connected. Quietly, slowly, and with sincerity, we get there working side by side, piling small things up until they're big.

Acknowledgments

We are, as always, indebted to our families and especially grateful for their support during the book's final, frazzled push. Thank you. Thank you, as well, to the friends, guides, and sounding boards who help keep us rooted: M&V, Everett, Stevie, Maple, D&C, Kato, Wesley, Anne, Mark, Theresa, Ashley, Joanne, Kelly, Sophie, Sarah F, Jo, LB, Ang, Cheryl, Wendy, Janet, D&C, El, Cal, S&R, John, Jeff, Cate B, Kate, A, AG, D&A, M&E, Becky, E&M, R&L, Sarah, S, G, and P. We are deeply grateful to the thinkers who have contributed to this project in various ways, particularly danah boyd, Jessica Beyer, Alice Marwick, Becca Lewis, Claire Wardle, Danielle Citron, Shireen Mitchell, Joan Donovan, Jason Koebler, Abby Ohlheiser, April Glaser, Brandy Zadrozny, Ezra Klein, Gabriella Coleman, Nikki Usher, Daniel Kreiss, and the book's reviewers. Dan Engber, Phillips's editor at *Wired*, is similarly excellent. Patrick Davison, Mike Rugnetta, and Stephen Bruckert, who offered such unflinching reflections in chapter 2, deserve special recognition and many thanks. The project has unfolded organically through countless conversations with journalists and scholars in the United States and abroad. Thank you to all, with special thanks to everyone at the Fluminense Federal University for being such gracious hosts—Viktor Chagas and Natalia Dias in particular. We are also extremely grateful for our dynamic, generous colleagues in the College of Charleston's Communication Department and Syracuse University's Communication and Rhetorical Studies Department; neither of us could say enough good things about our respective chairs, Jen Kopfman and Chuck Morris. And to our students, sheltered in place: thank you for your humor, grace, and patience. Our warmest thanks, as well, to Data & Society's Media Manipulation Initiative and its funders Craig Newmark Philanthropies, the Ford Foundation, and the News Integrity Initiative at the Craig Newmark Graduate School of Journalism at the City University of New York; Data & Society's MMI published Phillips's "The Oxygen of Amplification" report in 2018, and we've woven portions of that work into chapter 3. Big thanks, also, to the Knowledge Futures Group and the PubPub team, especially Catherine Ahearn and Quincy Childs, for giving the book an early home. And to everyone at the MIT Press: we are profoundly grateful for your care and concern and willingness to let the book meet the moment. María Garcia, Judy Feldmann, and William Henry, thank you. Gita Manaktala, you're our hero. Finally, Ryan, thank you. Whit, thank you.

Notes

INTRODUCTION

1. "Can Platforms Get It Right?" panel at "Disinfo 2020: Prepping the Press," cohosted by Columbia Journalism Review and the Tow Center for Digital Journalism, December 10, 2019, https://www.cjr.org/covering_the_election/disinformation-conference.php. Phillips spoke on an earlier panel at this event, with a focus on the climate/network crisis connection. During his panel, Steenfadt, who manages the Reporters without Borders' Journalism Trust Initiative, responded with this striking framing. It was so perfectly put that Phillips nearly fell off her chair, and during revisions, we restructured the opening of the introduction with those insights as the centerpiece. Needless to say, we are deeply grateful for his contribution.

2. Yochai Benkler, Robert Faris, and Hal Roberts, *Network Propaganda: Manipulation, Disinformation, and Radicalization in American Politics* (Oxford: Oxford University Press, 2018).

3. Anne Nelson, *Shadow Network: Media, Money, and the Secret Hub of the Radical Right* (New York: Bloomsbury, 2019).

4. Lee McIntyre, *Post-Truth* (Cambridge, MA: MIT Press, 2018); Francesca Tripodi, "Searching for Alternative Facts: Analyzing Scriptural Inference in Conservative News Practices," Data & Society Research Institute, May 16, 2017, https://datasociety.net/output/searching-for-alternative-facts; Safiya Noble, *Algorithms of Oppression: How Search Engines Reinforce Racism* (New York: NYU Press, 2018).

5. Ezra Klein, *Why We're Polarized* (New York: Simon and Schuster, 2020).

6. Claire Wardle and Hossein Derakhshan, "Information Disorder: Toward an Interdisciplinary Framework for Research and Policymaking," Council of Europe research report, Shorenstein Center on Media, Politics, and Public Policy, October 31, 2017, https://shorensteincenter.org/information-disorder-framework-for-research-and-policymaking.

7. Zeynep Tufekci, "It's the (Democracy-Poisoning) Golden Age of Free Speech," *Wired*, January 16, 2018, https://www.wired.com/story/free-speech-issue-tech-turmoil-new-censorship;

Danielle Citron, "How Deepfakes Undermine Truth and Threaten Democracy," TEDSummit 2019, July 2019, https://www.ted.com/talks/danielle_citron_how_deepfakes_under mine_truth_and_threaten_democracy.

8. Wilson Gomes, keynote delivered to the #MuseudeMEMES symposium at the Republic Museum, hosted by Fluminense Federal University, May 31, 2019.

9. For an early articulation of environmental justice issues, see Robert D. Bullard and Beverly H. Wright, "The Politics of Pollution: Implications for the Black Community," *Phylon* 47, no. 1 (1986): 71–78; Robert D. Bullard and Beverly H. Wright, "Environmental Justice for All: Community Health Perspectives on Health and Research Needs," *Toxicology and Industrial Health* 9, no. 5 (1993): 821–842.

10. Clifford C. Christians, John Ferré, and P. Mark Fackler, *Good News: Social Ethics and the Press* (Oxford: Oxford University Press, 1993).

11. Robin Wall Kimmerer, *Braiding Sweetgrass: Indigenous Wisdom, Scientific Knowledge, and the Teachings of Plants* (Minneapolis: Milkweed Editions, 2013), 30.

12. A vast corpus of cross-disciplinary literature is devoted to media ecology, broadly divided, Anthony Nadler explains, between studies that approach media as environments and studies that approach media as species. Our study follows its own path, though sociologist Amos Hawley's articulation of human ecology, which draws from the lexicon of the environmental sciences to emphasize ecosystems over individual actions and relationships over individual actors, is probably closest in spirit to our own. For more on the twists and turns of the media ecology tradition, see Amos H. Hawley, *Human Ecology: A Theoretical Essay* (New York: Ronald Press, 1950); Lance Strate, *Media Ecology: An Approach to Understanding the Human Condition* (New York: Peter Lang, 2017); Anthony Nadler, "Nature's Economy and News Ecology," *Journalism Studies* 20, no. 6 (2019): 823–839; Carloa A. Scolari, "Media Ecology: Exploring the Metaphor to Expand the Theory," *Communication Theory* 22, no. 2 (2012): 204–225.

13. A prominent critique of the media ecology metaphor is that, ironically, it obscures the environmental consequences of information networks; see Niall Stephens, "Toward a More Substantive Media Ecology: Postman's Metaphor versus Posthuman Futures," *International Journal of Communication* 8 (2014): 2027–2045; Timothy B. Morris and Todd Suomela, "Information in the Ecosystem: Against the 'Information Ecosystem,'" *First Monday* 22, no. 9 (2017), https://journals.uic.edu/ojs/index.php/fm/article/view/6847/6530. Other scholars argue that the metaphor is often woefully apolitical, normalizing the existence of particular media environments by framing them as being somehow "natural" and therefore separable from contemporary social dynamics, power structures, and political economies. See Nadler, "Nature's Economy and News Ecology." We have done our best to avoid both pitfalls; in particular, wariness of framing media environments as "natural" is one of the reasons we liked the symbolism of the Arcata Marsh, a wholly constructed ecosystem.

14. Kimmerer, *Braiding Sweetgrass.*

15. This framing aligns with actor network theory as described by Bruno Latour in *Reassembling the Social: An Introduction to Actor Network Theory* (Oxford: Oxford University Press, 2005).

16. Julia Carrie Wong, "The Debate over Facebook's Political Ads Ignores 90% of Its Global Users," *Guardian*, November 1, 2019, https://www.theguardian.com/technology/2019/nov/01/facebook-free-speech-democracy-claims.

17. See Viktor Chagas, Fernanda Freire, Daniel Rios, and Dandara Magalhães, "Political Memes and the Politics of Memes: A Methodological Proposal for Content Analysis of Online Political Memes," *First Monday* 24, no. 2 (2019), https://firstmonday.org/ojs/index.php/fm/article/view/7264; Viktor Chagas, "The Outbreak of Political Memes," *FAMECOS* 25, no. 1 (2018): 1–33; João Guilherme Bastos dos Santos and Viktor Chagas, "Fucking Right-Wing," *MATRIZes* 12, no. 3 (2018): 189–214.

CHAPTER 1

1. Abby Ohlheiser, "No, John Podesta Didn't Drink Bodily Fluids at a Secret Satanist Dinner," *Washington Post*, November 4, 2016, https://wapo.st/2fl2d8P.

2. Susan Faludi, "How Hillary Clinton Met Satan," *New York Times*, October 29, 2016, https://nyti.ms/2dYtb1y.

3. Tina Nguyen, "Ben Carson Doubles Down on Satan-Clinton Connection," *Vanity Fair*, July 20, 2016, https://www.vanityfair.com/news/2016/07/ben-carson-clinton-lucifer.

4. James T. Richardson, Joel Best, and David G. Bromley, eds., *The Satanism Scare* (New York: Taylor & Francis, 1991); Jeffrey S. Victor, *Satanic Panic: The Creation of a Contemporary Legend* (Chicago: Open Court Publishing, 1993); Bill Ellis, *Raising the Devil: Satanism, New Religions, and the Media* (Lexington: University Press of Kentucky, 2000); Kier-La Janisse and Paul Corupe, eds., *Satanic Panic: Pop-Cultural Paranoia in the 1980s* (Surrey: FAB Press, 2015).

5. Erving Goffman, *Frame Analysis: An Essay on the Organization of Experience* (Cambridge, MA: Harvard University Press, 1974); Victor, *Satanic Panic*; Ellis, *Raising the Devil*; George Lakoff and Mark Johnson, *Metaphors We Live By* (Chicago: University of Chicago Press, 1980).

6. Lakoff and Johnson, *Metaphors We Live By*; George Lakoff, *Don't Think of an Elephant! Know Your Values and Frame the Debate* (White River Junction, VT: Chelsea Green, 2004).

7. Sandra Harding, "Rethinking Standpoint Epistemology: What Is 'Strong Objectivity'?" *Centennial Review* 36, no. 3 (1992): 437–470.

8. Arlie Russell Hochschild, *Strangers in Their Own Land: Anger and Mourning on the American Right* (New York: New Press, 2016).

9. Ryan M. Milner, *The World Made Meme: Public Conversations and Participatory Media* (Cambridge, MA: MIT Press, 2016); Richard Dawkins, *The Selfish Gene* (Oxford: Oxford University Press, 1974).

10. Victor, *Satanic Panic*.

11. Interview with Ingersoll, quoted in Anna Merlan, *Republic of Lies: American Conspiracy Theorists and Their Surprising Rise to Power* (New York: Metropolitan Books, 2019), 15.

12. For more on the resonance of "them" within conspiratorial thinking, see Jon Ronson's appropriately titled *Them: Adventures with Extremists* (New York: Simon and Schuster, 2003).

13. Victor, *Satanic Panic*.

14. Victor, *Satanic Panic*.

15. Kembrew McLeod, *Pranksters: Making Mischief in the Modern World* (New York: NYU Press, 2014).

16. Ellis, *Raising the Devil*.

17. Ellis, *Raising the Devil*.

18. Ellis, *Raising the Devil*; McLeod, *Pranksters*.

19. Ellis, *Raising the Devil*.

20. Pat Robertson, *The New World Order* (Dallas, TX: Word Publishing, 1991), 185.

21. Victor, *Satanic Panic*.

22. Ellis, *Raising the Devil*.

23. Phillips Stevens Jr., "The Demonology of Satan: An Anthropological View," in *The Satanism Scare*, ed. James T. Richardson, Joel Best, and David G. Bromley (New York: Taylor & Francis, 1991), 21–40.

24. Yvonne Chireau, "Conjure and Christianity in the Nineteenth Century: Religious Elements in African American Magic," *Religion and American Culture* 7, no. 2 (1997): 225–246.

25. Chireau, "Conjure and Christianity."

26. Ellis, *Raising the Devil*.

27. Victor, *Satanic Panic*.

28. Tara Brach, "Real but Not True: Freeing Ourselves from Harmful Beliefs," Tarabrach.com, June 1, 2016, https://www.tarabrach.com/real-not-true.

29. Richard Hofstadter, *The Paranoid Style in American Politics and Other Essays* (New York: Alfred A. Knopf, 1965). In chapter 4 we revisit what Hofstadter called the "paranoid style of American politics."

30. Merlan, *Republic of Lies*.

31. Victor, *Satanic Panic*.

32. Ellis, *Raising the Devil*; McLeod, *Pranksters*.

33. Mary McGill, "Wicked W.I.T.C.H: The 60s Feminist Protestors Who Hexed Patriarchy," *Vice*, October 28, 2016, https://broadly.vice.com/en_us/article/43gd8p/wicked-witch-60s -feminist-protestors-hexed-patriarchy.

34. Ellis, *Raising the Devil*. At the time, far-right critics attributed the influence of "hippie cults" to the catchall boogeyman of communism, as the communism/Satanism transmutation had not yet been codified.

35. Ellis, *Raising the Devil*; McLeod, *Pranksters*.

36. McLeod, *Pranksters*.

37. Kier-La Janisse, "Introduction: Could It Be . . . Satan?" in *Satanic Panic: Pop-Cultural Para-noia in the 1980s*, ed. Kier-La Janisse and Paul Corupe (Surrey: FAB Press, 2015), 13–18.

38. Marcello Truzzi, "The Occult Revival as Popular Culture: Some Random Observations on the Old and the Nouveau Witch," *Sociological Quarterly* 13, no. 1 (1972): 16–36; "The Occult Revival: A Substitute Faith," *Time* 99, no. 25 (June 19, 1972), http://content.time .com/time/magazine/article/0,9171,877779,00.html.

39. Janisse, "Could It Be . . . Satan?"

40. Referenced in Janisse, "Could It Be . . . Satan?"

41. McLeod, *Pranksters*; Paul Corupe, "20-Sided Sins: How Jack T. Chick Was Drawn into the RPG War," in *Satanic Panic: Pop-Cultural Paranoia in the 1980s*, ed. Kier-La Janisse and Paul Corupe (Surrey: FAB Press, 2015), 69–82.

42. Victor, *Satanic Panic*.

43. McLeod, *Pranksters*, 207.

44. Victor, *Satanic Panic*.

45. Ellis, *Raising the Devil*.

46. Mike Warnke, *The Satan Seller* (Plainfield, NJ: Logos International, 1972).

47. Ellis, *Raising the Devil*.

48. Michelle Smith, *Michelle Remembers* (New York: Pocket, 1980).

49. Victor, *Satanic Panic*.

50. Victor, *Satanic Panic*.

51. Victor, *Satanic Panic*.

52. Alexandra Heller-Nicholas, "'The Only Word in the World Is Mine': Remembering *Michelle Remembers*," in *Satanic Panic: Pop-Cultural Paranoia in the 1980s*, ed. Kier-La Janisse and Paul Corupe (Surrey: FAB Press, 2015), 19–32; Philip Jenkins and Daniel Maier-Katkin, "Occult Survivors: The Making of a Myth," in *The Satanism Scare*, ed. James T. Richardson, Joel Best, and David G. Bromley (New York: Taylor & Francis, 1991), 127–144; Ellis, *Raising the Devil*.

53. Sherrill Mulhern, "Satanism and Psychotherapy: A Rumor in Search of an Inquisition," in *The Satanism Scare*, ed. James T. Richardson, Joel Best, and David G. Bromley (New York: Taylor & Francis, 1991), 145–174; Robert D. Hicks, "The Police Model of Satanism Crime," in *The Satanism Scare*, ed. James T. Richardson, Joel Best, and David G. Bromley (New York: Taylor & Francis, 1991), 175–190; Jenkins and Maier-Katkin, "Occult Survivors."

54. Quoted in Victor, *Satanic Panic*, 38.

55. Ellis, *Raising the Devil*.

56. Victor, *Satanic Panic*.

57. Nancy K. Baym, *Personal Connections in the Digital Age*, 2nd ed. (Malden, MA: Polity Press, 2015).

58. David G. Bromley, "Satanism: The New Cult Scare," in *The Satanism Scare*, ed. James T. Richardson, Joel Best, and David G. Bromley (New York: Taylor & Francis, 1991), 69.

59. Victor, *Satanic Panic*; McLeod, *Pranksters*.

60. James T. Richardson, Joel Best, and David G. Bromley, "Satanism as a Social Problem," in *The Satanism Scare*, ed. James T. Richardson, Joel Best, and David G. Bromley (New York: Taylor & Francis, 1991), 3–20; Debbie Nathan, "Satanism and Child Molestation: Constructing the Ritual Abuse Scare," in *The Satanism Scare*, ed. James T. Richardson, Joel Best, and David G. Bromley (New York: Taylor & Francis, 1991), 75–94.

61. Ellis, *Raising the Devil*.

62. American Psychiatric Association, *Diagnostic and Statistical Manual of Mental Disorders: DSM-IV-TR* (Washington, DC: American Psychiatric Association, 2000).

63. Joel Paris, "The Rise and Fall of Dissociative Identity Disorder," *Journal of Nervous and Mental Disease* 200, no. 12 (2012): 1076–1079.

64. Heller-Nicholas, "The Only Word in the World Is Mine."

65. Victor, *Satanic Panic*.

66. Victor, *Satanic Panic*; Mulhern, "Satanism and Psychotherapy"; Jenkins and Maier-Katkin, "Occult Survivors."

67. Mulhern, "Satanism and Psychotherapy," 158.

68. Joshua Benjamin Graham, "Masters of the Imagination: Fundamentalist Readings of the Occult in Cartoons of the 1980s," in *Satanic Panic: Pop-Cultural Paranoia in the 1980s*, ed. Kier-La Janisse and Paul Corupe (Surrey: FAB Press, 2015), 83–96.

69. Phil Phillips, *Turmoil in the Toy Box* (Lancaster, PA: Starburst Publishers, 1990); Phil Phillips, *Saturday Morning Mind Control* (Nashville, TN: Oliver-Nelson Books, 1991).

70. Victor, *Satanic Panic*.

71. Jack Chick, *Spellbound?* (Ontario, CA: Chick Publications, 1978).

72. Liisa Ladouceur, "The Filthy 15: When Venom and King Diamond Met the Washington Wives," in *Satanic Panic: Pop-Cultural Paranoia in the 1980s*, ed. Kier-La Janisse and Paul Corupe (Surrey: FAB Press, 2015), 159–172.

73. Daniel Martin and Gary Allen Fine, "Satanic Cultures, Satanic Play: Is Dungeons & Dragons a Breeding Ground for the Devil?" in *The Satanism Scare*, ed. James T. Richardson, Joel Best, and David G. Bromley (New York: Taylor & Francis, 1991), 107–126; Corupe, "20-Sided Sins."

74. Martin and Fine "Satanic Cultures, Satanic Play."

75. Corupe, "20-Sided Sins."

76. Ellis, *Raising the Devil*.

77. Hunter S. Thompson, *Kingdom of Fear: Loathsome Secrets of a Star-Crossed Child in the Final Days of the American Century* (New York: Penguin, 2003).

78. Ellis, *Raising the Devil*.

79. McLeod, *Pranksters*; Wm. Conley, "The Tracking of Evil: Home Video and the Proliferation of Satanic Panic," in *Satanic Panic: Pop-Cultural Paranoia in the 1980s*, ed. Kier-La Janisse and Paul Corupe (Surrey: FAB Press, 2015), 231–246.

80. Ellis, *Raising the Devil*.

81. Ellis, *Raising the Devil*; Jesse Walker, *United States of Paranoia: A Conspiracy Theory* (New York: Harper Perennial, 2013).

82. Ellis, *Raising the Devil*.

83. McLeod, *Pranksters*.

84. Nelson, *Shadow Network*.

85. Heather Hendershot, *What's Fair on the Air? Cold War Right-Wing Broadcasting and Public Interest* (Chicago: University of Chicago Press, 2011).

86. Jeffrey K. Hadden and Anson D. Shupe, *Televangelism: Power and Politics on God's Frontier* (New York: H. Holt, 1988).

87. Nelson, *Shadow Network*.

88. Hendershot, *What's Fair on the Air?*

89. Hendershot, *What's Fair on the Air?*

90. Hendershot, *What's Fair on the Air?*

91. Nelson, *Shadow Network*.

92. Hendershot, *What's Fair on the Air?*

93. Nelson, *Shadow Network*.

94. Nelson, *Shadow Network*.

95. Nelson, *Shadow Network*.

96. Richardson, Best, and Bromley, "Satanism as a Social Problem."

97. Nelson, *Shadow Network*, 23.

98. Nelson, *Shadow Network*.

99. Ben Crouch and Kelly Damphousse, "Law Enforcement and the Satanism-Crime Connection: A Survey of 'Cult Cops,'" in *The Satanism Scare*, ed. James T. Richardson, Joel Best, and David G. Bromley (New York: Taylor & Francis, 1991), 191–204.

100. Hicks, "Police Model of Satanism Crime."

101. Ellis, *Raising the Devil*.

102. Victor, *Satanic Panic*.

103. Victor, *Satanic Panic*, 226.

104. Richardson, Best, and Bromley, "Satanism as a Social Problem."

105. Nelson, *Shadow Network*.

106. Nelson, *Shadow Network*.

107. Victor, *Satanic Panic*.

108. Victor, *Satanic Panic*.

109. Viktor Chagas, keynote delivered to the #MuseudeMEMES symposium at the Republic Museum, hosted by Fluminense Federal University, May 29, 2019.

110. Eric Levitz, "Report: Clinton Linked to Satanic Rituals Involving Kidnapped Children and Marina Abramovic," *New York Magazine*, November 4, 2016, http://nymag.com/intelligencer/2016/11/spirit-cooking-explained-satanic-ritual-or-fun-dinner.html.

111. Philip Bump, "Oh, Cool, Now the Campaign Is All about Charges of Satanism," *Washington Post*, November 4, 2016, https://www.washingtonpost.com/news/the-fix/wp/2016/11/04/oh-cool-now-the-campaign-is-all-about-charges-of-satanism.

CHAPTER 2

1. Perhaps counterintuitively, liberalism is the core of much conservative thinking. So much so that libertarian-leaning conservatives will often call themselves "classical liberals," a philosophy articulated in David Conway, *Classical Liberalism: The Unvanquished Ideal* (New York: St. Martin's, 1995). For more on how liberalism informs modern conservatism, see Michael J. Lee, *Creating Conservatism: Postwar Words That Made an American Movement* (East Lansing: Michigan State University Press, 2014).

2. Clifford C. Christians, John Ferré, and P. Mark Fackler, *Good News: Social Ethics and the Press* (Oxford: Oxford University Press, 1993). Also see Sun-Ha Hong, *Technologies of Speculation: The Limits of Knowledge in a Data-Driven Society* (New York: NYU Press, 2020), for

a discussion of the ideal Enlightenment subject and how modern citizens are—in Hong's words—being trolled by and with the Enlightenment.

3. Steven Levy, *Hackers: Heroes of the Computer Revolution* (New York: Doubleday, 1984).

4. Bruce Sterling, "A Short History of the Internet," *Magazine of Fantasy and Science Fiction*, February 1993, http://sodacity.net/system/files/Bruce_Sterling_A_Short_History_of_the _Internet.pdf.

5. Meredith Broussard, *Artificial Unintelligence: How Computers Misunderstand the World* (Cambridge, MA: MIT Press, 2018).

6. "Mark Zuckerberg, Moving Fast and Breaking Things," *Business Insider*, October 14, 2010, https://www.businessinsider.com/mark-zuckerberg-2010-10.

7. April Glaser, "Another Network Is Possible," *Logic*, August 3, 2019, https://logicmag.io /bodies/another-network-is-possible.

8. Danah boyd, "Facing the Great Reckoning Head-On," *Apophenia*, September 15, 2019, https://www.zephoria.org/thoughts/archives/2019/09/15/facing-the-great-reckoning -head-on.html.

9. John Perry Barlow, "A Declaration of the Independence of Cyberspace," Electronic Frontier Foundation, February 8, 1996, https://www.eff.org/cyberspace-independence.

10. Whitney Phillips, *This Is Why We Can't Have Nice Things: Mapping the Relationship between Online Trolling and Mainstream Culture* (Cambridge, MA: MIT Press, 2015); Whitney Phillips and Ryan M. Milner, *The Ambivalent Internet: Mischief, Oddity, and Antagonism Online* (Cambridge: Polity Press, 2017). Phillips first introduced this concept in the context of trolls in *This Is Why We Can't Have Nice Things*; this sense of the fetish borrows from Karl Marx's commodity fetish, in which the "magic of capitalism" renders invisible all the infrastructural logistics, ecological impacts, and exploitative labor practices that make consumer culture possible. All consumers see, all they are intended to see, is the item they are purchasing.

11. Boyd, "Facing the Great Reckoning Head-On."

12. Whitney Phillips and Kate Miltner, "The Meme Election: Clicktivism, the BuzzFeed Effect and Corporate Meme-Jacking," *The Awl*, November 2, 2012, https://www.theawl .com/2012/11/the-meme-election-clicktivism-the-buzzfeed-effect-and-corporate-meme -jacking.

13. Chapter 3 takes up the evolution of the term *trolling* and how it has mapped onto Trump- era violent white supremacy.

14. "The Team," ROFLCon.org, April 30, 2010, https://web.archive.org/web/201004302 34306/http://roflcon.org/the-team; "The Team," ROFLCon.org, April 29, 2012, https:// web.archive.org/web/20120429041427/http://roflcon.org/the-team. Poole also attended the 2008 event, but under a pseudonym; see Tim Hwang and Christina Xu, "'Lurk More':

An Interview with the Founders of ROFLCon," *Journal of Visual Culture* 13, no. 3 (2014): 376–387.

15. Danah boyd, "Hacking the Attention Economy," *Data & Society Points*, January 5, 2017, https://points.datasociety.net/hacking-the-attention-economy-9fa1daca7a37.

16. "Mainstreaming the Web: Complete Video," ROFLCon.org, May 24, 2010, https://web.archive.org/web/20130308131320/http://roflcon.org/2010/05/24/mainstreaming-the-web-complete-video.

17. Nick Douglas, "It's Supposed to Look like Shit: The Internet Ugly Aesthetic," *Journal of Visual Culture* 13, no. 3 (2014): 314–339.

18. Douglas, "It's Supposed to Look like Shit," 314.

19. Douglas, "It's Supposed to Look like Shit."

20. Mike Rugnetta, "How Does Glitchy Art Show Us Broken Is Beautiful?" *PBS Idea Channel*, July 24, 2013, https://www.youtube.com/watch?v=7MCmBHPqz6I.

21. Douglas, "It's Supposed to Look like Shit."

22. Quoted in Alexis Lothian, "DML2011 Liveblog: The Politics of User-Generated Content," *Humanities, Arts, Science, and Technology Alliance and Collaboratory*, March 5, 2011, https://www.hastac.org/blogs/alexislothian/2011/03/05/dml2011-liveblog-politics-user-generated-content.

23. Gabriella Coleman, *Hacker, Hoaxer, Whistleblower, Spy: The Many Faces of Anonymous* (London: Verso, 2014).

24. Phillips, *This Is Why We Can't Have Nice Things*.

25. We will dive into this apparent contradiction in chapter 3.

26. Douglas, "It's Supposed to Look like Shit," 316.

27. Whitney Phillips, "So Bad It's Good: The *Kuso* Aesthetic in *Troll 2*," *Transformative Works and Cultures*, no. 14 (2013), https://journal.transformativeworks.org/index.php/twc/article/view/480/357.

28. Phillips, "So Bad It's Good," 1.2.

29. See Phillips and Milner, *The Ambivalent Internet*, for more on the affordances of digital media.

30. Siva Vaidhyanathan, *Antisocial Media: How Facebook Disconnects Us and Undermines Democracy* (Oxford: Oxford University Press, 2018).

31. Siva Vaidhyanathan, "Mark Zuckerberg Doesn't Understand Free Speech in the 21st Century," *Guardian*, October 18, 2019, https://www.theguardian.com/commentisfree/2019/oct/18/mark-zuckerberg-free-speech-21st-century.

32. Boyd, "Facing the Great Reckoning Head-On."

33. Ev Williams, Twitter, May 22, 2019, https://twitter.com/ev/status/1131258493162311680.

34. Charlie Warzal, "'A Honeypot for Assholes': Inside Twitter's 10-Year Failure to Stop Harassment," *BuzzFeed News*, August 11, 2016, https://www.buzzfeednews.com/article/charlie warzel/a-honeypot-for-assholes-inside-twitters-10-year-failure-to-s.

35. Tarleton Gillespie, *Custodians of the Internet: Platforms, Content Moderation, and the Hidden Decisions That Shape Social Media* (New Haven, CT: Yale University Press, 2018).

36. Maeve Duggan and Joanna Brenner, "Social Networking Site Users," Pew Research Center, February 14, 2013, https://www.pewinternet.org/2013/02/14/social-networking-site-users.

37. Hwang and Xu, "'Lurk More.'"

38. The "i can haz dream? Race and the Internet" panel during the 2010 conference did address race online but focused more on how people perform race in digitally mediated spaces. It did not change the sea of white faces in the audience.

39. Hwang and Xu, "'Lurk More,'" 384.

40. Hwang and Xu, "'Lurk More.'"

41. The cover of the program featured a collage of popular memes and did include a cartoon representation of one Black person—the rapper Xzibit, who became a meme in 2009 thanks to his MTV reality show *Pimp My Ride* and catchphrase "Yo dawg . . . ," which white people found hilarious.

42. André Brock, "From the Blackhand Side: Twitter as a Cultural Conversation," *Journal of Broadcasting and Electronic Media* 56, no. 4 (2012): 529–549. Brock expanded this analysis, along with additional chapters exploring a variety of black cybercultures, in his book *Distributed Blackness: African American Cybercultures* (New York: NYU Press, 2020).

43. People of color have long contributed to the development of network cultures and computing technologies, evidenced by the work of the indigenous Mexican activists, described by April Glaser, who laid the groundwork for anticapitalist grassroots networks in the 1990s (Glaser, "Another Network Is Possible"). Media historian Charlton McIlwain similarly chronicles the broad contributions of Black technologists and activists in his book *Black Software: The Internet and Racial Justice, from the AfroNet to Black Lives Matter* (Oxford: Oxford University Press, 2019).

44. Brock, "From the Blackhand Side," 542; Nick Douglas, "Micah's 'Black People on Twitter' Theory," *Too Much Nick*, August 21, 2009, https://toomuchnick.com/post/168222309/micahs-black-people-on-twitter-theory.

45. For examples, see Donna Haraway, *Simians, Cyborgs, and Women: The Reinvention of Nature* (New York: Routledge, 1991); Lisa Nakamura, *Cybertypes: Race, Ethnicity, and Identity on the Internet* (London: Routledge, 2002); Wendy Chun, *Control and Freedom: Power and Paranoia in the Age of Fiber Optics* (Cambridge, MA: MIT Press).

46. For examples, see Anita Say Chan, *Networking Peripheries: Technological Futures and the Myth of Digital Universalism* (Cambridge, MA: MIT Press, 2014); Ethan Zuckerman, *Digital Cosmopolitans: Why We Think the Internet Connects Us, Why It Doesn't, and How to Rewire*

It (New York: Norton, 2013); An Xiao Mina, *Memes to Movements: How the World's Most Viral Media Is Changing Social Protest and Power* (Boston, MA: Beacon Press, 2019).

47. For examples, see Kishonna L. Gray, "'They're Just Too Urban': Black Gamers Streaming on Twitch," in *Digital Sociologies*, ed. Jessie Daniels, Karen Gregory, and Tressie McMillan Cottom (Chicago: University of Chicago Press, 2016), 355–368; Meredith Clark, "Black Twitter: Building Connection through Cultural Conversations," in *Hashtag Publics: The Power and Politics of Discursive Networks*, ed. Nathan Rambukkana (New York: Peter Lang, 2015), 205–218; Keeanga-Yamahtta Taylor, *From #BlackLivesMatter to Black Liberation* (Chicago: Haymarket Press, 2016); Moya Bailey, "Redefining Representation: Black Trans and Queer Women's Digital Media Production," *Screen Bodies* 1, no. 1 (2016): 71–86; Craig S. Watkins and Alexander Cho, *The Digital Edge: How Black and Latino Youth Navigate Digital Inequality* (New York: NYU Press, 2018); Elizabeth LaPensée, "Games as Enduring Presence," in "Indigenous Art: New Media and the Digital," special issue, *PUBLIC* 54 (2016): 178–186.

48. Brock, quoted in André Wheeler, "Ten Years of Black Twitter: A Merciless Watchdog for Problematic Behavior," *Guardian*, December 23, 2019, https://www.theguardian.com /technology/2019/dec/23/ten-years-black-twitter-watchdog.

49. Cheris Kramarae, *Women and Men Speaking: Frameworks for Analysis* (Rowley, MA: Newbury House, 1981); Marsha Houston and Cheris Kramarae, "Speaking from Silence: Methods of Silencing and of Resistance," *Discourse and Society* 2, no. 4 (1991): 387–400; Mark P. Orbe, "From the Standpoint(s) of Traditionally Muted Groups: Explicating a Co-cultural Communication Theoretical Model," *Communication Theory* 8, no. 1 (1998): 1–26.

50. Moya Bailey and Trudy, "On Misogynoir: Citation, Erasure, and Plagiarism," *Feminist Media Studies* 18, no. 4 (2018): 762–768.

51. Clark, quoted in Wheeler, "Ten Years of Black Twitter."

52. Joe R. Feagin, *The White Racial Frame: Centuries of Racial Framing and Counter-Framing*, 2nd ed. (New York: Routledge, 2013).

53. For more on structural and symbolic forms of white supremacy, see Carol Anderson, *White Rage: The Unspoken Truth of Our Racial Divide* (New York: Bloomsbury, 2016); Elizabeth Gillespie McRae, *Mothers of Massive Resistance: White Women and the Politics of White Supremacy* (Oxford: Oxford University Press, 2018); George Lipsitz, *The Possessive Investment in Whiteness: How White People Profit from Identity Politics*, 2nd ed. (Philadelphia, PA: Temple University Press, 2006).

54. For more on how structural white supremacy does not need a single violent racist to replicate itself, see Eduardo Bonilla-Silva, *Racism without Racists: Color-Blind Racism and the Persistence of Racial Inequality in the United States* (Lanham, MD: Rowman and Littlefield, 2006).

55. Richard Dyer, *White: Essays on Race and Culture* (London: Routledge, 1997).

56. Tressie McMillan Cottom, "The Problem with Obama's Faith in White America," *Atlantic*, December 13, 2016, https://www.theatlantic.com/politics/archive/2016/12/obamas-faith-in-white-america/510503.

57. Patrick Davison, email interview with the authors, March 12, 2019. As part of that conversation, Davison attached a new introduction to a chapter he had written back in 2009, titled "The Language of Internet Memes." In 2009, Davison explained, the chapter was outright celebratory of internet memes and made not a single reference to race, gender, or harassment. He had recently been asked to include the chapter in an edited volume on internet memes, to be translated by Viktor Chagas into Portuguese, but did not feel comfortable submitting it without retrospective comment. So, in that new introduction, Davison explains that his thinking on the subject has shifted significantly over the last ten years, including his attitude toward the dehumanizing elements of many internet memes, and asks readers to keep that in mind as they read the body text.

58. Mike Rugnetta, email interview with the authors, July 15–17, 2019.

59. Stephen Bruckert, email interview with the authors, July 16, 2019.

60. Patrick Davison, email interview with the authors, July 16, 2019.

61. We aren't suggesting that Harvard University, or any Ivy League school, or any university, or any institution, is somehow above the structural white supremacist fray. The point is the easy-breeziness with which racist messaging flew under so many people's radars, including those who otherwise would have described themselves as liberal antiracists.

62. Mike Rugnetta, email interview with the authors.

63. Patrick Davison, email interview with the authors, July 2019.

64. Christy Wampole, "How to Live without Irony," *New York Times*, November 17, 2012, https://opinionator.blogs.nytimes.com/2012/11/17/how-to-live-without-irony.

65. "How the Facebook Ads That Targeted Voters Centered on Black American Culture: Voter Suppression Was the End Game," Stop Online Violence against Women, 2019, http://stoponlinevaw.com/wp-content/uploads/2018/10/Black-ID-Target-by-Russia-Report-SOVAW.pdf.

66. Rachelle Hampton, "The Black Feminists Who Saw the Alt-Right Threat Coming," *Slate*, April 23, 2019, https://slate.com/technology/2019/04/black-feminists-alt-right-twitter-gamergate.html.

67. Mina, *Memes to Movements*.

68. These platforms differ somewhat from their English-speaking counterparts owing to pervasive censorship efforts on the Chinese internet.

69. Discussion with coLAB research group at Fluminense Federal University, Rio de Janeiro, Brazil, May 29, 2019.

70. Wampole, "How to Live without Irony."

71. Hwang and Xu, "'Lurk More,'" 379.

72. Hwang and Xu, "'Lurk More,'" 379.

73. Phillips, *This Is Why We Can't Have Nice Things.*

CHAPTER 3

1. Portions of this chapter are based on Whitney Phillips, "The Oxygen of Amplification: Better Practices for Reporting on Extremists, Bigots, and Manipulators," Data & Society Research Institute, May 22, 2018, https://datasociety.net/output/oxygen-of-amplification. The project was funded and published by Data & Society's Media Manipulation Initiative. We are deeply grateful to Data & Society for allowing us to build on this work; from the MMI team to the communications team to all the amazing people Phillips worked with on the project, with danah boyd, Joan Donovan, and Patrick Davison deserving honorable mention, Phillips extends her thanks in every direction. Many thanks, as well, to MMI's funders, including Craig Newmark Philanthropies, the Ford Foundation, and the News Integrity Initiative at the Craig Newmark Graduate School of Journalism at the City University of New York, for supporting the project.

2. "Dust Storm in Morton County, Kansas," Kansas Historical Society, ca. 1935, https://www.kansasmemory.org/item/211239.

3. Clifford R. Hope, "Kansas in the 1930s," *Kansas History: A Journal of the Central Plains* 36, no. 1 (1970): 1–12; Ken Burns, *The Dust Bowl* (PBS, 2012); "Dust Bowl," Kansas Historical Society, June 2003, https://www.kshs.org/kansapedia/dust-bowl/12040.

4. Hope, "Kansas in the 1930s."

5. George Hawley, *Making Sense of the Alt-Right* (Chichester, NY: Columbia University Press, 2017).

6. Hawley, *Making Sense of the Alt-Right.*

7. Jacob Davey and Julia Ebner, "The Fringe Insurgency: Connectivity, Convergence, and Mainstreaming of the Extreme Right," Institute for Strategic Dialogue research paper, 2017, http://www.isdglobal.org/wp-content/uploads/2017/10/The-Fringe-Insurgency-221017.pdf.

8. Alice Marwick and Becca Lewis, "Media Manipulation and Disinformation Online," Data & Society Research Institute, May 15, 2017, https://datasociety.net/output/media-manipulation-and-disinfo-online.

9. Marwick and Lewis, "Media Manipulation," 3.

10. Heather Suzanne Woods and Leslie A. Hahner, *Make America Meme Again: The Rhetoric of the Alt-Right* (New York: Peter Lang, 2019).

11. Ashley Feinberg, "This Is the Daily Stormer's Playbook," *Huffington Post*, December 13, 2017, https://www.huffingtonpost.com/entry/daily-stormer-nazi-style-guide_us_5a2ece19e4 b0ce3b344492f2.

12. Aja Romano, "How the Alt-Right Uses Internet Trolling to Confuse You into Dismissing Its Ideology," *Vox*, January 11, 2017, https://www.vox.com/2016/11/23/13659634/alt-right-trolling.

13. Woods and Hahner, *Make America Meme Again.*

14. Jesse Singal, "How Internet Trolls Won the 2016 Presidential Election," *New York Magazine*, September 16, 2016, http://nymag.com/selectall/2016/09/how-internet-trolls-won-the-2016-presidential-election.html.

15. Angela Nagle, *Kill All Normies* (Winchester: Zero Books, 2017).

16. The outlets we are calling "center-left" media here are variously also called "mainstream," "legacy," or "liberal" media. Many people, particularly on the right, just call them "the media" (as if center-left outlets are a united monolith and as if conservative media outlets don't count as "media"). Depending on how a person feels about any of those terms, each can be used pejoratively, neutrally, or positively. For us, the most accurate, if unwieldy, descriptor for these outlets is "establishment, center-left news media," which conveys their prominence within the news ecosystem, situates them politically, and emphasizes their extraordinary power to amplify information across the nation and globe.

17. Chip Somodevilla, "Court Hearing for James Alex Fields, Suspect Who Drove Car into Group of Activists Protesting after White Supremacists Rally," Getty Images, August 14, 2017, https://www.gettyimages.com/detail/news-photo/matthew-heinbach-of-the-white-nationalist-traditionalist-news-photo/831329068.

18. Yochai Benkler, Robert Faris, and Hal Roberts, *Network Propaganda: Manipulation, Disinformation, and Radicalization in American Politics* (Oxford: Oxford University Press, 2018).

19. Phillips's study focused, as we do here, on print and online news outlets that produce written stories first and foremost, even if they also produce audiovisual content. There is, of course, a great deal to say about television and radio news, but as so much reporting begins with written journalism, and because written commentary is essential to center-left political conversations online, we focus there.

20. Benkler, Faris, and Roberts, *Network Propaganda.*

21. Alan Rappeport, "Hillary Clinton Denounces the 'Alt-Right,' and the Alt-Right Is Thrilled," *New York Times*, August 26, 2016, https://www.nytimes.com/2016/08/27/us/politics/alt-right-reaction.html.

22. Gaby Del Valle, "How Should the Alt-Right Be Covered?" *Outline*, October 10, 2017, https://theoutline.com/post/2381/how-should-the-alt-right-be-covered.

23. Lois Beckett, "How Leftwing Media Focus on Far Right Groups Is Helping to Normalize Hate," *Guardian*, March 5, 2017, https://www.theguardian.com/world/2017/mar/05/left-wing-media-far-right-normalize-hate-trump.

24. In a roundtable hosted on June 14, 2019, by the Shorenstein Center at Harvard University, Jessie Daniels shared this example; we thank her for it. For more on the incident, see Justin

Carissimo, "CNN Slammed for Running 'If Jews Are People' Headline," *Independent*, November 22, 2019, https://www.independent.co.uk/arts-entertainment/tv/news/cnn -slammed-for-running-if-jews-are-people-headline-a7432146.html.

25. Paul Starobin, *Madness Rules the Hour: Charleston, 1860, and the Mania for War* (New York: Public Affairs, 2017).

26. Starobin, *Madness Rules the Hour*, 176.

27. Elaine Frantz Parsons, *Ku Klux: The Birth of the Klan during Reconstruction* (Chapel Hill, NC: University of North Carolina Press, 2015).

28. Parsons, *Ku Klux*.

29. Parsons, *Ku Klux*.

30. Parsons, *Ku Klux*.

31. Parsons *Ku Klux*, 305.

32. Juan González and Joseph Torres, *News for All the People: The Epic Story of Race and the American Media* (New York: Verso, 2011).

33. Richard M. Perloff, "The Press and Lynchings of African Americans," *Journal of Black Studies* 30, no. 3 (2000): 315–330. The capitalization of "Whites" is as printed.

34. Felix Harcourt, *Ku Klux Kulture: America and the Klan in the 1920s* (Chicago: University of Chicago Press, 2017).

35. Harcourt, *Ku Klux Kulture*.

36. Harcourt, *Ku Klux Kulture*.

37. Joan Donovan, "How Hate Groups' Secret Sound System Works," *Atlantic*, March 17, 2019, https://www.theatlantic.com/ideas/archive/2019/03/extremists-understand-what-tech -platforms-have-built/585136.

38. Quoted in Harcourt, *Ku Klux Kulture*, 26.

39. Frederick J. Simonelli, *American Fuehrer: George Lincoln Rockwell and the American Nazi Party* (Urbana: University of Illinois Press, 1999); danah boyd and Joan Donovan, "The Case for Quarantining Extremist Ideas," *Guardian*, June 1, 2018, https://www.theguardian .com/commentisfree/2018/jun/01/extremist-ideas-media-coverage-kkk.

40. Aniko Bodroghkozy, *Equal Time: Television and the Civil Rights Movement* (Champaign: University of Illinois Press, 2012).

41. Bodroghkozy, *Equal Time*.

42. Boyd and Donovan, "Case for Quarantining Extremist Ideas."

43. "Covering the South: A National Symposium on the Media and the Civil Rights Movement," DVD recording of 1987 conference held at the University of Mississippi, courtesy of the University of Mississippi library special collections. Video transcribed by Kinjal Dave; we are grateful for the share.

44. Richard M. Perloff, "The Press and Lynchings of African Americans," *Journal of Black Studies* 30, no. 3 (2000): 315–330, 318.

45. Jessie Daniels, *White Lies: Race, Class, Gender and Sexuality in White Supremacist Discourse* (New York: Routledge, 1997).

46. Because of the radioactivity of their messaging, white supremacists have long been some of the savviest early adopters of new media. See Jessie Daniels, *Cyber Racism: White Supremacy Online and the New Attack on Civil Rights* (New York: Rowman and Littlefield, 2009).

47. For more on the persistent influence of institutional media, see Robert M. Entman and Nikki Usher, "Framing in a Fractured Democracy: Impacts of Digital Technology on Ideology, Power and Cascading Network Activation," *Journal of Communication* 68, no. 2 (2018): 298–308.

48. Mike Ananny, "Breaking News Pragmatically: Some Reflections on Silence and Timing in Networked Journalism," *Nieman Lab*, April 23, 2013, https://www.niemanlab.org/2013/04/breaking-news-pragmatically-some-reflections-on-silence-and-timing-in-networked-journalism.

49. Jessica Beyer, *Expect Us: Online Communities and Political Mobilization* (London: Oxford University Press, 2014); Gabriella Coleman, *Hacker, Hoaxer, Whistleblower, Spy: The Many Faces of Anonymous* (London: Verso, 2014); Whitney Phillips, *This Is Why We Can't Have Nice Things: Mapping the Relationship between Online Trolling and Mainstream Culture* (Cambridge, MA: MIT Press, 2015). All illustrate that while early hacking and trolling spaces were often pointed in their transgressions and dehumanizations, these communities were not uniform in those transgressions and dehumanizations—at least not initially. Coleman focuses in particular on the leftist turn taken by Anonymous in response to the Occupy Wall Street protests—an outcome that was puzzling as it began happening in 2011, and has only grown more mysterious in the Trump era, as the same subcultural stock that gave rise to left-leaning, activist Anonymous also gave rise to violently racist, reactionary abuse.

50. Shira Chess and Adrienne Shaw, "A Conspiracy of Fishes, or How We Learned to Stop Worrying about #GamerGate and Embrace Hegemonic Masculinity," *Journal of Broadcasting and Electronic Media* 59, no. 1 (2015): 208–220.

51. Sarah Banet-Weiser and Kate M. Miltner, "#MasculinitySoFragile: Culture, Structure, and Networked Misogyny," *Feminist Media Studies* 16, no. 1 (2016): 171–174.

52. Shireen Mitchell, Twitter Moments, April 22, 2018, https://twitter.com/i/moments/988069560921284608. Additional interview with Mitchell conducted on June 15, 2019, at Harvard University.

53. Joan Donovan, "First They Came for the Black Feminists," *New York Times*, August 15, 2019, https://www.nytimes.com/interactive/2019/08/15/opinion/gamergate-twitter.html.

54. "GamerGate—Moot Responds to GamerGate Deletions," Know Your Meme, September 14, 2014, http://knowyourmeme.com/photos/832349-gamergate.

55. "God Emperor Trump," Know Your Meme, February 11, 2019, https://knowyourmeme.com/memes/god-emperor-trump.

56. April Glaser, "El Paso Shows 8chan Is a Normal Part of Shootings Now," *Slate*, August 4, 2019, https://slate.com/technology/2019/08/el-paso-8chan-4chan-mass-shootings-manifesto.html.

57. Reporter A, Skype interview with Phillips, September 6, 2017.

58. Reporter B, phone interview with Phillips, September 13, 2017.

59. Reporter C, phone interview with Phillips, September 13, 2017.

60. Reporter D, phone interview with Phillips, September 7, 2017.

61. Ashley Feinberg, "This Is the Daily Stormer's Playbook."

62. Joseph Bernstein, "Alt-White: How the Breitbart Machine Laundered Racist Hate," *BuzzFeed News*, October 5, 2017, https://www.buzzfeednews.com/article/josephbernstein/heres-how-breitbart-and-milo-smuggled-white-nationalism.

63. Reporter C, phone interview with Phillips, September 13, 2017.

64. Reporter E, phone interview with Phillips, September 12, 2017.

65. Reporter F, Skype interview with Phillips, October 10, 2017. For a first-person account written by a Black female reporter describing the role that embodied identity played during the 2016 election, see Farai Chideya, "The Reconstruction of American Journalism in the Age of Culture War," *Medium*, August 5, 2019, https://medium.com/@faraic/culturewar journalism-e3db60ae725f.

66. Debra Walker King, *African Americans and the Culture of Pain* (Charlottesville: University of Virginia Press, 2008).

67. "Dust Bowl," Kansas Historical Society.

CHAPTER 4

1. Bruno Latour makes a similar point using actor-network theory, which describes how seemingly singular, seemingly self-contained things—like scientific knowledge—are, in fact, ever-evolving assemblages of countless other things, whether people or animals or objects or weather patterns. These things are *actors* in the sense that they act on something else. The *network* in actor-network theory refers to all the actors and all their effects, which, taken together, make up the overall life cycle of the narrative or object or theory in question. See Bruno Latour, *Reassembling the Social: An Introduction to Actor-Network Theory* (Oxford: Oxford University Press, 2005).

2. Kathryn Olmsted, *Real Enemies: Conspiracy Theories and American Democracy, World War I to 9/11* (Oxford: Oxford University Press, 2009).

3. Anna Merlan, *Republic of Lies: American Conspiracy Theorists and Their Surprising Rise to Power* (New York: Metropolitan Books, 2019).

4. Jesse Walker, *The United States of Paranoia: A Conspiracy Theory* (New York: Harper Perennial, 2013).

5. Walker, *United States of Paranoia*.

6. Olmsted, *Real Enemies*; Merlan, *Republic of Lies*.

7. Peter Knight, "Introduction: A Nation of Conspiracy Theorists," in *Conspiracy Nation: The Politics of Paranoia in Postwar America*, ed. Peter Knight (New York: NYU Press), 7.

8. Richard Hofstadter, *The Paranoid Style in American Politics and Other Essays* (New York: Alfred A. Knopf, 1964), 1. Contemporary historians have since challenged Hofstadter's analysis on the grounds that it collapses too many beliefs under too broad an umbrella. Kathryn Olmsted makes such a case, though she concedes that elements of Hofstadter's argument remain salient to analyzing precisely the sort of far-right MAGA theories we're focused on here. See "A Conspiracy So Dense," *Baffler* 42 (2018), https://thebaffler.com /salvos/a-conspiracy-so-dense-olmsted.

9. Jon Ronson, *Them: Adventures with Extremists* (New York: Simon and Schuster, 2003).

10. Olmsted, *Real Enemies*.

11. Hofstadter, *Paranoid Style*, 1.

12. Olmsted, *Real Enemies*.

13. Olmsted, *Real Enemies*.

14. Adam Serwer, "Trump Tells America What Kind of Nationalist He Is," *Atlantic*, July 15, 2019, https://www.theatlantic.com/ideas/archive/2019/07/trumps-white-nationalist-attack -four-congresswomen/594019.

15. Jason Sokol, *There Goes My Everything: White Southerners in the Age of Civil Rights* (New York: Vintage Books, 2007).

16. Hofstadter, *Paranoid Style*.

17. Arlie Russell Hochschild, *Strangers in Their Own Land: Anger and Mourning on the American Right* (New York: New Press, 2016).

18. Carol Anderson, *White Rage: The Unspoken Truth of Our Racial Divide* (New York: Bloomsbury, 2017).

19. Meagan Flynn, "Trump's Spiritual Adviser Seeks His Protection from 'Demonic Networks' at Reelection Rally, *Washington Post*, June 19, 2019, https://www.washingtonpost.com/nation /2019/06/19/paula-white-donald-trump-orlando-rally-demonic-networks.

20. Yochai Benkler, Robert Faris, and Hal Roberts, *Network Propaganda: Manipulation, Disinformation, and Radicalization in American Politics* (Oxford: Oxford University Press, 2018).

21. Anne Nelson, *Shadow Network: Media, Money, and the Secret Hub of the Radical Right* (New York: Bloomsbury, 2019).

22. Nelson, *Shadow Network*.

23. Abigail Tracy, "George W. Bush Finally Says What He Thinks about Trump," *Vanity Fair*, October 19, 2017, https://www.vanityfair.com/news/2017/10/george-w-bush-donald-trump.

24. Michael Isikoff, "The True Origins of the Seth Rich Conspiracy Theory," *Yahoo! News*, July 9, 2019, https://news.yahoo.com/exclusive-the-true-origins-of-the-seth-rich-conspiracy-a-yahoo-news-investigation-100000831.html.

25. "Donald Trump's Statements on Putin/Russia/Fake News Media," *Lawfare*, https://www.lawfareblog.com/donald-trumps-statements-putinrussiafake-news-media.

26. Merlan, *Republic of Lies*.

27. Stephen Battaglio and David Ng, "Sean Hannity: 'I Am Not Going to Stop Trying to Find the Truth,'" *Los Angeles Times*, May 23, 2017, https://www.latimes.com/business/hollywood/la-fi-ct-seth-rich-hannity-fox-20170523-story.html.

28. Dan Friedman, "Michael Flynn's Deep State Strategy Is Failing in Court. He May Not Care," *Mother Jones*, September 11, 2019, https://www.motherjones.com/politics/2019/09/michael-flynns-deep-state-strategy-is-failing-in-court-he-may-not-care; Philip Ewing, "Roger Stone, Trump Friend and Alleged Tie to WikiLeaks, Faces Trial in Washington," *NPR*, November 5, 2019, https://www.npr.org/2019/11/05/776121411/roger-stone-trump-friend-and-alleged-tie-to-wikileaks-faces-trial-in-washington.

29. Anna Merlan deserves credit for her use of the disturbingly evocative phrase "conspiracy entrepreneurship" in *Republic of Lies*. For more on the cottage industry of QAnon merch, see Brandy Zadrozny and Ben Collins, "Like the Fringe Conspiracy Theory QAnon? There's Plenty of Merch for Sale on Amazon," *NBC News*, July 18, 2018, https://www.nbcnews.com/business/business-news/fringe-conspiracy-theory-qanon-there-s-plenty-merch-sale-amazon-n892561.

30. John Soloman and Buck Sexton, "Trump Doesn't Like the Term 'Deep State' Because 'It Sounds So Conspiratorial,'" *The Hill*, September 19, 2018, https://thehill.com/hilltv/rising/407406-trump-doesnt-like-the-term-deep-state-because-it-sounds-so-conspiratorial.

31. Dana Farrington, "READ: The Mueller Report, with Redactions," *NPR*, April 18, 2019, https://www.npr.org/2019/04/18/708850903/read-the-full-mueller-report-with-redactions.

32. Quoted in Allie Conti, "The Jeffrey Epstein Story Is Fanning the Flames of Far-Right Pedophilia Panic," *Vice*, December 6, 2018, https://www.vice.com/en_us/article/pa5zyv/the-jeffrey-epstein-story-is-fanning-the-flames-of-far-right-pedophilia-panic.

33. Andrew Prokop, "Jeffrey Epstein's Connections to Bill Clinton and Donald Trump, Explained," *Vox*, July 17, 2019, https://www.vox.com/2019/7/9/20686347/jeffrey-epstein-trump-bill-clinton.

34. Dylan Matthews, "The Conspiracy Theories about the Clintons and Jeffrey Epstein's Death, Explained," *Vox*, November 14, 2019, https://www.vox.com/2019/8/10/20800195/clinton-bodycount-conspiracy-theory-jeffrey-epstein.

35. Matt Wilstein, "Fox News Mainstreams Conspiracy Theory about Parkland Students," *Daily Beast*, February 21, 2018, https://www.thedailybeast.com/fox-news-mainstreams-conspiracy -theory-about-parkland-students.

36. Michael Blackmon, "Roseanne Barr Deleted a Tweet Accusing a Parkland Survivor of Giving a Nazi Salute," *BuzzFeed News*, March 29, 2018, https://www.buzzfeednews.com /article/michaelblackmon/roseanne-barr-david-hogg-parkland-nazi-tweets; John Lynch, "Roseanne Barr Is under Fire for Appearing to Promote a Conspiracy Theory about a Parkland Student Activist," *Business Insider*, March 29, 2018, https://www.businessinsider.com /roseanne-barr-under-fire-for-nazi-salute-tweet-conspiracy-theory-parkland-student-david-hogg-2018-3; Anna Menta, "Tom Arnold Slams Ex-Wife Roseanne Barr for Tweeting 'Nazi Salute' at Parkland Survivor," *Newsweek*, March 30, 2018, https://www .newsweek.com/tom-arnold-slams-ex-wife-roseanne-barr-tweeting-nazi-salute-parkland -survivor-867294.

37. Benjamin Decker compiled this research as part of a fellowship at the Shorenstein Center at the Harvard Kennedy School. He sent these findings to Phillips on November 27, 2018.

38. Kelly Weill, "Roseanne Keeps Promoting QAnon, the Pro-Trump Conspiracy Theory That Makes Pizzagate Look Tame," *Daily Beast*, March 30, 2018, https://www.thedailybeast .com/roseanne-keeps-promoting-qanon-the-pro-trump-conspiracy-theory-that-makes -pizzagate-look-tame.

39. Julia Reinstein, "Let Us Break Down the Bizarre Right-Wing Conspiracy Theory Roseanne Barr Has Tweeted About," *BuzzFeed News*, March 31, 2018, https://www.buzzfeednews .com/article/juliareinstein/roseanne-qanon-explainer#.kb1Q4LJkr.

40. Weill, "Roseanne Keeps Promoting"; Devan Cole, "Roseanne Tweets Support of Trump Conspiracy Theory, Confuses Twitter," *CNN*, March 31, 2018, https://www.cnn.com /2018/03/31/politics/roseanne-barr-conspiracy-tweets/index.html; David Weigel, "The Conspiracy Theory behind a Curious Roseanne Barr Tweet, Explained," *Washington Post*, March 31, 2018, https://www.washingtonpost.com/news/the-fix/wp/2018/03/31/the-con spiracy-theory-behind-a-curious-roseanne-barr-tweet-explained.

41. Paris Martineau, "The Storm Is the New Pizzagate—Only Worse," *New York Magazine*, December 19, 2017, http://nymag.com/intelligencer/2017/12/qanon-4chan-the-storm -conspiracy-explained.html. The phrase "the storm" references one of Q's early 4chan posts, "The Calm before the Storm," which itself references a cryptic comment made by Trump. On October 5, 2017, Trump was smiling for a photo op and mumbled to reporters, "You guys know what this represents? Maybe it's the calm before the storm." When the reporters asked Trump to clarify, he only said, "You'll find out."

42. "QAnon," Know Your Meme, December 12, 2017, https://knowyourmeme.com/memes /qanon.

43. Sopan Deb, "Roseanne Barr's Tweets Didn't Come Out of Nowhere," *New York Times*, May 29, 2018, https://nyti.ms/2LBefZf.

44. Roseanne Barr, Twitter, June 20, 2018, https://twitter.com/therealroseanne/status/100933 0826553667584?s=20.

45. Whitney Phillips, "How Journalists Should Not Cover an Online Conspiracy Theory," *Guardian*, August 6, 2018, https://www.theguardian.com/commentisfree/2018/aug/06/ online-conspiracy-theory-journalism-qanon.

46. Brandy Zadronzny and Ben Collins, "How Three Conspiracy Theorists Took 'Q' and Sparked QAnon," *NBC News*, August 14, 2018, https://www.nbcnews.com/tech/tech-news /how-three-conspiracy-theorists-took-q-sparked-qanon-n900531.

47. Benjamin Decker, "QAnon Claims Victory after Mainstream Media Coverage of Trump Rally," research report, Shorenstein Center on Media, Politics, and Public Policy at Harvard Kennedy School, August 2018; Benjamin Decker, "QAnon Background Beginnings," research report, Shorenstein Center on Media, Politics, and Public Policy, August 2018.

48. Decker, "QAnon Claims Victory."

49. Jane Coaston, "#QAnon, the Scarily Popular Pro-Trump Conspiracy Theory, Explained," *Vox*, August 2, 2018, https://www.vox.com/policy-and-politics/2018/8/1/17253444/qanon -trump-conspiracy-theory-reddit; Justin Bank, Liam Stack, and Daniel Victor, "What Is QAnon: Explaining the Internet Conspiracy Theory That Showed Up at a Trump Rally," *New York Times*, August 1, 2018, https://www.nytimes.com/2018/08/01/us/politics /what-is-qanon.html; Luke Darby, "What the Hell Is QAnon? The Right-Wing Conspiracy, Explained," *GQ*, August 7, 2018, https://www.gq.com/story/what-the-hell-is-qanon; Julia Carrie Wong, "What Is QAnon? Explaining the Bizarre Rightwing Conspiracy Theory," *Guardian*, July 30, 2018, https://www.theguardian.com/technology/2018/jul/30 /qanon-4chan-rightwing-conspiracy-theory-explained-trump.

50. Ben Collins, "What Is QAnon? A Guide to the Conspiracy Theory Taking Hold among Trump Supporters," *NBC News*, August 3, 2018, https://www.nbcnews.com/tech/tech -news/what-qanon-guide-conspiracy-theory-taking-hold-among-trump-supporters-n897 271; Brandon Carter, "What Is QAnon? The Conspiracy Theory Tiptoeing into Trump World," *NPR*, August 2, 2018, https://www.npr.org/2018/08/02/634749387/what-is -qanon-the-conspiracy-theory-tiptoeing-into-trump-world; Ryan Bort, "As QAnon Goes Mainstream, Trump's Rallies Are Turning Darker," *Rolling Stone*, August 1, 2018, https:// www.rollingstone.com/politics/politics-news/trump-qanon-705425.

51. Andrew Griffin, "What Is QAnon? The Origins of Bizarre Conspiracy Theory Spreading Online," *Independent*, March 29, 2019, https://www.independent.co.uk/life-style/gadgets -and-tech/news/qanon-explained-what-is-trump-russia-investigation-pizzagate-a8845226 .html; "How the False, Fringe 'QAnon' Conspiracy Theory Aims to Protect Trump," *PBS NewsHour*, August 1, 2018, https://www.pbs.org/newshour/show/how-the-false-fringe -qanon-conspiracy-theory-aims-to-protect-trump; Paul Waldman, "Why the GOP Is So Easily Infiltrated by Bonkers Conspiracy Theorists," *Washington Post*, August 6, 2018, https:// www.washingtonpost.com/blogs/plum-line/wp/2018/08/06/why-the-gop-is-so-easily-infil trated-by-bonkers-conspiracy-theorists; Isaac Stanley-Becker, "'We Are Q': A Deranged

Conspiracy Cult Leaps from the Internet to the Crowd at Trump's 'MAGA' Tour," *Washington Post*, August 1, 2018, https://www.washingtonpost.com/news/morning-mix/wp/2018/08/01/we-are-q-a-deranged-conspiracy-cult-leaps-from-the-internet-to-the-crowd-at-trumps-maga-tour.

52. Phillips, "How Journalists Should Not."

53. Abby Ohlheiser, "You'll Never Guess How the QAnon Conspiracy Theorists Feel about All This Media Coverage," *Washington Post*, August 3, 2018, https://www.washingtonpost.com/news/the-intersect/wp/2018/08/03/this-is-the-moment-how-a-wave-of-media-coverage-gave-qanon-conspiracy-theorists-their-best-week-ever.

54. Will Sommer, "In a First, Lawmaker Cites QAnon Conspiracy from City Council Floor," *Daily Beast*, December 13, 2018, https://www.thedailybeast.com/in-a-first-lawmaker-cites-qanon-conspiracy-from-city-council-floor.

55. Ben Collins, Twitter, March 28, 2019, https://twitter.com/oneunderscore__/status/1111487028980523008?s=20.

56. Betsy Woodruff, "Twitter Suspends Conspiracy Account after Trump Retweet," *Daily Beast*, July 30, 2019, https://www.thedailybeast.com/twitter-suspends-conspiracy-account-after-trump-retweet.

57. Alex Kaplan, "The FBI Calls QAnon a Domestic Terror Threat: Trump Has Amplified QAnon Supporters on Twitter More Than 20 Times," *Media Matters for America*, August 1, 2019, https://www.mediamatters.org/twitter/fbi-calls-qanon-domestic-terror-threat-trump-has-amplified-qanon-supporters-twitter-more-20.

58. Philip Bump, "Hours after an FBI Warning about QAnon Is Published, a QAnon Slogan Turns Up at Trump's Rally," *Washington Post*, August 2, 2019, https://www.washingtonpost.com/politics/2019/08/02/hours-after-an-fbi-warning-about-qanon-is-published-qanon-slogan-turns-up-trumps-rally.

59. David Jackson and John Fritze, "Donald Trump Defends His Jeffrey Epstein, Bill Clinton Conspiracy Retweet," *USA Today*, August 13, 2019, https://www.usatoday.com/story/news/politics/2019/08/13/donald-trump-defends-jeffrey-epstein-bill-clinton-conspiracy-retweet/1996632001.

60. Sarah Posner, "The Army of Prayer Warriors Fighting Trump's Impeachment," *Huffington Post*, December 19, 2019, https://www.huffpost.com/entry/white-evangelicals-trump-impeachment_n_5df950c6e4b08083dc5ae146.

61. Will Sommer, "Rudy Giuliani Teams Up with a Seth Rich Conspiracy Theorist to Save Trump," *Daily Beast*, December 5, 2019, https://www.thedailybeast.com/rudy-giuliani-teams-up-with-seth-rich-conspiracy-theorist-chanel-rion-to-save-trump.

62. Ryan Broderick, "Republicans' Conspiracy Theory–Ridden Counterprogramming to Impeachment Is Working," *BuzzFeed News*, November 20, 2019, https://www.buzzfeednews.com/article/ryanhatesthis/republican-conspiracy-theory-counterprogramming.

63. Tom McKay, "GOP Rep. Paul Gosar Inserts 'Epstein Didn't Kill Himself' Conspiracy Theory into Impeachment Tweets," *Gizmodo*, November 13, 2019, https://gizmodo.com/gop-rep-paul-gosar-inserts-epstein-didnt-kill-himself-1839844491.

64. Matt Shuham, "Trump's Latest Twitter Meme Is Music to the Ears of QAnon Adherents," *Talking Points Memo* (March 9, 2020) https://talkingpointsmemo.com/news/qanon-satanic-cabal-obsession-donald-trump-dan-scavino-nothing-can-stop-whats-coming.

65. Paul Farhi and Sarah Ellison, "On Fox News, Suddenly a Very Different Tune about the Coronavirus," *Washington Post* (Mach 16, 2020), https://www.washingtonpost.com/lifestyle/media/on-fox-news-suddenly-a-very-different-tune-about-the-coronavirus/2020/03/16/7a7637cc-678f-11ea-9923-57073adce27c_story.html.

66. Olmstead, *Real Enemies*.

67. Kate Starbird, "Information Wars: A Window into the Alternative Media Ecosystem," *Medium*, March 14, 2017, https://medium.com/hci-design-at-uw/information-wars-a-window-into-the-alternative-media-ecosystem-a1347f32fd8f; Kate Starbird, Ahmer Arif, Tom Wilson, Katherine Van Koevering, Katya Yefimova, and Danial Scarnecchia, "Ecosystem or Echo-System? Exploring Content Sharing across Alternative Media Domains," Twelfth International AAAI Conference on Web and Social Media, 2018.

68. Merlan, *Republic of Lies*.

69. Nelson, *Shadow Network*.

70. Cailin O'Connor and James Owen Weatherall, *The Misinformation Age: How False Beliefs Spread* (New Haven, CT: Yale University Press, 2019).

71. Olmstead, *Real Enemies*.

72. Monica Alba and Ben Collins, "Trump Touts the 'Power' of Extremist Social Media Activists at White House Summit," *NBC News*, July 11, 2019, https://www.nbcnews.com/politics/white-house/trump-touts-power-controversial-social-media-activists-white-house-summit-n1029036.

73. Merlan, *Republic of Lies*.

74. Safiya Noble, *Algorithms of Oppression: How Search Engines Reinforce Racism* (New York: NYU Press, 2018).

75. Page rankings are essentially an internal upvoting process, reflecting which pages are most frequently linked to across the Web.

76. Tarleton Gillespie, *Custodians of the Internet: Platforms, Content Moderation, and the Hidden Decisions That Shape Social Media* (New Haven, CT: Yale University Press, 2018).

77. Danielle Citron, "Cyber Mobs, Disinformation, and Death Videos: The Internet as It Is (and as It Should Be)," *Michigan Law Review*, August 13, 2019, http://dx.doi.org/10.2139/ssrn.3435200.

78. Becca Lewis, "Alternative Influence: Broadcasting the Reactionary Right on YouTube," Data & Society Research Institute, September 18, 2018, https://datasociety.net/wp-content /uploads/2018/09/DS_Alternative_Influence.pdf. Zeynep Tufekci has also written on YouTube's reactionary rabbit holes; see "YouTube, the Great Radicalizer," *New York Times*, March 10, 2018, https://www.nytimes.com/2018/03/10/opinion/sunday/youtube-politics -radical.html.

79. Manoel Horta Ribeiro, Raphael Ottoni, Robert West, Virgílio A. F. Almeida, and Wagner Meira, "Auditing Radicalization Pathways on YouTube," Cornell University, arXiv, arXiv:1908.08313 [cs.CY], 1–18.

80. Taylor Lorenz, "Instagram Is the Internet's New Home for Hate," *Atlantic*, March 21, 2019, https://www.theatlantic.com/technology/archive/2019/03/instagram-is-the-internets -new-home-for-hate/585382.

81. Lewis, "Alternative Influence."

82. Danah boyd, "Media Manipulation, Strategic Amplification, and Responsible Journalism," *Data & Society Points*, September 18, 2018, https://points.datasociety.net/media-manipu lation-strategic-amplification-and-responsible-journalism-95f4d611f462.

CHAPTER 5

1. Renee Hobbs and Sandra McGee, "Teaching about Propaganda: An Examination of the Historical Roots of Media Literacy," *Journal of Media Literacy Education* 6, no. 2 (2014): 56–67.

2. Hobbs and McGee, "Teaching about Propaganda."

3. Monica Bulger and Patrick Davison, "The Promises, Challenges, and Futures of Media Literacy," Data & Society Research Institute, February 21, 2018, https://datasociety.net/out put/the-promises-challenges-and-futures-of-media-literacy.

4. Hobbs and McGee, "Teaching about Propaganda."

5. Renee Hobbs, "Digital and Media Literacy: A Plan of Action," Aspen Institute and Knight Foundation report, 2010, https://knightfoundation.org/reports/digital-and-media-literacy -plan-action.

6. "Media Literacy Defined," National Association for Media Literacy Education, https:// namle.net/publications/media-literacy-definitions.

7. Richard Campbell, Christopher Martin, and Bettina Fabos, *Media Essentials: A Brief Introduction*, 2nd ed. (New York: Bedford/St. Martin's, 2018), 28.

8. Cristina Tardáguila, "Don't Be the One Spreading False News about Mass Shootings: Here Are Some Tips from Fact-Checkers," *Poynter*, August 5, 2019, https://www.poynter.org /fact-checking/2019/dont-be-the-one-spreading-false-news-about-mass-shootings-here -are-some-tips-from-fact-checkers.

9. For more on the contours of liberalism, particularly in the context of journalism, see Clifford C. Christians, John Ferré, and P. Mark Fackler, *Good News: Social Ethics and the Press* (Oxford: Oxford University Press, 1993). For a refresher on how liberalism as a political philosophy factors into a great deal of conservative thinking, see chapter 2.

10. John Milton, "Areopagitica: A Speech of Mr. John Milton for the Liberty of Unlicenc'd Printing, to the Parlament of England" (1644), https://www.bl.uk/collection-items/areo pagitica-by-john-milton-1644; John Stuart Mill, *On Liberty, Utilitarianism and Other Essays* (1859; Cambridge: Cambridge World Classics, 2015).

11. Louis Brandeis, "Concurring Opinion, *Whitney v. California*" (May 16, 1927), https://www.law.cornell.edu/supremecourt/text/274/357.

12. Bulger and Davison, "Promises, Challenges, and Futures."

13. Mary Anne Franks, *The Cult of the Constitution* (Stanford, CA: Stanford University Press, 2019).

14. Clifford C. Christians, John Ferré, and P. Mark Fackler, *Good News: Social Ethics and the Press* (Oxford: Oxford University Press, 1993), 26.

15. Bulger and Davison, "Promises, Challenges, and Futures."

16. Danah boyd, "You Think You Want Media Literacy . . . Do You?" *Data & Society Points*, March 9, 2018, https://points.datasociety.net/you-think-you-want-media-literacy-do-you -7cad6af18ec2.

17. Siva Vaidhyanathan, "Why Conservatives Allege Big Tech Is Muzzling Them," *Atlantic*, July 28, 2019, https://www.theatlantic.com/ideas/archive/2019/07/conservatives-pretend -big-tech-biased-against-them/594916.

18. Donald J. Trump, Twitter, July 14, 2019, https://twitter.com/realDonaldTrump/status /1150381394234941448?s=20.

19. Katie Rogers and Nicholas Fandos, "Trump Tells Congresswomen to 'Go Back' to the Countries They Came From," *New York Times*, July 14, 2019, https://www.nytimes.com /2019/07/14/us/politics/trump-twitter-squad-congress.html.

20. Aaron Rupar, "Trump Says He's Not Concerned about Being Racist Because 'Many People Agree' with Him," *Vox*, July 15, 2019, https://www.vox.com/2019/7/15/20694986/trump -racist-tweet-ilhan-omar-al-qaeda.

21. Jeremy W. Peters, Annie Karni, and Maggie Haberman, "Trump Sets the 2020 Tone: Like 2016, Only This Time 'the Squad' Is Here," *New York Times*, July 16, 2019, https://www .nytimes.com/2019/07/16/us/politics/trump-election-squad.html.

22. "Trump Voter: How Is That Racist?" *CNN*, July 20, 2019, https://www.cnn.com/videos /politics/2019/07/20/trump-voters-2016-wisconsin-kaye-pkg-vpx.cnn.

23. Adam Serwer, "Trump Tells America What Kind of Nationalist He Is," *Atlantic*, July 15, 2019, https://www.theatlantic.com/ideas/archive/2019/07/trumps-white-nationalist-attack -four-congresswomen/594019.

24. Jessica Vitak, "The Impact of Context Collapse and Privacy on Social Network Site Disclosures," *Journal of Broadcasting and Electronic Media* 56, no. 4 (2012): 451–470.

25. Ryan M. Milner, *The World Made Meme: Public Conversations and Participatory Media* (Cambridge, MA: MIT Press, 2016); Whitney Phillips and Ryan M. Milner, *The Ambivalent Internet: Mischief, Oddity, and Antagonism Online* (Cambridge: Polity Press, 2017).

26. Poe's Law can only go so far when describing Trump, however; whatever the man might say on Twitter, when it comes to White House policy, cruelty against marginalized groups, from immigrants to trans people, is clear and consistent. That cruelty lays bare the answer to the question "what does this mean?" even when Trump's short-term motives are inscrutable.

27. Ioanna Noula, "I Do Want Media Literacy . . . and More," London School of Economics and Political Science Media Policy Project, June 21, 2018, https://blogs.lse.ac.uk/medialse/2018/06/21/i-do-want-media-literacy-and-more-a-response-to-danah-boyd.

28. Francesca Tripodi, "Searching for Alternative Facts: Analyzing Scriptural Inference in Conservative News Practices," Data & Society Research Institute, May 16, 2017, https://datasociety.net/output/searching-for-alternative-facts.

29. Tripodi, "Searching for Alternative Facts."

30. Boyd, "You Think You Want Media Literacy."

31. Louis Brandeis, "Chapter V: What Publicity Can Do," in *Other People's Money*, Louis D. Brandeis School of Law Library, https://louisville.edu/law/library/special-collections/the-louis-d.-brandeis-collection/other-peoples-money-chapter-v.

32. Rolf Reichardt and Deborah Louise Cohen, "Light against Darkness: The Visual Representations of a Central Enlightenment Concept," *Representations* 61 (1998): 95–148.

33. Whitney Phillips, "Unpredictable Light with Unpredictable Outcomes: A Cultural and Rhetorical History of the Term 'Light Disinfects,'" *Georgetown Law and Technology Review* (forthcoming).

34. Jay Rosen, "The View from Nowhere: Questions and Answers," *PressThink*, November 10, 2010, https://pressthink.org/2010/11/the-view-from-nowhere-questions-and-answers/.

35. Christians, Ferré, and Fackler, *Good News*, 30–37.

36. "The 1619 Project," *New York Times*, August 14, 2019, https://www.nytimes.com/interactive/2019/08/14/magazine/1619-america-slavery.html. Although the light of social justice is less common within majority white establishment newsrooms, it has a long and rich history in the context of advocacy journalism within the minority press. See Juan González and Joseph Torres, *News for All the People: The Epic Story of Race and the American Media* (New York: Verso Press, 2011).

37. Nabiha Syed, "Real Talk about Fake News: Nabiha Syed in Conversation with Claire Wardle and Joan Donovan," *Data & Society Databites* (February 28, 2018), https://listen.datasociety.net/real-talk-fake-news/.

38. Elaine Frantz Parsons, *Ku Klux: The Birth of the Klan during Reconstruction* (Chapel Hill: University of North Carolina Press, 2015); Felix Harcourt, *Ku Klux Kulture: America and the Klan in the 1920s* (Chicago: University of Chicago Press, 2017).

39. Phillips, "Unpredictable Light with Unpredictable Outcomes."

40. Brian Barrett, "The Wrong Way to Talk about a Shooter's Manifesto," *Wired*, August 4, 2019, https://www.wired.com/story/wrong-way-talk-about-shooter-manifesto.

41. Michael Calderone, "Black Journalists Push Media to Cover 'Hyper-racial' Moment in Politics," *Politico*, July 29, 2019, https://www.politico.com/story/2019/07/29/black-journalists-racial-politics-1440628.

42. Barrett, "Wrong Way to Talk."

43. Chris Hayes, "Ta-Nehisi Coates Defends His Hometown of Baltimore," *MSNBC*, August 2, 2019, https://www.msnbc.com/all-in/watch/ta-nehisi-coates-defends-his-hometown-of-baltimore-65209413938; Justin Baragona, "CNN Anchor Chokes Up while Defending Baltimore from Trump's Racist Attacks," *Daily Beast*, July 27, 2019, https://www.thedailybeast.com/cnn-anchor-victor-blackwell-chokes-up-while-defending-baltimore-from-trumps-racist-attacks.

44. Simon Romero, Caitlin Dickerson, Miriam Jordan, and Patricia Mazzei, "'It Feels like Being Hunted': Latinos across U.S. in Fear after El Paso Massacre," *New York Times*, August 6, 2019, https://www.nytimes.com/2019/08/06/us/el-paso-shooting-latino-anxiety.html.

45. Michael Kunzelman and Astrid Galvan, "Trump Words Linked to More Hate Crime? Some Experts Think So," *Associated Press*, August 7, 2019, https://apnews.com/7d0949974b1648a2bb592cab1f85aa16.

46. Ken Meyer, "Beto O'Rourke Loses It on Reporter Asking about Trump's Handling of Shootings: 'Press, What the F*ck!?'" *Mediaite*, August 5, 2019, https://www.mediaite.com/tv/beto-orourke-rips-reporter-asking-how-trump-can-make-the-situation-better-after-mass-shootings-what-the-fck.

47. For a journalistic take on these tensions, see Ezra Klein, "Trump's Racist Tweets: Is the Media Part of the Problem?" *Vox*, August 2, 2019, https://www.vox.com/policy-and-politics/2019/8/2/20702029/donald-trump-racism-squad-tweets-media-2020. Phillips would also like to thank Klein for catalyzing her thinking on the light of liberalism/social justice binary.

48. Alice Marwick, "Why Do People Share Fake News? A Sociotechnical Model of Media Effects," *Georgetown Law Technology Review* 2 (2018): 1–39.

49. Michael Barthel, Amy Mitchell, and Jesse Holcomb, "Many Americans Believe Fake News Is Sowing Confusion," Pew Research Center, December 15, 2016, https://www.journalism.org/2016/12/15/many-americans-believe-fake-news-is-sowing-confusion.

50. Boyd, "You Think You Want Media Literacy."

51. Brendan Nyhan and Jason Reifler, "When Corrections Fail: The Persistence of Political Misperceptions," *Political Behavior* 32 (2010): 303–330, https://doi.org/10.1007/s11109 -010-9112-2.

52. Thomas Wood and Ethan Porter. "The Elusive Backfire Effect: Mass Attitudes' Steadfast Factual Adherence," *Political Behavior* 41 (2019): 135–163, https://link.springer.com/article /10.1007/s11109-018-9443-y.

53. Brendan Nyhan and Jason Reifler, "Displacing Misinformation about Events: An Experimental Test of Causal Corrections," *Journal of Experimental Political Science* 2, no. 1 (2015): 81–93.

54. Elmie Nekmat, "Nudge Effect of Fact-Check Alerts: Source Influence and Media Skepticism on Sharing of News Misinformation," *Social Media + Society* (January 2020), https:// doi.org/10.1177/2056305119897322.

55. Ryan Broderick, "QAnon Supporters and Anti-Vaxxers Are Spreading a Hoax that Bill Gates Created the Coronavirus," *Buzzfeed News*, January 23, 2020. https://www.buzzfeed news.com/article/ryanhatesthis/qanon-supporters-and-anti-vaxxers-are-spreading-a-hoax -that.

56. Ryan Broderick, "Trump's Biggest Supporters Think the Coronavirus Is a Deep State Plot," *BuzzFeed News*, February 26, 2020, https://www.buzzfeednews.com/article/ryanhatesthis /trump-supporters-coronavirus-deep-state-qanon.

57. Lynn Hasher, David Goldstein, and Thomas Toppino, "Frequency and the Conference of Referential Validity," *Journal of Verbal Learning and Verbal Behavior* 16, no. 1 (1977): 107– 112.

58. Lisa K. Fazio, Nadia M. Brashier, B. Keith Payne, and Elizabeth J. Marsh, "Knowledge Does Not Protect against Illusory Truth," *Journal of Experimental Psychology* 144, no. 5 (2015): 993–1002.

59. Ian Skurnik, Carolyn Yoon, Denise C. Park, and Norbert Schwarz, "How Warnings about False Claims Become Recommendations," *Journal of Consumer Research* 31, no. 4 (2005): 713–724.

60. Brendan Nyhan and Jason Reifler, "Displacing Misinformation about Events: An Experimental Test of Causal Corrections," *Journal of Experimental Political Science* 2, no. 1 (2015): 81–93.

61. Hugo Mercier and Dan Sperber, "Why Do Humans Reason? Arguments for an Argumentative Theory," *Behavioral and Brain Sciences* 34, no. 2 (2011): 57–74; Lewandowsky et al., "Misinformation and Its Correction."

62. Stephan Lewandowsky, Ullrich Ecker, Colleen M. Seifert, Norbert Schwarz, and John Cook, "Misinformation and Its Correction: Continued Influence and Successful Debiasing," *Psychological Science in the Public Interest* 13, no. 3 (2012): 106–131.

63. Stephan Lewandowsky, Ullrich Ecker, Colleen M. Seifert, Norbert Schwarz, and John Cook, "Misinformation and Its Correction: Continued Influence and Successful Debiasing," *Psychological Science in the Public Interest* 13, no. 3 (2012): 106–131.

64. Boyd, "You Think You Want Media Literacy."

65. Brian Sternthal, Ruby Dholakia, and Clark Leavitt, "The Persuasive Effect of Source Credibility: Tests of Cognitive Response," *Journal of Consumer Research* 4, no. 4 (1978): 252–260.

66. D. J. Flynn., Brendan Nyhan, and Jason Reifler, "The Nature and Origins of Misperceptions: Understanding False and Unsupported Beliefs about Politics," *Advances in Political Psychology* 38 (2017): 127–150, https://doi.org/10.1111/pops.12394.

67. Flynn, Nyhan, and Reifler, "The Nature and Origins of Misperceptions."

68. Robin Wall Kimmerer, *Braiding Sweetgrass: Indigenous Wisdom, Scientific Knowledge, and the Teachings of Plants* (Minneapolis: Milkweed Editions, 2013), 16.

69. Sarah Banet-Weiser and Kate Miltner, "#MasculinitySoFragile: Culture, Structure, and Networked Misogyny," *Feminist Media Studies* 16, no. 1 (2016): 171–174.

70. Jessie Daniels, *Cyber Racism: White Supremacy Online and the New Attack on Civil Rights* (New York: Rowman and Littlefield, 2009); Jessie Daniels, "Twitter and White Supremacy: A Love Story," *Dame Magazine*, October 9, 2017, https://www.damemagazine.com/2017/10/19/twitter-and-white-supremacy-love-story/.

71. Boyd, "You Think You Want Media Literacy."

72. Christians, Ferré, and Fackler, *Good News*.

73. Carol Gilligan, *In a Different Voice: Psychological Theory and Women's Development* (Cambridge, MA: Harvard University Press, 1982). In this work, Gilligan was describing the presumed differences between men and women—thus essentializing certain traits as "natural" to both genders and in the process implicitly asserting that there are only two options, male or female. Gender is, in reality, fluid and contextual. That said, Gilligan's breakdown holds some truth; within the liberal tradition, ideals of self-sufficiency, rugged individualism, and cool rationality (which have historically been gendered male) are privileged over ideals of intimacy, reciprocity, and emotional expression (which have historically been gendered female). The liberal frame looks the way it does, values the kinds of behaviors it does, and rewards the kinds of people it does because of these essentialized gender assumptions, even if gender itself is much more complicated.

74. Kimmerer, *Braiding Sweetgrass*.

75. Kimmerer, *Braiding Sweetgrass*, 30.

76. Virginia Held, *The Ethics of Care: Personal, Political, and Global* (Oxford: Oxford University Press, 2006), 151.

CHAPTER 6

1. April Glaser, "Communities Rally around One Another—and Google Docs—to Bring Coronavirus Aid," *NBC News* (March 20, 2020), https://www.nbcnews.com/tech/tech-news/communities-rally-around-each-other-google-docs-bring-coronavirus-aid-n1164126.

2. A growing corpus of studies has explored how bias is baked into the technologies we use. For studies of the inequality encoded into algorithms, see Cathy O'Neil, *Weapons of Math Destruction: How Big Data Increases Inequality and Threatens Democracy* (New York: Random House, 2016); Safiya Noble, *Algorithms of Oppression: How Search Engines Reinforce Racism* (New York: NYU Press, 2018); and Virginia Eubanks, *Automating Inequality: How High-Tech Tools Profile, Police, and Punish the Poor* (New York: St. Martin's, 2018).

3. Whitney Phillips and Ryan M. Milner, *The Ambivalent Internet: Mischief, Oddity, and Antagonism Online* (Cambridge: Polity Press, 2017).

4. We borrow this framing from anthropologist Gregory Bateson's popularization of the play frame. See his *Steps to an Ecology of Mind: Collected Essays in Anthropology, Psychiatry, Evolution, and Epistemology* (Chicago: University of Chicago Press, 1972). We've previously applied this concept to online jokes in Whitney Phillips and Ryan M. Milner, "Putting Jokes in Scare Quotes: How Sparkle Hair Scully Reveals What's New and What's Not about Humor Online," *Flow Journal*, October 2, 2017, https://www.flowjournal.org/2017/10/putting-jokes-in-scare-quotes.

5. The COVID-19 crisis has moved the needle slightly, at least when it comes to false and misleading medical information; following the World Health Organization's designation of COVID-19 as a global pandemic on March 11, 2020, platforms like Facebook and Twitter began aggressively moderating clear-cut lies about the virus and other exploitative advertising content. Some of these efforts have been downright communitarian. But they're also very limited, as they've allowed—for example—QAnon and other Deep State theories to persist on-site, even as they've taken down—for example—false coronavirus cures. Given their track record on the subject, how long it took them to intervene (COVID-19 pollution flourished for months between the initial outbreak in Wuhan and the WHO declaration), as well as the sites' binary cleaving between health information and political information (as if those two things don't feed into each other), it seems unlikely that the decisive measures taken by the platforms will extend to political speech as well. The fact that the sites are employing any communitarian thought at all, however, provides some hope, and a foothold for further, more sweeping, intervention.

6. Patrick Davison, email interview with the authors, July 16, 2019.

7. Addressing in 2014 the growing tendency to conflate trolling with violent antagonism, ROFLCon cofounder Christina Xu made an uncanny prediction about equating deliberate harms with online play. "I feel there are a lot of dangerous things happening around that conflation, brewing under the surface, and they will bite us in the ass in five years or something," she explained. Bite us in the ass they did indeed. See Tim Hwang and Christina Xu,

"'Lurk More': An Interview with the Founders of ROFLCon," *Journal of Visual Culture* 13, no. 3 (2014): 376–387.

8. For their case supporting strategic silence in newsrooms, see danah boyd and Joan Donovan, "The Case for Quarantining Extremist Ideas," *Guardian*, June 1, 2018, https://www.theguardian.com/commentisfree/2018/jun/01/extremist-ideas-media-coverage-kkk.

9. J. Nathan Matias, "Preventing Harassment and Increasing Group Participation through Social Norms in 2,190 Online Science Discussions," *PNAS* 116, no. 20 (2019): 9785–9789, https://doi.org/10.1073/pnas.1813486116.

10. Debra Walker King, *African Americans and the Culture of Pain* (Charlottesville: University of Virginia Press, 2008).

11. Stephan Lewandowsky, Ullrich Ecker, Colleen M. Seifert, Norbert Schwarz, and John Cook, "Misinformation and Its Correction: Continued Influence and Successful Debiasing," *Psychological Science in the Public Interest* 13, no. 3 (2012): 106–131; Brendan Nyhan and Jason Reifler, "Displacing Misinformation about Events: An Experimental Test of Causal Corrections," *Journal of Experimental Political Science* 2, no. 1 (2015): 81–93.

12. Lewandowsky et al., "Misinformation and Its Correction."

13. George Lipsitz, *The Possessive Investment in Whiteness: How White People Profit from Identity Politics*, 2nd ed. (Philadelphia, PA: Temple University Press, 2006).

14. Robin Wall Kimmerer, *Braiding Sweetgrass: Indigenous Wisdom, Scientific Knowledge, and the Teachings of Plants* (Minneapolis: Milkweed Editions, 2013), 16.

Bibliography

Alba, Monica, and Ben Collins. "Trump Touts the 'Power' of Extremist Social Media Activists at White House Summit." *NBC News*, July 11, 2019. https://www.nbcnews.com/politics/white -house/trump-touts-power-controversial-social-media-activists-white-house-summit-n1029036.

American Psychiatric Association. *Diagnostic and Statistical Manual of Mental Disorders: DSM-IV-TR*. Washington, DC: American Psychiatric Association, 2000.

Ananny, Mike. "Breaking News Pragmatically: Some Reflections on Silence and Timing in Networked Journalism." *Nieman Lab*, April 23, 2013. https://www.niemanlab.org/2013/04/breaking -news-pragmatically-some-reflections-on-silence-and-timing-in-networked-journalism.

Anderson, Carol. *White Rage: The Unspoken Truth of Our Racial Divide*. New York: Bloomsbury, 2016.

Bailey, Moya. "Redefining Representation: Black Trans and Queer Women's Digital Media Production." *Screen Bodies* 1, no. 1 (2016): 71–86.

Bailey, Moya, and Trudy. "On Misogynoir: Citation, Erasure, and Plagiarism." *Feminist Media Studies* 18, no. 4 (2018): 762–768.

Banet-Weiser, Sarah, and Kate M. Miltner. "#MasculinitySoFragile: Culture, Structure, and Networked Misogyny." *Feminist Media Studies* 16, no. 1 (2016): 171–174.

Bank, Justin, Liam Stack, and Daniel Victor. "What Is QAnon: Explaining the Internet Conspiracy Theory That Showed Up at a Trump Rally." *New York Times*, August 1, 2018. https://www .nytimes.com/2018/08/01/us/politics/what-is-qanon.html.

Baragona, Justin. "CNN Anchor Chokes Up while Defending Baltimore from Trump's Racist Attacks." *Daily Beast*, July 27, 2019. https://www.thedailybeast.com/cnn-anchor-victor-blackwell -chokes-up-while-defending-baltimore-from-trumps-racist-attacks.

Barlow, John Perry. "A Declaration of the Independence of Cyberspace." Electronic Frontier Foundation, February 8, 1996. https://www.eff.org/cyberspace-independence.

Barr, Roseanne. Twitter, June 20, 2018. https://twitter.com/therealroseanne/status/1009330826 553667584?s=20.

Barrett, Brian. "The Wrong Way to Talk about a Shooter's Manifesto." *Wired*, August 4, 2019. https://www.wired.com/story/wrong-way-talk-about-shooter-manifesto.

Bateson, Gregory. *Steps to an Ecology of Mind: Collected Essays in Anthropology, Psychiatry, Evolution, and Epistemology*. Chicago: University of Chicago Press, 1972.

Battaglio, Stephen, and David Ng. "Sean Hannity: 'I Am Not Going to Stop Trying to Find the Truth.'" *Los Angeles Times*, May 23, 2017. https://www.latimes.com/business/hollywood/la-fi-ct-seth-rich-hannity-fox-20170523-story.html.

Baym, Nancy K. *Personal Connections in the Digital Age*. 2nd ed. Malden, MA: Polity Press, 2015.

Beckett, Lois. "How Leftwing Media Focus on Far Right Groups Is Helping to Normalize Hate." *Guardian*, March 5, 2017. https://www.theguardian.com/world/2017/mar/05/left-wing-media-far-right-normalize-hate-trump.

Benkler, Yochai, Robert Faris, and Hal Roberts. *Network Propaganda: Manipulation, Disinformation, and Radicalization in American Politics*. Oxford: Oxford University Press, 2018.

Bernstein, Joseph. "Alt-White: How the Breitbart Machine Laundered Racist Hate." *BuzzFeed News*, October 5, 2017. https://www.buzzfeednews.com/article/josephbernstein/heres-how-breitbart-and-milo-smuggled-white-nationalism.

Beyer, Jessica. *Expect Us: Online Communities and Political Mobilization*. London: Oxford University Press, 2014.

Blackmon, Michael. "Roseanne Barr Deleted a Tweet Accusing a Parkland Survivor of Giving a Nazi Salute." *BuzzFeed News*, March 29, 2018. https://www.buzzfeednews.com/article/michaelblackmon/roseanne-barr-david-hogg-parkland-nazi-tweets.

Bodroghkozy, Aniko. *Equal Time: Television and the Civil Rights Movement*. Champaign: University of Illinois Press, 2012.

Bonilla-Silva, Eduardo. *Racism without Racists: Color-Blind Racism and the Persistence of Racial Inequality in the United States*. Lanham, MD: Rowman and Littlefield, 2006.

Bort, Ryan. "As QAnon Goes Mainstream, Trump's Rallies Are Turning Darker." *Rolling Stone*, August 1, 2018. https://www.rollingstone.com/politics/politics-news/trump-qanon-705425.

boyd, danah. "Facing the Great Reckoning Head-On." *Apophenia*, September 15, 2019. https://www.zephoria.org/thoughts/archives/2019/09/15/facing-the-great-reckoning-head-on.html.

boyd, danah. "The Fragmentation of Truth." *Data & Society Points*, April 24, 2019. https://points.datasociety.net/the-fragmentation-of-truth-3c766ebb74cf.

boyd, danah. "Hacking the Attention Economy." *Data & Society Points*, January 5, 2017. https://points.datasociety.net/hacking-the-attention-economy-9fa1daca7a37.

boyd, danah. "Media Manipulation, Strategic Amplification, and Responsible Journalism." *Data & Society Points*, September 18, 2018. https://points.datasociety.net/media-manipulation-strategic-amplification-and-responsible-journalism-95f4d611f462.

boyd, danah. "You Think You Want Media Literacy . . . Do You?" *Data & Society Points*, March 9, 2018. https://points.datasociety.net/you-think-you-want-media-literacy-do-you-7cad6af18ec2.

boyd, danah, and Joan Donovan. "The Case for Quarantining Extremist Ideas." *Guardian*, June 1, 2018. https://www.theguardian.com/commentisfree/2018/jun/01/extremist-ideas-media-coverage-kkk.

Brach, Tara. "Real but Not True: Freeing Ourselves from Harmful Beliefs." Tarabrach.com, June 1, 2016. https://www.tarabrach.com/real-not-true.

Brandeis, Louis. "Chapter V: What Publicity Can Do." Louis D. Brandeis School of Law Library. https://louisville.edu/law/library/special-collections/the-louis-d.-brandeis-collection/other-peoples-money-chapter-v.

Brandeis, Louis. "Concurring Opinion, *Whitney v. California*" (May 16, 1927). https://www.law.cornell.edu/supremecourt/text/274/357.

Brock, André. *Distributed Blackness: African American Cybercultures*. New York: NYU Press, 2020.

Brock, André. "From the Blackhand Side: Twitter as a Cultural Conversation." *Journal of Broadcasting and Electronic Media* 56, no. 4 (2012): 529–549.

Broderick, Ryan. "QAnon Supporters and Anti-Vaxxers Are Spreading a Hoax that Bill Gates Created the Coronavirus." *Buzzfeed News*, January 23, 2020. https://www.buzzfeednews.com/article/ryanhatesthis/qanon-supporters-and-anti-vaxxers-are-spreading-a-hoax-that.

Broderick, Ryan. "Republicans' Conspiracy Theory–Ridden Counterprogramming to Impeachment Is Working." *BuzzFeed News*, November 20, 2019. https://www.buzzfeednews.com/article/ryanhatesthis/republican-conspiracy-theory-counterprogramming.

Broderick, Ryan. "Trump's Biggest Supporters Think the Coronavirus Is a Deep State Plot," *BuzzFeed News*, February 26, 2020. https://www.buzzfeednews.com/article/ryanhatesthis/trump-supporters-coronavirus-deep-state-qanon.

Bromley, David G. "Satanism: The New Cult Scare." In *The Satanism Scare*, ed. James T. Richardson, Joel Best, and David G. Bromley, 49–74. New York: Taylor & Francis, 1991.

Broussard, Meredith. *Artificial Unintelligence: How Computers Misunderstand the World*. Cambridge, MA: MIT Press, 2018.

Bruckert, Stephen. Interview with authors, email, July 15–18, 2019.

Bulger, Monica, and Patrick Davison. "The Promises, Challenges, and Futures of Media Literacy." Data & Society Research Institute. February 21, 2018. https://datasociety.net/output/the-promises-challenges-and-futures-of-media-literacy.

Bullard, Robert D., and Beverly H. Wright. "Environmental Justice for All: Community Health Perspectives on Health and Research Needs." *Toxicology and Industrial Health* 9, no. 5 (1993): 821–842.

Bullard, Robert D., and Beverly H. Wright. "The Politics of Pollution: Implications for the Black Community." *Phylon* 47, no. 1 (1986): 71–78.

Bump, Philip. "Hours After an FBI Warning about QAnon Is Published, a QAnon Slogan Turns Up at Trump's Rally." *Washington Post*, August 2, 2019. https://www.washingtonpost.com/poli tics/2019/08/02/hours-after-an-fbi-warning-about-qanon-is-published-qanon-slogan-turns-up -trumps-rally.

Bump, Philip. "Oh, Cool, Now the Campaign Is All about Charges of Satanism." *Washington Post*, November 4, 2016. https://www.washingtonpost.com/news/the-fix/wp/2016/11/04/oh-cool -now-the-campaign-is-all-about-charges-of-satanism.

Burns, Ken. *The Dust Bowl*. PBS, 2012.

Calderone, Michael. "Black Journalists Push Media to Cover 'Hyper-racial' Moment in Politics." *Politico*, July 29, 2019. https://www.politico.com/story/2019/07/29/black-journalists-racial-poli tics-1440628.

Campbell, Richard, Christopher Martin, and Bettina Fabos. *Media Essentials: A Brief Introduction*. 2nd ed. New York: Bedford / St. Martin's, 2018.

"Can Platforms Get It Right?" Panel at "Disinfo 2020: Prepping the Press." Cohosted by Columbia Journalism Review and the Tow Center for Digital Journalism. December 10, 2019. https:// www.cjr.org/covering_the_election/disinformation-conference.php.

Carissimo, Justin. "CNN Slammed for Running 'If Jews Are People' Headline." *Independent*, November 22, 2019. https://www.independent.co.uk/arts-entertainment/tv/news/cnn-slammed -for-running-if-jews-are-people-headline-a7432146.html.

Carter, Brandon. "What Is QAnon? The Conspiracy Theory Tiptoeing into Trump World." *NPR*, August 2, 2018. https://www.npr.org/2018/08/02/634749387/what-is-qanon-the-conspiracy -theory-tiptoeing-into-trump-world.

Chagas, Viktor. Keynote delivered to the #MuseudeMEMES symposium at the Republic Museum. Hosted by Fluminense Federal University. May 29, 2019.

Chagas, Viktor. "The Outbreak of Political Memes." *FAMECOS* 25, no. 1 (2018): 1–33.

Chagas, Viktor, Fernanda Freire, Daniel Rios, and Dandara Magalhães. "Political Memes and the Politics of Memes: A Methodological Proposal for Content Analysis of Online Political Memes." *First Monday* 24, no. 2 (2019). https://firstmonday.org/ojs/index.php/fm/article/view/7264.

Chan, Anita Say. *Networking Peripheries: Technological Futures and the Myth of Digital Universalism*. Cambridge, MA: MIT Press, 2014.

Chess, Shira, and Adrienne Shaw. "A Conspiracy of Fishes, or How We Learned to Stop Worrying about #GamerGate and Embrace Hegemonic Masculinity." *Journal of Broadcasting and Electronic Media* 59, no. 1 (2015): 208–220.

Chick, Jack. *Spellbound?* Ontario, CA: Chick Publications, 1978.

Chideya, Farai. "The Reconstruction of American Journalism in the Age of Culture War." *Medium*, August 5, 2019. https://medium.com/@faraic/culturewarjournalism-e3db60ae725f.

Chireau, Yvonne. "Conjure and Christianity in the Nineteenth Century: Religious Elements in African American Magic." *Religion and American Culture* 7, no. 2 (1997): 225–246.

"Christian Identity." Southern Poverty Law Center. https://www.splcenter.org/fighting-hate/extremist-files/ideology/christian-identity.

Christians, Clifford C., John Ferré, and P. Mark Fackler. *Good News: Social Ethics and the Press.* Oxford: Oxford University Press, 1993.

Chun, Wendy. *Control and Freedom: Power and Paranoia in the Age of Fiber Optics.* Cambridge, MA: MIT Press, 2008.

Citron, Danielle. "Cyber Mobs, Disinformation, and Death Videos: The Internet as It Is (and as It Should Be)." *Michigan Law Review*, August 13, 2019. http://dx.doi.org/10.2139/ssrn.3435200.

Citron, Danielle. "How Deepfakes Undermine Truth and Threaten Democracy." TEDSummit 2019, July 2019. https://www.ted.com/talks/danielle_citron_how_deepfakes_undermine_truth_and_threaten_democracy.

Clark, Meredith. "Black Twitter: Building Connection through Cultural Conversations." In *Hashtag Publics: The Power and Politics of Discursive Networks*, ed. Nathan Rambukkana, 205–218. New York: Peter Lang, 2015.

Coaston, Jane. "#QAnon, the Scarily Popular Pro-Trump Conspiracy Theory, Explained." *Vox*, August 2, 2018. https://www.vox.com/policy-and-politics/2018/8/1/17253444/qanon-trump-conspiracy-theory-reddit.

Cole, Devan. "Roseanne Tweets Support of Trump Conspiracy Theory, Confuses Twitter." *CNN*, March 31, 2018. https://www.cnn.com/2018/03/31/politics/roseanne-barr-conspiracy-tweets/index.html.

Coleman, Gabriella. *Hacker, Hoaxer, Whistleblower, Spy: The Many Faces of Anonymous.* London: Verso, 2014.

Collins, Ben. Twitter, March 28, 2019. https://twitter.com/oneunderscore__/status/1111487028980523008?s=20.

Collins, Ben. "What Is Qanon? A Guide to the Conspiracy Theory Taking Hold among Trump Supporters." *NBC News*, August 3, 2018. https://www.nbcnews.com/tech/tech-news/what-qanon-guide-conspiracy-theory-taking-hold-among-trump-supporters-n897271.

Conley, Wm. "The Tracking of Evil: Home Video and the Proliferation of Satanic Panic." In *Satanic Panic: Pop-Cultural Paranoia in the 1980s*, ed. Kier-La Janisse and Paul Corupe, 231–246. Surrey: FAB Press, 2015.

Conti, Allie. "The Jeffrey Epstein Story Is Fanning the Flames of Far-Right Pedophilia Panic." *Vice*, December 6, 2018. https://www.vice.com/en_us/article/pa5zyv/the-jeffrey-epstein-story-is-fanning-the-flames-of-far-right-pedophilia-panic.

Conway, David. *Classical Liberalism: The Unvanquished Ideal*. New York: St. Martin's, 1995.

Corupe, Paul. "20-Sided Sins: How Jack T. Chick Was Drawn into the RPG War." In *Satanic Panic: Pop-Cultural Paranoia in the 1980s*, ed. Kier-La Janisse and Paul Corupe, 69–82. Surrey: FAB Press, 2015.

"Covering the South: A National Symposium on the Media and the Civil Rights Movement." DVD recording of 1987 conference held at the University of Mississippi. Courtesy of University of Mississippi Library Special Collections.

Crouch, Ben, and Kelly Damphousse. "Law Enforcement and the Satanism-Crime Connection: A Survey of 'Cult Cops.'" In *The Satanism Scare*, ed. James T. Richardson, Joel Best, and David G. Bromley, 191–204. New York: Taylor & Francis, 1991.

Daniels, Jessie. *Cyber Racism: White Supremacy Online and the New Attack on Civil Rights*. New York: Rowman and Littlefield, 2009.

Daniels, Jessie. "Twitter and White Supremacy: A Love Story." *Dame Magazine*, October 9, 2017. https://www.damemagazine.com/2017/10/19/twitter-and-white-supremacy-love-story/.

Daniels, Jessie. *White Lies: Race, Class, Gender and Sexuality in White Supremacist Discourse*. New York: Routledge, 1997.

Darby, Luke. "What the Hell Is QAnon? The Right-Wing Conspiracy, Explained." *GQ*, August 7, 2018. https://www.gq.com/story/what-the-hell-is-qanon.

Davey, Jacob, and Julia Ebner. "The Fringe Insurgency: Connectivity, Convergence, and Mainstreaming of the Extreme Right." Institute for Strategic Dialogue research paper. 2017. http://www.isdglobal.org/wp-content/uploads/2017/10/The-Fringe-Insurgency-221017.pdf.

Davison, Patrick. Interview with authors, email, March 12, 2019, and July 15–18, 2019.

Dawkins, Richard. *The Selfish Gene*. Oxford: Oxford University Press, 1974.

Deb, Sopan. "Roseanne Barr's Tweets Didn't Come Out of Nowhere." *New York Times*, May 29, 2018. https://nyti.ms/2LBefZf.

Decker, Benjamin. "QAnon Background Beginnings." Research report. Shorenstein Center on Media, Politics, and Public Policy at Harvard Kennedy School. August 2018.

Decker, Benjamin. "QAnon Claims Victory after Mainstream Media Coverage of Trump Rally." Research report. Shorenstein Center on Media, Politics, and Public Policy at Harvard Kennedy School. August 2018.

Del Valle, Gaby. "How Should the Alt-Right Be Covered?" *Outline*, October 10, 2017. https://theoutline.com/post/2381/how-should-the-alt-right-be-covered.

"Donald Trump's Statements on Putin/Russia/Fake News Media." *Lawfare*. https://www.lawfareblog.com/donald-trumps-statements-putinrussiafake-news-media.

Donovan, Joan. "First They Came for the Black Feminists." *New York Times*, August 15, 2019. https://www.nytimes.com/interactive/2019/08/15/opinion/gamergate-twitter.html.

Donovan, Joan. "How Hate Groups' Secret Sound System Works." *Atlantic*, March 17, 2019. https://www.theatlantic.com/ideas/archive/2019/03/extremists-understand-what-tech-platforms-have-built/585136.

dos Santos, João Guilherme Bastos, and Viktor Chagas. "Fucking Right-Wing." *MATRIZes* 12, no. 3 (2018): 189–214.

Douglas, Nick. "It's Supposed to Look like Shit: The Internet Ugly Aesthetic." *Journal of Visual Culture* 13, no. 3 (2014): 314–339.

Douglas, Nick. "Micah's 'Black People on Twitter' Theory." *Too Much Nick*, August 21, 2009. https://toomuchnick.com/post/168222309/micahs-black-people-on-twitter-theory.

Duggan, Maeve, and Joanna Brenner. "Social Networking Site Users." Pew Research Center, February 14, 2013. https://www.pewinternet.org/2013/02/14/social-networking-site-users.

"Dust Bowl." Kansas Historical Society. June 2003. https://www.kshs.org/kansapedia/dust-bowl/12040.

"Dust Storm in Morton County, Kansas." Kansas Historical Society. Ca. 1935. https://www.kansasmemory.org/item/211239.

Dyer, Richard. *White: Essays on Race and Culture*. London: Routledge, 1997.

Ellis, Bill. *Raising the Devil: Satanism, New Religions, and the Media*. Lexington: University Press of Kentucky, 2000.

Entman, Robert M., and Nikki Usher. "Framing in a Fractured Democracy: Impacts of Digital Technology on Ideology, Power and Cascading Network Activation." *Journal of Communication* 68, no. 2 (2018): 298–308.

Eubanks, Virginia. *Automating Inequality: How High-Tech Tools Profile, Police, and Punish the Poor*. New York: St. Martin's, 2018.

Ewing, Philip. "Roger Stone, Trump Friend and Alleged Tie to WikiLeaks, Faces Trial in Washington." *NPR*, November 5, 2019. https://www.npr.org/2019/11/05/776121411/roger-stone-trump-friend-and-alleged-tie-to-wikileaks-faces-trial-in-washington.

Faludi, Susan. "How Hillary Clinton Met Satan." *New York Times*, October 29, 2016. https://nyti.ms/2dYtb1y.

Farhi, Paul and Ellison, Sarah. "On Fox News, Suddenly a Very Different Tune about the Coronavirus." *Washington Post*, Mach 16, 2020. https://www.washingtonpost.com/lifestyle/media/on-fox-news-suddenly-a-very-different-tune-about-the-coronavirus/2020/03/16/7a7637cc-678f-11ea-9923-57073adce27c_story.html.

Farrington, Dana. "READ: The Mueller Report, with Redactions." *NPR*, April 18, 2019. https://www.npr.org/2019/04/18/708850903/read-the-full-mueller-report-with-redactions.

Fazio, Lisa K., Nadia M. Brashier, B. Keith Payne, and Elizabeth J. Marsh. "Knowledge Does Not Protect against Illusory Truth." *Journal of Experimental Psychology* 144, no. 5 (2015): 993–1002.

Feagin, Joe R. *The White Racial Frame: Centuries of Racial Framing and Counter-Framing*. 2nd ed. New York: Routledge, 2013.

Feinberg, Ashley. "This Is the Daily Stormer's Playbook." *Huffington Post*, December 13, 2017. https://www.huffingtonpost.com/entry/daily-stormer-nazi-style-guide_us_5a2ece19e4b0ce3b 344492f2.

Flynn, J. D., Brendan Nyhan, and Jason Reifler. "The Nature and Origins of Misperceptions: Understanding False and Unsupported Beliefs about Politics." *Advances in Political Psychology* 38 (2017): 127–150. https://doi.org/10.1111/pops.12394.

Flynn, Meagan. "Trump's Spiritual Adviser Seeks His Protection from 'Demonic Networks' at Reelection Rally." *Washington Post*, June 19, 2019. https://www.washingtonpost.com/nation /2019/06/19/paula-white-donald-trump-orlando-rally-demonic-networks.

Mary Anne. *The Cult of the Constitution*. Stanford, CA: Stanford University Press, 2019.

Friedman, Dan. "Michael Flynn's Deep State Strategy Is Failing in Court. He May Not Care." *Mother Jones*, September 11, 2019. https://www.motherjones.com/politics/2019/09/michael -flynns-deep-state-strategy-is-failing-in-court-he-may-not-care.

"GamerGate—Moot Responds to GamerGate Deletions." Know Your Meme, September 14, 2014. http://knowyourmeme.com/photos/832349-gamergate.

Gillespie, Tarleton. *Custodians of the Internet: Platforms, Content Moderation, and the Hidden Decisions That Shape Social Media*. New Haven, CT: Yale University Press, 2018.

Gilligan, Carol. *In a Different Voice: Psychological Theory and Women's Development*. Cambridge, MA: Harvard University Press, 1982.

Glaser, April. "Another Network Is Possible." *Logic*, August 3, 2019. https://logicmag.io/bodies /another-network-is-possible.

Glaser, April. "Communities Rally around One Another—and Google Docs—to Bring Coronavirus Aid." NBC News, March 20, 2020. https://www.nbcnews.com/tech/tech-news/communi ties-rally-around-each-other-google-docs-bring-coronavirus-aid-n1164126.

Glaser, April. "El Paso Shows 8chan Is a Normal Part of Shootings Now." *Slate*, August 4, 2019. https://slate.com/technology/2019/08/el-paso-8chan-4chan-mass-shootings-manifesto.html.

"God Emperor Trump." Know Your Meme, February 11, 2019. https://knowyourmeme.com /memes/god-emperor-trump.

Goffman, Erving. *Frame Analysis: An Essay on the Organization of Experience*. Cambridge, MA: Harvard University Press, 1974.

Gomes, Wilson. Keynote delivered to the #MuseudeMEMES symposium at the Republic Museum. Hosted by Fluminense Federal University. May 31, 2019.

González, Juan, and Joseph Torres. *News for All the People: The Epic Story of Race and the American Media*. New York: Verso, 2011.

Graham, Joshua Benjamin. "Masters of the Imagination: Fundamentalist Readings of the Occult in Cartoons of the 1980s." In *Satanic Panic: Pop-Cultural Paranoia in the 1980s*, ed. Kier-La Janisse and Paul Corupe, 83–96. Surrey: FAB Press, 2015.

Gray, Kishonna L. "'They're Just Too Urban': Black Gamers Streaming on Twitch." In *Digital Sociologies*, ed. Jessie Daniels, Karen Gregory, and Tressie McMillan Cottom, 355–368. Chicago: University of Chicago Press, 2016.

Green, Emma. "A Resolution Condemning White Supremacy Causes Chaos at the Southern Baptist Convention." *Atlantic*, June 14, 2017. https://www.theatlantic.com/politics/archive/2017/06/the-southern-baptist-convention-alt-right-white-supremacy/530244.

Griffin, Andrew. "What Is QAnon? The Origins of Bizarre Conspiracy Theory Spreading Online." *Independent*, March 29, 2019. https://www.independent.co.uk/life-style/gadgets-and-tech/news/qanon-explained-what-is-trump-russia-investigation-pizzagate-a8845226.html.

Hadden, Jeffrey K., and Anson D. Shupe. *Televangelism: Power and Politics on God's Frontier*. New York: H. Holt, 1988.

Hampton, Rachelle. "The Black Feminists Who Saw the Alt-Right Threat Coming." *Slate*, April 23, 2019. https://slate.com/technology/2019/04/black-feminists-alt-right-twitter-gamergate.html.

Haraway, Donna. *Simians, Cyborgs, and Women: The Reinvention of Nature*. New York; Routledge, 1991.

Harcourt, Felix. *Ku Klux Kulture: America and the Klan in the 1920s*. Chicago: University of Chicago Press, 2017.

Harding, Sandra. "Rethinking Standpoint Epistemology: What Is 'Strong Objectivity'?" *Centennial Review* 36, no. 3 (1992): 437–470.

Hasher, Lynn, David Goldstein, and Thomas Toppino. "Frequency and the Conference of Referential Validity." *Journal of Verbal Learning and Verbal Behavior* 16, no. 1 (1977): 107–112.

Hawley, Amos H. *Human Ecology: A Theoretical Essay*. New York: Ronald Press, 1950.

Hawley, George. *Making Sense of the Alt-Right*. Chichester, NY: Columbia University Press, 2017.

Hayes, Chris. "Ta-Nehisi Coates Defends His Hometown of Baltimore." *MSNBC*, August 2, 2019. https://www.msnbc.com/all-in/watch/ta-nehisi-coates-defends-his-hometown-of-baltimore-65209413938.

Held, Virginia. *The Ethics of Care: Personal, Political, and Global*. Oxford: Oxford University Press, 2006.

Heller-Nicholas, Alexandra. "'The Only Word in the World Is Mine': Remembering *Michelle Remembers*." In *Satanic Panic: Pop-Cultural Paranoia in the 1980s*, ed. Kier-La Janisse and Paul Corupe, 19–32. Surrey: FAB Press, 2015.

Hendershot, Heather. *What's Fair on the Air? Cold War Right-Wing Broadcasting and Public Interest*. Chicago: University of Chicago Press, 2011.

Hicks, Robert D. "The Police Model of Satanism Crime." In *The Satanism Scare*, ed. James T. Richardson, Joel Best, and David G. Bromley, 175–190. New York: Taylor & Francis, 1991.

Hobbs, Renee. "Digital and Media Literacy: A Plan of Action." Aspen Institute and Knight Foundation Report. 2010. https://knightfoundation.org/reports/digital-and-media-literacy-plan -action.

Hobbs, Renee, and Sandra McGee. "Teaching about Propaganda: An Examination of the His-torical Roots of Media Literacy." *Journal of Media Literacy Education* 6, no. 2 (2014): 56–67.

Hochschild, Arlie Russell. *Strangers in Their Own Land: Anger and Mourning on the American Right*. New York: New Press, 2016.

Hofstadter, Richard. *The Paranoid Style in American Politics and Other Essays*. New York: Alfred A. Knopf, 1965.

Hong, Sun-Ha. *Technologies of Speculation: The Limits of Knowledge in a Data-Driven Society*. New York: NYU Press, 2020.

Hope, Clifford R. "Kansas in the 1930s." *Kansas History: A Journal of the Central Plains* 36, no. 1 (1970): 1–12.

Houston, Marsha, and Cheris Kramarae. "Speaking from Silence: Methods of Silencing and of Resistance." *Discourse and Society* 2, no. 4 (1991): 387–400.

"How the Facebook Ads That Targeted Voters Centered on Black American Culture: Voter Sup-pression Was the End Game." Stop Online Violence against Women. 2019. http://stoponline vaw.com/wp-content/uploads/2018/10/Black-ID-Target-by-Russia-Report-SOVAW.pdf.

"How the False, Fringe 'QAnon' Conspiracy Theory Aims to Protect Trump." *PBS NewsHour*, August 1, 2018. https://www.pbs.org/newshour/show/how-the-false-fringe-qanon-conspiracy -theory-aims-to-protect-trump.

Hwang, Tim, and Christina Xu. "'Lurk More': An Interview with the Founders of ROFLCon." *Journal of Visual Culture* 13, no. 3 (2014): 376–387.

Introne, Joshua, Irem Gokce Yildirim, Luca Iandoli, Julia DeCook, and Shaima Elzeini. "How People Weave Online Information into Pseudoknowledge." *Social Media and Society* (2018). https://doi.org/10.1177/2056305118785639.

Isikoff, Michael. "The True Origins of the Seth Rich Conspiracy Theory." *Yahoo! News*, July 9, 2019. https://news.yahoo.com/exclusive-the-true-origins-of-the-seth-rich-conspiracy-a-yahoo -news-investigation-100000831.html.

Jackson, David, and John Fritze. "Donald Trump Defends His Jeffrey Epstein, Bill Clin-ton Conspiracy Retweet." *USA Today*, August 13, 2019. https://www.usatoday.com/story /news/politics/2019/08/13/donald-trump-defends-jeffrey-epstein-bill-clinton-conspiracy -retweet/1996632001.

Janisse, Kier-La. "Introduction: Could It Be . . . Satan?" In *Satanic Panic: Pop-Cultural Paranoia in the 1980s*, ed. Kier-La Janisse and Paul Corupe, 13–18. Surrey: FAB Press, 2015.

Janisse, Kier-La, and Paul Corupe, eds. *Satanic Panic: Pop-Cultural Paranoia in the 1980s*. Surrey: FAB Press, 2015.

Jenkins, Philip, and Daniel Maier-Katkin. "Occult Survivors: The Making of a Myth." In *The Satanism Scare*, ed. James T. Richardson, Joel Best, and David G. Bromley, 127–144. New York: Taylor & Francis, 1991.

Kaplan, Alex. "The FBI Calls QAnon a Domestic Terror Threat: Trump Has Amplified QAnon Supporters on Twitter More than 20 Times." *Media Matters for America*, August 1, 2019. https://www.mediamatters.org/twitter/fbi-calls-qanon-domestic-terror-threat-trump-has-amplified-qanon-supporters-twitter-more-20.

Kimmerer, Robin Wall. *Braiding Sweetgrass: Indigenous Wisdom, Scientific Knowledge, and the Teachings of Plants*. Minneapolis: Milkweed Editions, 2013.

King, Debra Walker. *African Americans and the Culture of Pain*. Charlottesville: University of Virginia Press, 2008.

Klein, Ezra. "Trump's Racist Tweets: Is the Media Part of the Problem?" *Vox*, August 2, 2019. https://www.vox.com/policy-and-politics/2019/8/2/20702029/donald-trump-racism-squad-tweets-media-2020.

Klein, Ezra. *Why We're Polarized*. New York: Simon and Schuster, 2020.

Knight, Peter. "Introduction: A Nation of Conspiracy Theorists." In *Conspiracy Nation: The Politics of Paranoia in Postwar America*, ed. Peter Knight, 1–20. New York: NYU Press.

Kramarae, Cheris. *Women and Men Speaking: Frameworks for Analysis*. Rowley, MA: Newbury House, 1981.

Kunzelman, Michael, and Astrid Galvan. "Trump Words Linked to More Hate Crime? Some Experts Think So." *Associated Press*, August 7, 2019. https://apnews.com/7d0949974b1648a2b b592cab1f85aa16.

Ladouceur, Liisa. "The Filthy 15: When Venom and King Diamond Met the Washington Wives." In *Satanic Panic: Pop-Cultural Paranoia in the 1980s*, ed. Kier-La Janisse and Paul Corupe, 159–172. Surrey: FAB Press, 2015.

Lakoff, George. *Don't Think of an Elephant! Know Your Values and Frame the Debate*. White River Junction, VT: Chelsea Green, 2004.

Lakoff, George, and Mark Johnson. *Metaphors We Live By*. Chicago: University of Chicago Press, 1980.

LaPensée, Elizabeth. "Games as Enduring Presence." In "Indigenous Art: New Media and the Digital," special issue, *PUBLIC* 54 (Winter 2016): 178–186.

Latour, Bruno. *Reassembling the Social: An Introduction to Actor Network Theory*. Oxford: Oxford University Press, 2005.

Lee, Michael J. *Creating Conservatism: Postwar Words That Made an American Movement*. East Lansing: Michigan State University Press, 2014.

Levitz, Eric. "Report: Clinton Linked to Satanic Rituals Involving Kidnapped Children and Marina Abramovic." *New York Magazine*, November 4, 2016. http://nymag.com/intelligencer /2016/11/spirit-cooking-explained-satanic-ritual-or-fun-dinner.html.

Levy, Steven. *Hackers: Heroes of the Computer Revolution.* New York: Doubleday, 1984.

Lewandowsky, Stephan, Ullrich Ecker, Colleen M. Seifert, Norbert Schwarz, and John Cook. "Misinformation and Its Correction: Continued Influence and Successful Debiasing." *Psychological Science in the Public Interest* 13, no. 3 (2012): 106–131.

Lewis, Becca. "Alternative Influence: Broadcasting the Reactionary Right on YouTube." Data & Society Research Institute. September 18, 2018. https://datasociety.net/wp-content/uploads /2018/09/DS_Alternative_Influence.pdf.

Lipsitz, George. *The Possessive Investment in Whiteness: How White People Profit from Identity Politics.* 2nd ed. Philadelphia, PA: Temple University Press, 2006.

Lorenz, Taylor. "Instagram Is the Internet's New Home for Hate." *Atlantic*, March 21, 2019. https://www.theatlantic.com/technology/archive/2019/03/instagram-is-the-internets-new -home-for-hate/585382.

Lothian, Alexis. "DML2011 Liveblog: The Politics of User-Generated Content." *Humanities, Arts, Science, and Technology Alliance and Collaboratory*, March 5, 2011. https://www.hastac.org /blogs/alexislothian/2011/03/05/dml2011-liveblog-politics-user-generated-content.

Lynch, John. "Roseanne Barr Is under Fire for Appearing to Promote a Conspiracy Theory about a Parkland Student Activist." *Business Insider*, March 29, 2018. https://www.businessinsider .com/roseanne-barr-under-fire-for-nazi-salute-tweet-conspiracy-theory-parkland-student-david -hogg-2018-3.

"Mainstreaming the Web: Complete Video." ROFLCon.org, May 24, 2010. https://web.archive .org/web/20130308131320/http://roflcon.org/2010/05/24/mainstreaming-the-web-complete -video.

"Mark Zuckerberg, Moving Fast and Breaking Things." *Business Insider*, October 14, 2010. https://www.businessinsider.com/mark-zuckerberg-2010-10.

Martin, Daniel, and Gary Allen Fine. "Satanic Cultures, Satanic Play: Is Dungeons & Dragons a Breeding Ground for the Devil?" In *The Satanism Scare*, ed. James T. Richardson, Joel Best, and David G. Bromley, 107–126. New York: Taylor & Francis, 1991.

Martineau, Paris. "The Storm Is the New Pizzagate—Only Worse." *New York Magazine*, December 19, 2017. http://nymag.com/intelligencer/2017/12/qanon-4chan-the-storm-conspiracy-explained.html.

Marwick, Alice. "Why Do People Share Fake News? A Sociotechnical Model of Media Effects." *Georgetown Law Technology Review* 2 (2018): 1–39.

Marwick, Alice, and Becca Lewis. "Media Manipulation and Disinformation Online." Data & Society Research Institute. May 15, 2017. https://datasociety.net/output/media-manipulation-and-disinfo-online.

Matthews, Dylan. "The Conspiracy Theories about the Clintons and Jeffrey Epstein's Death, Explained." *Vox*, November 14, 2019. https://www.vox.com/2019/8/10/20800195/clintonbody count-conspiracy-theory-jeffrey-epstein.

McGill, Mary. "Wicked W.I.T.C.H: The 60s Feminist Protestors Who Hexed Patriarchy." *Vice*, October 28, 2016. https://broadly.vice.com/en_us/article/43gd8p/wicked-witch-60s-feminist -protestors-hexed-patriarchy.

McIlwain, Charlton. *Black Software: The Internet and Racial Justice, from the AfroNet to Black Lives Matter*. Oxford: Oxford University Press, 2019.

McIntyre, Lee. *Post-Truth*. Cambridge, MA: MIT Press, 2018.

McKay, Tom. "GOP Rep. Paul Gosar Inserts 'Epstein Didn't Kill Himself' Conspiracy Theory into Impeachment Tweets." *Gizmodo*, November 13, 2019. https://gizmodo.com/gop-rep-paul -gosar-inserts-epstein-didnt-kill-himself-1839844491.

McLeod, Kembrew. *Pranksters: Making Mischief in the Modern World*. New York: NYU Press, 2014.

McMillan Cottom, Tressie. "The Problem with Obama's Faith in White America." *Atlantic*, December 13, 2016. https://www.theatlantic.com/politics/archive/2016/12/obamas-faith-in -white-america/510503.

McRae, Elizabeth Gillespie. *Mothers of Massive Resistance: White Women and the Politics of White Supremacy*. Oxford: Oxford University Press, 2018.

"Media Literacy Defined." National Association for Media Literacy Education. https://namle .net/publications/media-literacy-definitions.

Menta, Anna. "Tom Arnold Slams Ex-Wife Roseanne Barr for Tweeting 'Nazi Salute' at Parkland Survivor." *Newsweek*, March 30, 2018. https://www.newsweek.com/tom-arnold-slams-ex-wife -roseanne-barr-tweeting-nazi-salute-parkland-survivor-867294.

Mercier, Hugo, and Dan Sperber. "Why Do Humans Reason? Arguments for an Argumentative Theory." *Behavioral and Brain Sciences* 34, no. 2 (2011): 57–74.

Merlan, Anna. *Republic of Lies: American Conspiracy Theorists and Their Surprising Rise to Power*. New York: Metropolitan Books, 2019.

Meyer, Ken. "Beto O'Rourke Loses It on Reporter Asking about Trump's Handling of Shootings: 'Press, What the F*ck!?'" *Mediaite*, August 5, 2019. https://www.mediaite.com/tv/beto-orourke -rips-reporter-asking-how-trump-can-make-the-situation-better-after-mass-shootings-what-the -fck.

Mill, John Stuart. *On Liberty, Utilitarianism and Other Essays*. 1859. Cambridge: Cambridge World Classics, 2015.

Milner, Ryan M. *The World Made Meme: Public Conversations and Participatory Media*. Cambridge, MA: MIT Press, 2016.

Milton, John. "Areopagitica: A Speech of Mr. John Milton for the Liberty of Unlicenc'd Printing, to the Parlament of England." 1644. https://www.bl.uk/collection-items/areopagitica-by-john-milton-1644.

Mina, An Xiao. *Memes to Movements: How the World's Most Viral Media Is Changing Social Protest and Power.* Boston, MA: Beacon Press, 2019.

Mitchell, Shireen. Twitter Moments, April 22, 2018. https://twitter.com/i/moments/9880 69560921284608.

Morris, Timothy B., and Todd Suomela. "Information in the Ecosystem: Against the 'Information Ecosystem.'" *First Monday* 22, no. 9 (2017). https://journals.uic.edu/ojs/index.php/fm/article/view/6847/6530.

Mulhern, Sherrill. "Satanism and Psychotherapy: A Rumor in Search of an Inquisition." In *The Satanism Scare*, ed. James T. Richardson, Joel Best, and David G. Bromley, 145–174. New York: Taylor & Francis, 1991.

Nadler, Anthony. "Nature's Economy and News Ecology." *Journalism Studies* 20, no. 6 (2019): 823–839.

Nagle, Angela. *Kill All Normies*. Winchester: Zero Books, 2017.

Nakamura, Lisa. *Cybertypes: Race, Ethnicity, and Identity on the Internet.* London: Routledge, 2002.

Nathan, Debbie. "Satanism and Child Molestation: Constructing the Ritual Abuse Scare." In *The Satanism Scare*, ed. James T. Richardson, Joel Best, and David G. Bromley, 75–94. New York: Taylor & Francis, 1991.

Nekmat, Elmie. "Nudge Effect of Fact-Check Alerts: Source Influence and Media Skepticism on Sharing of News Misinformation." *Social Media + Society*, January 2020. https://doi.org/10.1177/2056305119897322.

Nelson, Anne. *Shadow Network: Media, Money, and the Secret Hub of the Radical Right.* New York: Bloomsbury, 2019.

Nguyen, Tina. "Ben Carson Doubles Down on Satan-Clinton Connection." *Vanity Fair*, July 20, 2016. https://www.vanityfair.com/news/2016/07/ben-carson-clinton-lucifer.

"The 1619 Project." *New York Times*, August 14, 2019. https://www.nytimes.com/interactive/2019/08/14/magazine/1619-america-slavery.html.

Noble, Safiya. *Algorithms of Oppression: How Search Engines Reinforce Racism.* New York: NYU Press, 2018.

Noula, Ioanna. "I Do Want Media Literacy . . . and More." London School of Economics and Political Science Media Policy Project. June 21, 2018. https://blogs.lse.ac.uk/medialse/2018/06/21/i-do-want-media-literacy-and-more-a-response-to-danah-boyd.

Nyhan, Brendan, and Jason Reifler. "Displacing Misinformation about Events: An Experimental Test of Causal Corrections." *Journal of Experimental Political Science* 2, no. 1 (2015): 81–93.

Nyhan, Brendan, and Jason Reifler. "When Corrections Fail: The Persistence of Political Misperceptions." *Political Behavior* 32 (2010): 303–330. https://doi.org/10.1007/s11109-010-9112-2.

"The Occult Revival: A Substitute Faith." *Time* 99, no. 25 (June 19, 1972). http://content.time.com/time/magazine/article/0,9171,877779,00.html.

O'Connor, Cailin, and James Owen Weatherall. *The Misinformation Age: How False Beliefs Spread*. New Haven, CT: Yale University Press, 2019.

Ohlheiser, Abby. "No, John Podesta Didn't Drink Bodily Fluids at a Secret Satanist Dinner." *Washington Post*, November 4, 2016. https://wapo.st/2fl2d8P.

Ohlheiser, Abby. "You'll Never Guess How the QAnon Conspiracy Theorists Feel about All This Media Coverage." *Washington Post*, August 3, 2018. https://www.washingtonpost.com/news/the-intersect/wp/2018/08/03/this-is-the-moment-how-a-wave-of-media-coverage-gave-qanon-conspiracy-theorists-their-best-week-ever.

Olmsted, Kathryn. *Real Enemies: Conspiracy Theories and American Democracy, World War I to 9/11*. Oxford: Oxford University Press, 2009.

O'Neil, Cathy. *Weapons of Math Destruction: How Big Data Increases Inequality and Threatens Democracy*. New York: Random House, 2016.

Orbe, Mark P. "From the Standpoint(s) of Traditionally Muted Groups: Explicating a Co-cultural Communication Theoretical Model." *Communication Theory* 8, no. 1 (1998): 1–26.

Paris, Joel. "The Rise and Fall of Dissociative Identity Disorder." *Journal of Nervous and Mental Disease* 200, no. 12 (2012): 1076–1079.

Parsons, Elaine Frantz. *Ku Klux: The Birth of the Klan during Reconstruction*. Chapel Hill: University of North Carolina Press, 2015.

Perloff, Richard M. "The Press and Lynchings of African Americans." *Journal of Black Studies* 30, no. 3 (2000): 315–30.

Peters, Jeremy W., Annie Karni, and Maggie Haberman. "Trump Sets the 2020 Tone: Like 2016, Only This Time 'the Squad' Is Here." *New York Times*, July 16, 2019. https://www.nytimes.com/2019/07/16/us/politics/trump-election-squad.html.

Phillips, Phil. *Saturday Morning Mind Control*. Nashville, TN: Oliver-Nelson Books, 1991.

Phillips, Phil. *Turmoil in the Toy Box*. Lancaster, PA: Starburst Publishers, 1990.

Phillips, Whitney. "Unpredictable Light with Unpredictable Outcomes: A Cultural and Rhetorical History of the Term 'Light Disinfects'" *Georgetown Law and Technology Review* (forthcoming).

Phillips, Whitney. "How Journalists Should Not Cover an Online Conspiracy Theory." *Guardian*, August 6, 2018. https://www.theguardian.com/commentisfree/2018/aug/06/online-conspiracy-theory-journalism-qanon.

Phillips, Whitney. "The Oxygen of Amplification: Better Practices for Reporting on Far Right Extremists, Antagonists, and Manipulators." Data & Society Research Institute. May 22, 2018. https://datasociety.net/output/oxygen-of-amplification.

Phillips, Whitney. "So Bad It's Good: The *Kuso* Aesthetic in *Troll 2*." *Transformative Works and Cultures*, no. 14 (2013). https://journal.transformativeworks.org/index.php/twc/article/view/480/357.

Phillips, Whitney. *This Is Why We Can't Have Nice Things: Mapping the Relationship between Online Trolling and Mainstream Culture*. Cambridge, MA: MIT Press, 2015.

Phillips, Whitney, and Ryan M. Milner. *The Ambivalent Internet: Mischief, Oddity, and Antagonism Online*. Cambridge: Polity Press, 2017.

Phillips, Whitney, and Ryan M. Milner. "Putting Jokes in Scare Quotes: How Sparkle Hair Scully Reveals What's New and What's Not about Humor Online." *Flow Journal*, October 2, 2017. https://www.flowjournal.org/2017/10/putting-jokes-in-scare-quotes.

Phillips, Whitney, and Kate Miltner. "The Meme Election: Clicktivism, the BuzzFeed Effect and Corporate Meme-Jacking." *The Awl*, November 2, 2012. https://www.theawl.com/2012/11/the-meme-election-clicktivism-the-buzzfeed-effect-and-corporate-meme-jacking.

Posner, Sarah. "The Army of Prayer Warriors Fighting Trump's Impeachment." *Huffington Post*, December 19, 2019. https://www.huffpost.com/entry/white-evangelicals-trump-impeachment_n_5df950c6e4b08083dc5ae146.

Prokop, Andrew. "Jeffrey Epstein's Connections to Bill Clinton and Donald Trump, Explained." *Vox*, July 17, 2019. https://www.vox.com/2019/7/9/20686347/jeffrey-epstein-trump-bill-clinton.

"QAnon." Know Your Meme, December 12, 2017. https://knowyourmeme.com/memes/qanon.

Rappeport, Alan. "Hillary Clinton Denounces the 'Alt-Right,' and the Alt-Right Is Thrilled." *New York Times*, August 26, 2016. https://www.nytimes.com/2016/08/27/us/politics/alt-right-reaction.html.

Reichardt, Rolf, and Deborah Louise Cohen. "Light against Darkness: The Visual Representations of a Central Enlightenment Concept." *Representations* 61 (1998): 95–148.

Reinstein, Julia. "Let Us Break Down the Bizarre Right-Wing Conspiracy Theory Roseanne Barr Has Tweeted About." *BuzzFeed News*, March 31, 2018. https://www.buzzfeednews.com/article/juliareinstein/roseanne-qanon-explainer#.kb1Q4LJkr.

Reporter A. Skype interview with Phillips, September 6, 2017.

Reporter B. Phone interview with Phillips, September 13, 2017.

Reporter C. Phone interview with Phillips, September 13, 2017.

Reporter D. Phone interview with Phillips, September 7, 2017.

Reporter E. Phone interview with Phillips, September 12, 2017.

Reporter F. Skype interview with Phillips, October 10, 2017.

Ribeiro, Manoel Horta, Raphael Ottoni, Robert West, Virgílio A. F. Almeida, and Wagner Meira. "Auditing Radicalization Pathways on YouTube." Cornell University, arXiv, arXiv:1908.08313 [cs.CY], 1–18.

Richardson, James T., Joel Best, and David G. Bromley. "Satanism as a Social Problem." In *The Satanism Scare*, ed. James T. Richardson, Joel Best, and David G. Bromley, 3–20. New York: Taylor & Francis, 1991.

Richardson, James T., Joel Best, and David G. Bromley, eds. *The Satanism Scare*. New York: Taylor & Francis, 1991.

Roberts, Sarah T. *Behind the Screen: Content Moderation in the Shadow of Social Media*. New Haven, CT: Yale University Press, 2019.

Robertson, Pat. *The New World Order*. Dallas, TX: Word Publishing, 1991.

Rogers, Katie, and Nicholas Fandos. "Trump Tells Congresswomen to 'Go Back' to the Countries They Came From." *New York Times*, July 14, 2019. https://www.nytimes.com/2019/07/14/us/politics/trump-twitter-squad-congress.html.

Romano, Aja. "How the Alt-Right Uses Internet Trolling to Confuse You into Dismissing Its Ideology." *Vox*, January 11, 2017. https://www.vox.com/2016/11/23/13659634/alt-right-trolling.

Romero, Simon, Caitlin Dickerson, Miriam Jordan, and Patricia Mazzei. "'It Feels like Being Hunted': Latinos across U.S. in Fear after El Paso Massacre." *New York Times*, August 6, 2019. https://www.nytimes.com/2019/08/06/us/el-paso-shooting-latino-anxiety.html.

Ronson, Jon. *Them: Adventures with Extremists*. New York: Simon and Schuster, 2003.

Rosen, Jay. "The View from Nowhere: Questions and Answers." *Press Think*, November 10, 2010. https://pressthink.org/2010/11/the-view-from-nowhere-questions-and-answers/.

Rugnetta, Mike. "How Does Glitchy Art Show Us Broken Is Beautiful?" *PBS Idea Channel*, July 24, 2013. https://www.youtube.com/watch?v=7MCmBHPqz6I.

Rugnetta, Mike. Interview with authors, email, July 15–18, 2019.

Rupar, Aaron. "Trump Says He's Not Concerned about Being Racist Because 'Many People Agree' with Him." *Vox*, July 15, 2019. https://www.vox.com/2019/7/15/20694986/trump-racist-tweet-ilhan-omar-al-qaeda.

Scolari, Carloa A. "Media Ecology: Exploring the Metaphor to Expand the Theory." *Communication Theory* 22, no. 2 (2012): 204–225.

Serwer, Adam. "Trump Tells America What Kind of Nationalist He Is." *Atlantic*, July 15, 2019. https://www.theatlantic.com/ideas/archive/2019/07/trumps-white-nationalist-attack-four-congresswomen/594019.

Simonelli, Frederick J. *American Fuehrer: George Lincoln Rockwell and the American Nazi Party*. Urbana: University of Illinois Press, 1999.

Singal, Jesse. "How Internet Trolls Won the 2016 Presidential Election." *New York Magazine*, September 16, 2016. http://nymag.com/selectall/2016/09/how-internet-trolls-won-the-2016-presidential-election.html.

Shuham, Matt. "Trump's Latest Twitter Meme Is Music to the Ears of QAnon Adherants." *Talking Points Memo*, March 9, 2020. https://talkingpointsmemo.com/news/qanon-satanic -cabal-obsession-donald-trump-dan-scavino-nothing-can-stop-whats-coming.

Skurnik, Ian, Carolyn Yoon, Denise C. Park, and Norbert Schwarz. "How Warnings about False Claims Become Recommendations." *Journal of Consumer Research* 31, no. 4 (2005): 713–724.

Smith, Michelle. *Michelle Remembers*. New York: Pocket, 1980.

Sokol, Jason. *There Goes My Everything: White Southerners in the Age of Civil Rights*. New York: Vintage Books, 2007.

Soloman, John, and Buck Sexton. "Trump Doesn't Like the Term 'Deep State' Because 'It Sounds So Conspiratorial.'" *The Hill*, September 19, 2018. https://thehill.com/hilltv/rising/407406 -trump-doesnt-like-the-term-deep-state-because-it-sounds-so-conspiratorial.

Sommer, Will. "How the Ilhan Omar Marriage Smear Went from Fever Swamp to Trump." *Daily Beast*, July 17, 2019. https://www.thedailybeast.com/how-the-ilhan-omar-marriage-smear-went -from-an-anonymous-post-on-an-obscure-forum-to-being-embraced-by-trump.

Sommer, Will. "In a First, Lawmaker Cites QAnon Conspiracy from City Council Floor." *Daily Beast*, December 13, 2018. https://www.thedailybeast.com/in-a-first-lawmaker-cites-qanon-con spiracy-from-city-council-floor.

Sommer, Will. "Rudy Giuliani Teams Up with a Seth Rich Conspiracy Theorist to Save Trump." *Daily Beast*, December 5, 2019. https://www.thedailybeast.com/rudy-giuliani-teams-up-with -seth-rich-conspiracy-theorist-chanel-rion-to-save-trump.

Somodevilla, Chip. "Court Hearing for James Alex Fields, Suspect Who Drove Car into Group of Activists Protesting after White Supremacists Rally." Getty Images. August 14, 2017. https:// www.gettyimages.com/detail/news-photo/matthew-heinbach-of-the-white-nationalist-tradi tionalist-news-photo/831329068.

Stanley-Becker, Isaac. "'We Are Q': A Deranged Conspiracy Cult Leaps from the Internet to the Crowd at Trump's 'MAGA' Tour." *Washington Post*, August 1, 2018. https://www.washington post.com/news/morning-mix/wp/2018/08/01/we-are-q-a-deranged-conspiracy-cult-leaps-from -the-internet-to-the-crowd-at-trumps-maga-tour.

Starbird, Kate. "Information Wars: A Window into the Alternative Media Ecosystem." *Medium*, March 14, 2017. https://medium.com/hci-design-at-uw/information-wars-a-window-in to-the-alternative-media-ecosystem-a1347f32fd8f.

Starbird, Kate, Ahmer Arif, Tom Wilson, Katherine Van Koevering, Katya Yefimova, and Danial Scarnecchia. "Ecosystem or Echo-System? Exploring Content Sharing across Alternative Media Domains." Paper presented at the Twelfth International AAAI Conference on Web and Social Media, 2018.

Starobin, Paul. *Madness Rules the Hour: Charleston, 1860, and the Mania for War*. New York: Public Affairs, 2017.

Stephens, Niall. "Toward a More Substantive Media Ecology: Postman's Metaphor versus Post-human Futures." *International Journal of Communication* 8 (2014): 2027–2045.

Sterling, Bruce. "A Short History of the Internet." *Magazine of Fantasy and Science Fiction*, February 1993. http://sodacity.net/system/files/Bruce_Sterling_A_Short_History_of_the_Internet.pdf.

Sternthal, Brian, Ruby Dholakia, and Clark Leavitt. "The Persuasive Effect of Source Credibility: Tests of Cognitive Response." *Journal of Consumer Research* 4, no. 4 (1978): 252–260.

Stevens, Phillips, Jr. "The Demonology of Satan: An Anthropological View." In *The Satanism Scare*, ed. James T. Richardson, Joel Best, and David G. Bromley, 21–40. New York: Taylor & Francis, 1991.

Strate, Lance. *Media Ecology: An Approach to Understanding the Human Condition*. New York: Peter Lang, 2017.

Syed, Nabiha. "Real Talk about Fake News: Nabiha Syed in Conversation with Claire Wardle and Joan Donovan." *Data & Society Databites*, February 28, 2018. https://listen.datasociety.net/real-talk-fake-news.

Tardáguila, Cristina. "Don't Be the One Spreading False News about Mass Shootings: Here Are Some Tips from Fact-Checkers." *Poynter*, August 5, 2019. https://www.poynter.org/fact-checking/2019/dont-be-the-one-spreading-false-news-about-mass-shootings-here-are-some-tips-from-fact-checkers.

Taylor, Keeanga-Yamahtta. *From #BlackLivesMatter to Black Liberation*. Chicago: Haymarket Books, 2016.

"The Team." ROFLCon.org. April 29, 2012. https://web.archive.org/web/20120429041427/http://roflcon.org/the-team.

"The Team." ROFLCon.org. April 30, 2010. https://web.archive.org/web/20100430234306/http://roflcon.org/the-team.

Thompson, Hunter S. *Kingdom of Fear: Loathsome Secrets of a Star-Crossed Child in the Final Days of the American Century*. New York: Penguin, 2003.

Tracy, Abigail. "George W. Bush Finally Says What He Thinks about Trump." *Vanity Fair*, October 19, 2017. https://www.vanityfair.com/news/2017/10/george-w-bush-donald-trump.

Tripodi, Francesca. "Searching for Alternative Facts: Analyzing Scriptural Inference in Conservative News Practices." Data & Society Research Institute. May 16, 2017. https://datasociety.net/output/searching-for-alternative-facts.

Trump, Donald J. Twitter, July 14, 2019. https://twitter.com/realDonaldTrump/status/1150381394234941448?s=20.

"Trump Voter: How Is That Racist?" *CNN*, July 20, 2019. https://www.cnn.com/videos/politics/2019/07/20/trump-voters-2016-wisconsin-kaye-pkg-vpx.cnn.

Truzzi, Marcello. "The Occult Revival as Popular Culture: Some Random Observations on the Old and the Nouveau Witch." *Sociological Quarterly* 13, no. 1 (1972): 16–36.

Tufekci, Zeynep. "It's the (Democracy-Poisoning) Golden Age of Free Speech." *Wired*, January 16, 2018. https://www.wired.com/story/free-speech-issue-tech-turmoil-new-censorship.

Tufekci, Zeynep. "YouTube, the Great Radicalizer." *New York Times*, March 10, 2018. https://www.nytimes.com/2018/03/10/opinion/sunday/youtube-politics-radical.html.

Vaidhyanathan, Siva. *Antisocial Media: How Facebook Disconnects Us and Undermines Democracy.* Oxford: Oxford University Press, 2018.

Vaidhyanathan, Siva. "Mark Zuckerberg Doesn't Understand Free Speech in the 21st Century." *Guardian*, October 18, 2019. https://www.theguardian.com/commentisfree/2019/oct/18/mark-zuckerberg-free-speech-21st-century.

Vaidhyanathan, Siva. "Why Conservatives Allege Big Tech Is Muzzling Them." *Atlantic*, July 28, 2019. https://www.theatlantic.com/ideas/archive/2019/07/conservatives-pretend-big-tech-biased-against-them/594916.

Victor, Jeffrey S. *Satanic Panic: The Creation of a Contemporary Legend.* Chicago: Open Court Publishing, 1993.

Vitak, Jessica. "The Impact of Context Collapse and Privacy on Social Network Site Disclosures." *Journal of Broadcasting and Electronic Media* 56, no. 4 (2012): 451–470.

Waldman, Paul. "Why the GOP Is So Easily Infiltrated by Bonkers Conspiracy Theorists." *Washington Post*, August 6, 2018. https://www.washingtonpost.com/blogs/plum-line/wp/2018/08/06/why-the-gop-is-so-easily-infiltrated-by-bonkers-conspiracy-theorists.

Walker, Jesse. *The United States of Paranoia: A Conspiracy Theory.* New York: Harper Perennial, 2013.

Wampole, Christy. "How to Live without Irony." *New York Times*, November 17, 2012. https://opinionator.blogs.nytimes.com/2012/11/17/how-to-live-without-irony.

Wardle, Claire, and Hossein Derakhshan. "Information Disorder: Toward and Interdisciplinary Framework for Research and Policymaking." Council of Europe research report. Shorenstein Center on Media, Politics, and Public Policy. October 31, 2017. https://shorensteincenter.org/information-disorder-framework-for-research-and-policymaking.

Warnke, Mike. *The Satan Seller.* Plainfield, NJ: Logos International, 1972.

Warzel, Charlie. "'A Honeypot for Assholes': Inside Twitter's 10-Year Failure to Stop Harassment." *BuzzFeed News*, August 11, 2016. https://www.buzzfeednews.com/article/charliewarzel/a-honeypot-for-assholes-inside-twitters-10-year-failure-to-s.

Watkins, Craig S., and Alexander Cho. *The Digital Edge: How Black and Latino Youth Navigate Digital Inequality.* New York: NYU Press, 2018.

Weigel, David. "The Conspiracy Theory behind a Curious Roseanne Barr Tweet, Explained." *Washington Post*, March 31, 2018. https://www.washingtonpost.com/news/the-fix/wp/2018/03/31/the-conspiracy-theory-behind-a-curious-roseanne-barr-tweet-explained.

Weill, Kelly. "Roseanne Keeps Promoting QAnon, the Pro-Trump Conspiracy Theory That Makes Pizzagate Look Tame." *Daily Beast*, March 30, 2018. https://www.thedailybeast.com/roseanne-keeps-promoting-qanon-the-pro-trump-conspiracy-theory-that-makes-pizzagate-look-tame.

Wells, Ida B. *Southern Horrors and Other Writings: The Anti-lynching Campaign of Ida B. Wells, 1892–1900*. Ed. Jacqueline Jones Royster. Boston, MA: Bedford/St. Martin's, 1997.

Wheeler, André. "Ten Years of Black Twitter: A Merciless Watchdog for Problematic Behavior." *Guardian*, December 23, 2019. https://www.theguardian.com/technology/2019/dec/23/ten-years-black-twitter-watchdog.

Williams, Ev. Twitter, May 22, 2019. https://twitter.com/ev/status/1131258493162311680.

Wilstein, Matt. "Fox News Mainstreams Conspiracy Theory about Parkland Students." *Daily Beast*, February 21, 2018. https://www.thedailybeast.com/fox-news-mainstreams-conspiracy-theory-about-parkland-students.

Wong, Julia Carrie. "The Debate over Facebook's Political Ads Ignores 90% of Its Global Users." *Guardian*, November 1, 2019. https://www.theguardian.com/technology/2019/nov/01/facebook-free-speech-democracy-claims.

Wong, Julia Carrie. "What Is QAnon? Explaining the Bizarre Rightwing Conspiracy Theory." *Guardian*, July 30, 2018. https://www.theguardian.com/technology/2018/jul/30/qanon-4chan-rightwing-conspiracy-theory-explained-trump.

Wood, Thomas, and Ethan Porter. "The Elusive Backfire Effect: Mass Attitudes' Steadfast Factual Adherence." *Political Behavior* 41 (2019): 135–163. https://link.springer.com/article/10.1007/s11109-018-9443-y.

Woodruff, Betsy. "Twitter Suspends Conspiracy Account after Trump Retweet." *Daily Beast*, July 30, 2019. https://www.thedailybeast.com/twitter-suspends-conspiracy-account-after-trump-retweet.

Woods, Heather Suzanne, and Leslie A. Hahner. *Make America Meme Again: The Rhetoric of the Alt-Right*. New York: Peter Lang, 2019.

Zadronzny, Brandy, and Ben Collins. "How Three Conspiracy Theorists Took 'Q' and Sparked Qanon." *NBC News*, August 14, 2018. https://www.nbcnews.com/tech/tech-news/how-three-conspiracy-theorists-took-q-sparked-qanon-n900531.

Zadrozny, Brandy, and Ben Collins. "Like the Fringe Conspiracy Theory Qanon? There's Plenty of Merch for Sale on Amazon." *NBC News*, July 18, 2018. https://www.nbcnews.com/business/business-news/fringe-conspiracy-theory-qanon-there-s-plenty-merch-sale-amazon-n892561.

Zuckerman, Ethan. *Digital Cosmopolitans: Why We Think the Internet Connects Us, Why It Doesn't, and How to Rewire It*. New York: Norton, 2013.

Index